BOTH SIDES *of the* TRACK

A Journey
through Trauma and
Adversity towards
Forgiveness
and Freedom

DIANA HYLTON

Hasmark
PUBLISHING
INTERNATIONAL

Hasmark Publishing
www.hasmarkpublishing.com

First Edition

Permission should be addressed in writing to
anaidempowerment@gmail.com

Editor: Harshita Sharma – harshita@hasmarkpublishing.com
Cover: Photograph by Joel Capillaire – www.Joelcapillaire.com
Layout Design by Anne Karklins – anne@hasmarkpublishing.com
Interior Layout: Amit Dey – amit@hasmarkpublishing.com

ISBN 13: 978-1-77482-164-0
ISBN 10: 1774821648

Hasmark
PUBLISHING
INTERNATIONAL

DEDICATION

Pierre, my darling husband, this book has been in my mind for many years, but it was not until you gave me your unwavering love, nurturing, encouragement, and support that I was able to finally write and complete it. You are my best friend, my rock, my always and forever, and I love you eternally.

To my wonderful children, Reace and Jessica, you gave me strength and you are the ones I always stayed strong for. I am so very proud of you both; I love you.

To my dearest brother Mark, thank you for always believing in me. I love you and I will always be here for you as you are for me.

To my little grandson Jamie, you are so precious. Nana loves you.

CONTENTS

PROLOGUE

Throughout my life, I can say I have genuinely worked hard, and I have been focused on achieving many goals. However, when thinking about writing this book, it would be true to say that I have procrastinated for years around the completion of it. I have often thought that the time is not right, or that I do not have the appropriate ending, and sometimes just contemplated about the point of even writing this book and whether it's worth it. The pain has been so deep and sometimes so raw that even now I ponder on what I will gain from baring my soul. Will anyone be interested? Will anyone care? These are questions I have asked myself countless times and somehow, I always come back to the same conclusion, that my story IS important. I believe it will not only give hope and possibly inspire, but that it will also contribute to supporting children and families who have experienced or are currently experiencing trauma and adversity, in ways I hope will continue long after I am no longer on this earth. Overall, if we all have a life purpose, then this is surely mine.

Another factor contributing to the lengthy time it has taken to complete this book has been fear, which, I must add, has been crippling at times. It has been my fear of baring myself to my loved ones, friends, and colleagues and its possible impact upon my professional reputation, and the need to protect certain individuals whilst aiming to expose others. I have also considered writing this book under a pseudonym. However, I have always known this would not be possible and that I need to be brave and forgiving towards myself. So, what is the point of telling my story, and why now?

Many children in the UK and worldwide have and continue to suffer traumatic, abusive, and neglectful childhoods. Such is the trauma that some individuals find their pain just too hard to overcome and often resort to numbing their existence through various addictions, be it drugs, alcohol, food, or sex, to name a few. Some people simply do not know how to change their family story, thus conforming to their own parents' way of life and perpetuating their family dynamic. Realistically, albeit sadly, we live in a world where we cannot stop abuse, neglect, and pain. So, if we cannot stop it, I have often thought what is it that I can do, with help of others, to at least ameliorate some of the repercussions of the abuse and the resulting trauma, to support children and assist parents to make and sustain changes that will lead to better outcomes for their children, and in turn, for our society overall.

There have been many people who have suffered childhood abuse and/or adult trauma and who have gone on to write their stories in beautiful and inspiring ways. I have never wanted to write a misery memoir, so to speak, and have always wanted my story to contribute to something tangible and long-lasting in some way. While I have always known my story is individual and at times, possibly shocking, I have sometimes lacked faith in my ability to write my story and have lacked confidence in its originality. There will be some things that even my nearest and dearest will come to know only through this book, that previously they did not. However, I am hoping that by writing this book, I will be able to show that you can overcome trauma and crisis with belief, determination, and support, and that it is possible to affect a sustainable change by concentrating on the right areas. I remain steadfast in my belief that some of the most damaged souls, with love and support, can turn the course of events and make life better and safer for their next generation.

However, this book does not claim that all damaged or traumatised individuals can survive and make positive changes. Sometimes, acceptance is the only way, and in this, I have had to accept that change may not always come, even after the sincerest of efforts have taken place. While saying this, I would like to say to my dear brother, "I love you, Mark, and I am always here for you." My story is my story. No one else can tell it; therefore, I must.

I have always been a dreamer. Some of my dreams and goals have been realised, and others have not yet. A long-held dream of mine is that this book will lead to the creation of something special, strong, and essential in supporting children and families. Therefore, this book will conclude with this overall goal, and I hope it will also galvanise support and action from all those who wish to be involved in the greater purpose.

I have been careful to protect the identity of some individuals and I have sought permission from others where I have felt it important to keep it real. There are some individuals and organisations whose permission has not been obtained. This is due to either it not being necessary, and/or the information already being widely available within the public domain. At points, I have made it clear that not all that was said is a verbatim account of what was actually said.

CHAPTER 1

On Christmas Eve, 1974, as darkness enveloped the evening, my mother left the filthy squat we inhabited. While leaving, her only words were, "Don't go out and don't open the door." I think I remember her looking at us in a funny way as she left, although this may just be my wistful thinking. I was four and a half, and my brother Mark was six. Apart from a brief sighting about a year or so later, this would be the last time I saw my mother for the next fifteen years.

The squat, a squalid, dark, dank, and smelly place, had a broken toilet and no furniture. My memories of my mother are of her being sad and depressed, not talking, not washing, and certainly not cleaning the 'home.' On reflection, I do acknowledge it would have been hard to take pride in such appalling conditions. Not being able to provide for us properly, she had often fed us Weetabix with plain water, which may explain why I cannot stand those horrid little brown wheat biscuits today. The broken toilet did not flush, so it quickly became overflowed with excrement and the like, and a putrid smell emanated from it.

Earlier that evening, my father had visited with his new young girlfriend, a tall and very fat white woman called Anne. They had made quite a spectacle, both dressed up to the nines in glitzy party clothes, as given the time of year, a party was most likely where they were going. My father brought with him a Christmas food hamper. Mark and I had squealed with excitement, almost forgetting our desperate situation. I can only imagine what was going through my mother's mind, as after they left, she again appeared distressed and would not talk to us, not that I remember her talking much to us anyway. When she walked out of the door on that fateful Christmas Eve evening, I was terrified. Prior to this, she had left us alone many times, and sometimes, strange men would come to the squat knocking. Even though I was scared, part of me was also excited, as it meant Mark and I were able to raid the food hamper that our father had left for us. At that time, this was our sole focus, and we thoroughly ransacked that hamper, gobbling down whatever items of food we could open. The tinned food in the hamper was tossed to the side in our haste to eat the accessible goodies.

The squat, while it did have electricity, which I guess was illegally sourced, had only one room with a working light. With the corrugated windows serving as curtains, it got dark very quickly. As the night deepened, my brother and I became increasingly frightened. We certainly did not understand the significance of it being Christmas Eve. We just knew that it was dark and cold and that we were on our own. In my fear, I said to Mark that we should try and get some help. I begged him to come with me, but he refused. I don't know why, and he was unable to say why he wouldn't either. However, this is likely to be due to what we now know to be his learning difficulties. In those days it was called, amongst many things, being mentally retarded and/or backward. Whatever the politically correct term is, Mark was a slow developer in all areas and especially in learning to speak and walk. Such was his case that I was the more advanced and, in many ways, I acted as the eldest.

As I opened the front door into the cold, dark night and ran along the communal walkway, I was petrified. I am pretty sure I had no idea of what to do, so I banged on numerous doors and cried out for help. A moment of relief swept over me when some people came out of their flats to see what was going on. I must have known this was different from the other times she had left us, as I whimpered, "I don't know where my mummy is" and words to the effect of, "She's gone." Those people must have known the danger I was in, as they called the police. When the police arrived to take me, I cried, "Please, please don't leave my brother. He is still in there," frantically pointing in the direction of the squat. I know now the police did go to the flat, but shockingly, Mark was not there. When they returned without him, I became hysterical and cried more for my brother at that time than I did for my mother.

The police were kind and sympathetic towards me. They must have felt sad to realise that I had been abandoned by my own mother on Christmas Eve. They must also have been focused on finding Mark, or at least I hope they were. I was taken to Bow Road Police Station, in the East End of London. It was a large Victorian building with looming steps up to a set of thick oak double doors. The police did their best to reassure me and gave me a drink, which I think may have been orange juice. I was also given a chocolate biscuit and a blanket to wrap around my tiny shivering little body. However, I was inconsolable in my distress at being parted from my brother and was disorientated, most likely out of sheer fear. I spent a few hours at the police station before being bundled into another police car in the early hours of that bleak and life-changing Christmas morning. This evening is forever imprinted in my psyche as it has caused me significant emotional pain and has irrevocably shaped my personality and life as an adult.

CHAPTER 2

Though in the present times, the UK has one of the fastest growing dual heritage populations in the world, during the 1960s and for several years after that, interracial relationships were considered repugnant and at the very least, extremely frowned upon. It was a period that was fraught with racism, discrimination, inequality, and social injustice. Tragically, on April 4, 1968, Dr. Martin Luther King was assassinated in Memphis, Tennessee, for his beliefs and life's work to end racial divide and injustice, and just sixteen days later, on April 20, 1968, Enoch Powell delivered his "Rivers of Blood" speech. He was a leading advocate and campaigner for segregation in the UK, and in this speech, he lamented that integration would be the downfall of humanity. These were the days when *'No Dogs, No Blacks, No Irish'* was the prevalent discourse within British society. It was in this context that my black Jamaican father and white British—but of Irish descent—mother met, got married, and had my brother Mark and me.

Some years earlier, in the winter of 1960, my father travelled to England, a few weeks short of his twentieth birthday. A part of the Windrush generation, the journey took twenty-eight days. He arrived in Liverpool with just the clothes he stepped off the boat in and his only possession a small, battered suitcase with his meagre but 'important to him' belongings. I know very little of my mother's history. I am aware only of what my father has told me and the little I have gleaned from a few others over the years. Her family was of Irish descent and had settled in the Hastings area. When was that? I have no idea. In his recounting of the story of their first meeting, my father tells it through a rose-tinted haze and in an almost laughable nostalgic manner. I say this wryly when considering the devastating consequences of their ill-fated union.

My parents met in 1967 at a Brook Benton soul concert, which took place in the West End of London. My father, being a keen soul lover and having a penchant for white women, found himself sitting next to my mother at the concert. He says he was in awe of her, especially as she seemed to indicate she was attracted to him, and as the years have unfolded and other secrets have been exposed, it is clear my mother also had penchants of her own. Theirs was a 'whirlwind romance,' and again, I say this tongue-in-cheek. I know little of the circumstances of their relationship prior to our births, and I only have the snippets of information. My mother used to work in the Post Office, was intelligent, and an avid reader. My father, being illiterate in those days, was most likely impressed. They got married in March 1968, at which point my mother was already pregnant with my brother, who arrived into the world eight months later, in November.

Mark weighed eleven pounds at birth, and it was a most difficult labour, resulting in my mother not being able to bond with him. Almost immediately, my parents struggled because my mother drank too much alcohol, and she did not nurture or attend to his needs. Nine months later, she became pregnant with me. I know nothing of her pregnancy with me and how she felt about having another child so soon after Mark. My father, who has not been able to shed much light on this, says he did most of the childcare, but it is hard to understand what is wholly true and what is not. However, I do believe him when he says the support from their respective extended families was nonexistent due to the strong opposition over their relationship. My mother's family had disowned her, and my father's family was extremely judgemental and critical of him marrying and having children with a white woman.

On the day of my birth, my mother had been drinking alcohol all day and all night, and while my father did not like her doing this, he was not able to stop her. During the evening of May 17, 1970, my mother took a bath and, complaining of back pain, had yet another shot of 'medicinal' whisky. Having gone to sleep early, my father awoke to find the bed covered in blood, with a scrawny little baby crying and screeching in the bloody mess. My father has enjoyed telling this story and will tell it in a similar vein to that of a horror story, all blood and gore. So, the story goes, in the early hours of May 18, 1970, I was born at 'home.' I have no idea of the time of my birth or other information such as my weight. I do know that 'home' was 11 Hudson House in Poplar (East London), an old prefab-built house constructed to meet the growing demand for social housing during those times.

I have no memory of what life was like at Hudson House or how my mother coped (or didn't cope) with motherhood in those early days. I do know we stayed in the East End of London and later moved to a flat on the seventh floor of a twenty-five-storey high-rise tenement block called Priestman Point in Bromley by Bow. I have only fleeting memories of this time. Mainly, these are of my parents constantly arguing, and a near constant feeling of fear overshadowing me, which at times was all-consuming. At the time, I could not have known why. I just know this was how I felt. My earliest memory of living in this flat is when I was about eighteen months old, or maybe slightly older. It's of being in my cot, screaming, most likely for someone to pick me up or comfort me. However, no one came to do so. I felt very scared, and through the opening of the door, I could see Mark manically running in and out of the bedroom and up and down the hall landing.

We were on our own at the time, and Mark, who was about three years old, must have been extremely frightened as well. I do have a clear recollection of him banging on the front door of the flat and of the door being broken in by a group of firemen. Of course, at that time I didn't know they were firemen. I found this out later from my father. It was during this commotion that my mother returned. My father says that he was out to 'work,' that he had left us in our mother's care, and that she had gone to another man's flat in the same block as ours to "have sex." He reveals that a neighbour had heard our cries and Mark's banging on the door, which had resulted in the door being broken in by the firemen. My father says this was the start of the unravelling of their relationship, and that he could not cope with her inability to look after us or to maintain a clean and functional home.

Another strong memory I have of that time is of my mother allowing some of the local kids on the estate to take Mark and me out to the park. At the time, we could have only been about two and three and a half years old, respectively. As I have stated, Mark was born with a mild learning disability, and as a result, according to my father, it seemed that my mother preferred me over Mark. I do remember having a feeling of her loving me and of her giving me hugs on occasion, so this may be true. However, she completely rejected Mark; therefore, it is hard to know whether his learning difficulties were perhaps due to lack of oxygen in view of his long and protracted birth, her excessive alcohol use and thereafter being compounded by a complete lack of nurturing, or whether he would have been 'slow' in any case. When my mother allowed the local children to take us out, they would often make fun of Mark due to his language difficulties and they would take great pleasure in running away from him and making him eat rotten food off the ground.

I seemed to invoke a more caring side from these children. I was treated similarly to a doll and was played with accordingly. They loved to push me around the council estate in a massive Silver Cross pram and they enjoyed pushing me on the swings. On one such day, we had all been playing together when the older kids thought it would be fun to encourage Mark to eat a piece of half-eaten cake off the dirty concrete floor. Maybe this wouldn't have been so bad, had the cake not been crawling alive with ants. I vividly remember Mark eating the cake, the tiny black ants escaping from his mouth. The children hysterically roared with laughter, and in my lack of understanding, I fear I may have joined in with them. My father was livid with my mother for allowing the children to take us out and for Mark to have been treated in this way. This incident only served to increase the already numerous volatile arguments between them.

I do have some brief—and possibly, dare I say, happy—memories of that time. One is of my mother cuddling me when I had a terrible earache that made me scream out loud for hours in pain. It is the only time I can recall her responding to me being in distress and reminds me that at some point, she must have cared. I also have some happy memories of my father's nephew, my cousin Paul, staying with us on occasion at the flat. Paul was much older than me and was already a young man by then. He would often read to me and would spend time making me laugh. I mention Paul now as he played such an important role in my life, and he will always have an enduring place in my heart. He was one of the few men in my family who tried, to the best of his ability, to provide some nurturing. The only other happy memory I have is when my mother took us to stay for a short while with her own grandmother who lived in Hastings. It seems my mother's grandmother was her only family member who did not reject her for taking up with a black man. My extremely hazy memory of my great-grandmother is of her being a short little old lady with pure white and wispy hair. She gave sweets to Mark and me, and she was very kind to us. I believe her house would have been cosy if it were not for the copious amount of daddy long-legs spiders that seemed to come out in full force at night, creepy crawling around the bathroom. Aside from being terrified of the spiders, I seem to remember a brief and fleeting feeling of safety whilst there.

This was not to last for long as my father said that my mother continued to be unfaithful to him, though he does not admit to his own infidelities around that period. However, their relationship finally imploded following him catching an STD from her. He has never elaborated on this, and I have never asked. My father left my mother in 1973. He moved out of Priestman Point and left us alone with her in the flat. I have no knowledge of his life in the early months of him leaving us. However, he says he gave her money to pay the rent and buy food. I do know that not long after leaving us, he moved to Leytonstone (East London) and bought a house. It seems my father leaving my mother was the start of a spiralling downfall that would beset her until her death many years later. My father says that despite him providing her with *"child maintenance,"* she did not pay the rent and as a result, we were evicted from Priestman Point.

I have some vague memories of the stress of the 'eviction' and of my father finding us our new 'home.' It was now either late 1973 or very early 1974, and I remember my father taking us to some flats on the Bow Road, right by the Bow Flyover. These flats were on a large council estate; they were brown and foreboding-looking buildings. The flat in which we were to live had corrugated iron at the windows and padlocks on the door. I know now this was a squat (an abandoned or unoccupied dwelling), and in her desperation at having nowhere to live, my father 'supported' her to break in and move into the squat. Why he didn't take us to his new house, even if just for a temporary period, I do not know.

My mother, clearly incapable of making rational decisions or providing us with the care we needed, would often go out, leaving Mark and me alone in the squat. As such, I was fairly 'grown up' even at the tender ages of three and four. Mark and I often played out in the communal area of the flats, and I do not remember any concern being expressed for our safety at the time. It may have been because it was the early 1970s, and the UK child protection system was simply not as developed in those days as it is today. Such was my adult-like behaviour that I would often take charge of Mark and boss him about. I would try to make food with whatever scraps were in the squat, and on one occasion, I remember attempting to exert my authority by saying he wasn't allowed to play with knives as they were sharp. In order to demonstrate the risk, I proceeded to cut my palm with a knife to show him just how sharp it was. Upon seeing my blood flowing from the cut, I became upset as any very young child would, and I think I may have been scared that I would get into trouble. As it happened, my mother was not as concerned as you may think she should have been, and upon her return, she simply bandaged my bleeding little hand with a dirty piece of material. Given the circumstances and the surroundings, I am sure we didn't have a first aid kit, or even a packet of plasters amid our sorry state of belongings.

Despite my father's unwavering rose-tinted insistence of my mother being intelligent and knowledgeable, I know now she most probably suffered mental health problems and I suspect she may have been on the ASD spectrum, although I cannot be sure. While I have no medical evidence to support this feeling, it is through the piecing together of her story and in my thinking about her life that I have come to this conclusion. The most desperate year for her was 1974, as she seemed to attract predatory and unscrupulous men. While I do not know for sure whether she was prostituting or simply being used and abused, in view of her obvious vulnerabilities, I sadly believe it was the latter. Strange men would come to the squat, and she would have sex on the floor, on a filthy dirty mattress, often with us present. I remember one smelly, horrible man with hardly any teeth giving me some pennies to go in another room, and then hearing them having sex. Of course, I did not realise at the time what they were doing. It was when I grew older that the awful realisation set in.

Such was her desperate situation that one day my distressed and crying mother took Mark and me on a bus to our father's new house in Leytonstone. I have a clear memory of her sobbing hysterically on his doorstep and of him finally letting us in after what seemed a long, painful, and unnecessary wait (I mean, we were his children after all). Soon after being let into 'his' house, I vividly remember seeing her on the upstairs toilet and hearing her screaming out loud in what seemed to be excruciating pain. I remember this clearly as I was terrified of her screams, and in my panic, I tried to help her. However, my small self simply did not know how to. It ended with her giving birth on the bathroom floor to a dead baby. The baby's head was large and a bluish/purplish colour. Shortly after giving birth, she was taken away in an ambulance. I don't know who looked after us and I do not remember being comforted in any way. I think I may have been traumatised by the horror of this incident, and most likely, I was. This was in September 1974. I know this from having researched ancestry.com and finding a baby, simply named Hylton Male, in the Waltham Forest death registry. My father denies any connection to this child, stating the baby would have been named Hylton to reflect her surname as they were not divorced at the time. Thereafter, it seems my mother's mental health deteriorated even further as from then on, our lives spiralled most certainly out of her control.

CHAPTER 3

I was a snivelling and pitiful little wreck who could not be comforted during the journey with the police to the first children's home I lived in. I was to be under the care of the London Borough of Tower Hamlets and the children's home I was placed in was called Langley House. It was situated in Lime House, East London, not too far from where we had been living with our mother. While I was deeply traumatised, I do remember being taken in by a kind man who gave me a strong and purposeful cuddle. He made me a cup of hot chocolate and tucked me into a small bed. The bed felt clean and smelt nice. It had fresh, crisp sheets and a warm, cosy blanket. It was at this point that I must have felt somewhat comforted, as in my exhaustion, I settled down to rest from the events that had taken place. The kind man stayed with me and stroked my hair. He also asked me what I wanted for Christmas. I don't think I even asked for Mark or my mother. I simply asked for a watch. Why? I do not know, as I do not even think I could tell the time. I then fell into a deep but fretful sleep.

I have no memories of Christmases prior to my mother abandoning me and I think this may have been because Christmas Day in 1974 was like no other I had experienced in my short life up until that point. Langley House was clean, warm, and there were lots of children and adults. I remember there being an air of excitement and lots of chattering and laughter. The other children were keen to talk to me, asking numerous questions such as "What is your name?" and "When and how did you get here?" They must have been just as perplexed by my Christmas arrival as I was. The staff were very kind to me and upon reflection, they must have felt a sense of sadness over my situation, which I would not be able to fully comprehend until many years later. Initially, I was happy because I had nice food to eat, had slept in a lovely clean bed and had even been given the watch that I had asked for. How that kind man had managed to fulfil my request, I don't know, but he did. However, the novelty of my new situation soon wore off, and I soon became distressed about my missing brother again. I don't remember much more of that Christmas Day other than that I cried often, and at times, hysterically. I was impossible to console. Later, during the afternoon, the kindly staff took me into a room and told me my brother had been found, and that he would soon be joining me at Langley House. I remember feeling happy and excited, and I kept asking, "When? When?" Oddly, I really can't remember if I even asked for my mother. I may have, but I just don't remember.

I will never forget when Mark was brought to Langley House during the evening of Christmas 1974, or my shock over the state that he was in. He was traumatised, couldn't or wouldn't speak, and he would not allow anyone to touch him, not even me. The sight of my poor severely distressed brother caused me again to become hysterical, as at the vulnerable age of four and a half, I simply couldn't comprehend what was happening. Mark has, over the years, been more able to talk about the horror he suffered during those hours he was 'missing.' I can say with his permission that one of my mother's male acquaintances—or should I say abusers—took him from the squat and defiled him in such a manner that he is still unable to express the true extent of what happened. This abuse has forever deeply scarred him, and I would say beyond repair.

When we have talked about what happened, we now know it was the horrid, scary, smelly man with hardly any teeth who caused my brother such fear and pain. Having read my social services records in my later years, I learned Mark had been found in a dishevelled and traumatised state near to the squat on Christmas Day. The full extent of what had happened to him was not known or was not reported in the records. However, it was recorded that he had most probably been sexually assaulted during those missing hours. Such was the trauma Mark had suffered that his behaviour became unmanageable, and the staff at Langley House found it impossible to look after him. He would have major temper tantrums and meltdowns which often resulted in him having to be held down and restrained in their attempts to calm him down.

I think it must have been due to his challenging behaviour that shortly after Mark joined me at Langley House, Social

Services moved him to Gorseway, a special needs boarding school in Hayling Island, which is near Portsmouth. This was one of the many separations we were to experience over the course of the following years. I am not sure whether it was my young age or the fact that I was assured I would see him again soon. However, on this first occasion, I accepted this separation with a fair amount of ease. I was also told that my father would be coming to see me soon. I am not sure if this made me feel happy or not. I think I just accepted that my life had changed for good. I am also unsure whether Mark had been moved prior to me seeing our father or not.

My father says it was not until Boxing Day, 1974, that he was informed of our abandonment, of Mark's trauma, and of us being taken into local authority care. He told me that he had been asleep at home with his girlfriend Anne, when they had been woken in the early hours of the morning by the police forcefully banging on his door. He said when the police informed him of our plight, he was upset, but moreover, angry with our mother for having left us. He has, over the years, conceded to the fact he should not have left us in 'her care' on that Christmas Eve, especially as he says he had a feeling she was going to go out. He has never said why he did not even attempt to see his children on Christmas Day, given the circumstances we were in. Although it is likely he felt extremely guilty, this is as much as he ever said about this time.

Despite the trauma of my mother's abandonment and the neglect I had suffered in her care, I did settle relatively well into my new life at Langley House. This was without my brother and my mother, and even though I was with complete strangers. I would not know of the trauma, or should I say I couldn't feel the deep emotional scars of being abandoned by my mother on Christmas Eve until I grew older. Langley House, the children's home, was a large Victorian house with two dormitories, one for the girls and one for the boys. The house was light and airy, or so I thought. It was most certainly lighter, airier, and cleaner than our familiar squat had been. I also remember the food being a new experience of fun and a source of enjoyment. Langley House had a dumb waiter, which is a small freight lift designed to carry food and objects. It was used to transport food from the downstairs kitchen to the upstairs dining room, and I was completely and totally fascinated by this. I thoroughly enjoyed helping the staff load and unload the dumb waiter and I often begged to be allowed to ride in it. Of course, even in those days, there were rules around health and safety. Therefore, to my utter dismay, I was never allowed to sit in the dumb waiter even though I am quite certain I could have fit in it.

Langley House, whilst a children's home, was also an assessment centre, and I was in the 'care' of the local authority, specifically the London Borough of Tower Hamlets. My father had requested Mark and I be placed in his care. However, an assessment of his ability to care for us had to take place first. The staff members at the Langley House were kind and friendly, and I think I must have found some temporary relief from the constant fearfulness I felt when in the so-called 'care' of my mother. I started my first school and I responded well to safety, structure, and attention.

My father visited regularly with Anne, and he was allowed to take me to see Mark at his boarding school. On these trips, my father drove to Portsmouth in his green Austin Morris Minor car, and it was like an adventure as we had to go on a ferry from Portsmouth over the sea to Hayling Island. On one such visit, I remember watching a film, *Peter and the Wolf*, and I remember being mesmerised by the story, with its haunting music. I also recall my cousin Paul, whom I spoke of earlier, coming to visit me at Langley House and of him encouraging me to learn to read. I was a bright child and I learned somehow to read early on. My love of reading followed me right through childhood, and at times, was my only source of escape from the nightmare world I found myself growing up in.

Overall, my memory of Langley House is positive, given the preceding events, as I was well cared for, kept safe, and even nurtured at points. However, there is one traumatising event that sticks out in my mind. It was an uneventful day, being taken to or from school. I was walking down the road holding hands with a member of staff. I would have been about five years old. Suddenly, I saw a shadowy but familiar figure of a woman in a battered and shabby brown coat on the other side of the road. In an instant, I recognised this figure to be my mother. I frantically tugged the staff member's hand and excitedly pointed at her, calling out, "Mummy, Mummy, it's me, it's me!" The shadowy figure looked over the road and directly at me. She then turned her head and walked away, at which point I collapsed to the ground, sobbing, "That's my mummy. Please, please get her for me." The poor staff member was left to struggle with an extremely distressed little girl wailing inconsolably for her mother on the side of the road.

While I cannot say for certain that the shabbily coated woman was my mother, I do know over the years I have convinced myself that she was, and I had a strong feeling of recognition at the time. Langley House was within the same area that we had lived, and as I say, she recognised me; I could actually feel it. I also know that it was at this point that the pain of my abandonment started to hit me, and from then on, it has never really left. I have learned how to cope with the pain, but I doubt I will ever be free of the deep scar of rejection. Even today, these feelings and my defence mechanisms regarding this have the power to influence my decision-making within my relationships. To put it simply, my default mechanism is, I would rather walk away no matter how much I love someone than be rejected or abandoned by them. I did not see my mother after that and no one ever spoke of her. She became a ghostlike figure in my memory, one which I mourned over, fantasised about, and yearned for from that day on until I saw her again some fifteen years later.

CHAPTER 4

The assessment of my father's 'parenting abilities' took eighteen months, and at the age of six, I was told I was going 'home' to live with him. Langley House staff were very happy for me, and I was made a big fuss of. At the time, I experienced difficulties with sleeping and developed narcolepsy, which is a neurological condition that affects the brain's capacity to regulate sleep. It is known that trauma can induce this disorder in young children. This condition affected me at school and in my everyday life. I would often fall asleep at tables and during periods when I should have been awake. I was given medication, although I do not know what it was and for how long I was treated. The relevance of this memory is important, as this was a condition that was no fault of my own, and which my stepmother Anne was going to be deeply antagonised by in her role of 'looking after' me. On the day of my leaving Langley House, I fondly bade farewell to the staff and to the other children. In my naivety, I was incredibly excited about my new life.

It was early 1976, and I was now at 'home.' Not a home I had lived in before, but still a home nonetheless. I had a new 'mother' (Anne), my father, and my brother, who joined me shortly after my leaving Langley House. I started going to a new school called Newport Primary, and

I must have hoped things were going to be okay. However, it very quickly became apparent that Anne was coming to resent her newfound responsibilities of caring for two children, particularly as one had sleeping difficulties like enuresis (bedwetting), and the other displayed challenging behaviour in the form of out-of-control temper tantrums. Mark and I could do nothing right, and Anne made us know it for sure.

My father seemed to think it was Anne's responsibility to look after us, and because he had to work as a long-distance lorry driver, he often left us for days on end in her 'care.' All I know is that every time he returned from a period of being away, she would constantly moan at him about our supposedly 'bad' behaviour. This resulted in us often being hit by him as his means of trying to discipline us. Mark would be hit more often than me, as he was clearly the more 'badly' behaved. My father would hit us with his belt around our legs, and another method of chastisement was to put us in a cold bath, which I hated and would then cry for hours afterwards, much to my father's annoyance. To this day, I thoroughly hate cold water and my preferred water temperature is extremely hot, some would say to the point of boiling. I just know the feeling of hot water is very comforting.

Anne, whom we were told, or should I say made, to call 'Mummy,' was a formidable woman to two young and emotionally damaged children. She clearly didn't like us and would always tell us so and act accordingly. I was called a cry-baby frequently and often told to stop snivelling. She was cruel and mean and she took great delight in using us as her little 'skivvies.' In the main, our task was to ensure the carpets were kept clean. For this, we each had our own dustpan and brush set which we had to use in our weekly cleaning of the house. Our job was to sweep the house from top to bottom and woe betide us if we missed a bit. Anne and my father would often get dressed up to go out, leaving us behind at home alone to complete our chores. On their way out the door, they would leave a biscuit on the bottom stair banister as a treat that we were not to eat until we had finished the sweeping. Of course, we always ate the biscuit first, and then we did the sweeping. On one occasion, they came back early and discovered we had eaten the 'treat' first, which resulted in us being punished severely.

As awful as it was, Mark and I would try to have some fun when they went out and left us on our own. I liked to pretend Mark was a horse, or perhaps a donkey. (If you knew him, you would know he could never have been a horse.) The fun element was to make him go up and down the stairs on all fours with me riding on his back. I would take great delight in pretending my feet were in stirrups and kicking him in his sides to make him go faster. At the time, he had a rather grand afro (standard in the 1970s), and I would use his afro or his ears as another mechanism to control my not-so-sturdy steed. We had many hours of fun playing this game, or at least I did. These 'fun' times, however, were few and far between.

As the months progressed, Anne became more and more resentful of her 'parental' responsibilities and her abusive behaviour towards us escalated. She did not ever hug us and the names she often called us would cause her to roar with laughter at her own jokes. She called Mark a mongrel, spastic, and stupid, and me a "Cry Baby Bunting" after the nursery rhyme of the same name. She never did so in front of my father. I don't think she would have dared. She knew how to manipulate the situation and it would not have been in her interest to mock us in front of our father, but she did mock us immensely in his absence. Prior to Mark and I being placed in our father's care, my cousin Paul had been living for a brief period in my father's house. During his short stay with my father, he slept in the bedroom that I was soon to occupy. Now my cousin Paul was a smoker, and I mention this as the only explanation I have for matches being found under my bed. Paul must have left them there. Anyhow, these matches were found by Anne, who flew into a ballistic white rage, accusing me of playing with them and trying to burn the house down. I knew these matches had nothing to do with me and that I had not been playing with them. However, she seemed to take great pleasure in taunting me and saying, "Just you wait until your father gets home." When he did, she could not wait to inform him of my alleged fire-starting actions.

My father, upon hearing that I was attempting to burn his house down, went absolutely mental. He grabbed my hand and dragged me towards the gas cooker in the kitchen, ignoring my pitiful and pleading cries of fear and distress. I don't remember his exact words; however, it went along the lines of "this will teach you to never play with matches." I was terrified as I knew what was going to happen and I even tried to struggle to get away. However, I was a tiny scrap of a kid, and at the time, he was huge in comparison. He lit the gas ring and placed my hand in the fire and held it there for at least five seconds. Then he pulled it out and to my horror, put it back on the fire again. The pain was excruciating, and in my terror, I wet myself and almost fainted. In the commotion and through my fear, I heard them both exclaim that I had wet myself.

I was in so much pain and I was so traumatised, I could not stop shaking or crying. My father left it to Anne to sort me out. At the time I was wearing a pair of bright red trousers, and the dye from my trousers ran onto my white socks, staining them a pale pink by my own urine. Anne made me take off my trousers and tried to make me wash my socks. However, this was impossible due to the pain I was in, so she dragged me by my hair and threw me into my bedroom. I remember crying through the night quietly to myself, trying to soothe my burnt hand that had rapidly blistered. They must have been worried about the repercussions, as the next day, both were very nice to me. However, I was not provided with any medical treatment, and I was kept off school until it had healed. I was told not to tell anyone of the deliberate burning, but if anyone asked, to say that I had fallen on the gas cooker. My father did not apologise until many years later, and I do not remember any teachers querying my hand. Strangely, though, I do remember developing a morbid fascination with matches and taking to playing with them when I was left to my own devices. I must have had some sort of death wish or something, as I really don't know why I took such a risk when I knew what the punishment could entail.

Life, as we had come to know it, went on with Anne being forced to be our main carer and her clearly resenting this. Even on occasions when she tried to be nice, she failed. I say this as once, on Mark's eighth birthday, she must have been trying to do something kind as she had a birthday cake made which was in the shape of a hedgehog. She made a big deal about the cake and said Mark was not supposed to look at it until his birthday, yet she simply left it covered over in the fridge. Now, how can you honestly expect a young child not to look at something you have told him not to look at? Suffice to say he did look at it, and on the day of his birthday, she said to him, "I bet you can't guess what your cake is." Mark, not being the smartest, said outright, "Oh, yes I can. It's a hedgehog." Thereafter her temper exploded, as it often did, and she proceeded to lock him in the cellar, throwing the cake in the bin. He was left in the cellar for hours and no amount of him screaming or kicking the door made her relent. This abuse only served to make his tempers worse.

Another example of Anne's failure in her attempt to be nice occurred. Being an avid reader, she attempted to encourage this in me. She did buy me some books, and one of my favourites was called *A Treasury of Poems*. It was a beautiful green hardback book full of beautiful, colourful illustrations. I especially loved the poems called "The Jumblies" and "The Raggle Taggle Gypsies." I just loved reading these poems over and over, and I was enthralled by the pictures of the bright, colourful, and beautiful characters. One day we were at the kitchen table eating, and on this occasion, she was engrossed in the book she was reading whilst eating her chips. I took this as a cue that I could also read whilst eating and proceeded to read my much-treasured book of poems. However, my mimicking of her actions simply sent her into one of her rages, and she grabbed the book out of my hands, screaming that it was "fucking rude to read at the table." Upon snatching the book, she threw it at my face, and it caught the side of my eye, painfully hitting the corner bone next to my eye socket.

As the familiar fat and salty tears rolled down my face, I could feel the swelling of my eye as it rapidly reddened, and then later, blackened. Later that evening, I gingerly looked in the hallway mirror at my eye. She rushed out of the living room to bark at me to go to my room, shouting that I wasn't going to school, and if I carried on snivelling, she would give me another black eye to match the shiner that had developed. True to her word, I was kept off school until my black eye had healed. In those days, I don't think educational welfare questioned children's poor attendance.

I do not remember any professionals questioning why I was absent so often, and I had become very good at hiding the truth and protecting Anne and my father from exposure.

In late 1976, Anne became pregnant with my half-sister. My main memory of her pregnancy was of her constantly making me run errands and do chores for her. Ruby, my little sister, was born in July 1977. My father, being the philanderer that he was, prior to and following her birth, had been staying away from the house even more. He didn't spend much time with my baby sister, and I have no real memories of being with her at home. She could have only been a couple of weeks old when they had an almighty argument, causing him to storm out of the house. I don't know whether it was the reality of her growing responsibilities or the fact that she now had her own child. What was evident, though, was that by now she had had enough. The situation culminated in another terrible incident that was to change the course of our childhoods, yet again.

It was early evening, and it must have still been sometime in July 1977, when Ruby was a tiny baby. My father and Anne's relationship had deteriorated further to the point where even though he was the father of a new-born baby, he did not come home, causing her to resent us even more. That evening, I had gone to the toilet. I was in mid flow when Anne rushed in, shouting, "I need to use the toilet." She then pulled me off the seat and threw me to the floor, causing me to wet myself. It was the very same toilet where

I had witnessed my mother in agony, giving birth to her dead baby a few years earlier. What Anne did not bank on was my father coming back to the house at this very moment and seeing her abusive behaviour towards me. I do not know what caused him to come to my defence, as this had not always been the case. However, he said something like, "Stop fucking treating her like this," and to my horror, punched her so hard in the face that she toppled over and fell down the stairs. The whole scene descended into chaos. She had blood pouring from her eye and again, like history repeating itself, an ambulance took her away. Soon after, Anne's mother, who also didn't like Mark or me, came and collected Ruby. My father was charged with assault and Anne was granted a court injunction against him. Social Services were informed of the situation, and while Anne told them about my father's ill treatment such as the burning of my hand, she omitted anything about her own extremely abusive behaviour. Anne simply disappeared, taking Ruby with her. I did not see either again during my childhood.

Shortly after this incident, a social worker, Mrs. Lincoln, attended the house with the police and informed us that she was taking Mark and me away for our own safety to live somewhere else. I do not remember being told where we were going. However, I do remember seeing my father standing in the kitchen with big fat tears rolling down his cheeks, and him wiping his tears with a dirty old tea towel. I had never seen my father cry and I did feel slightly sad for him. Although, I was overly happy and excited as we were finally getting away, and I thought that maybe I was being taken to my 'real mummy,' the mother whom I had started to develop a distinct and rather pitiful pining for. Silly me!

CHAPTER 5

I was seven years old and Mark was eight and a half when we were removed from our father's care and placed back into the 'care' of The London Borough of Tower Hamlets. I do not know why it was not Waltham Forest, given that we had been living in Leytonstone, although it is likely due to the fact we were still subject to monitoring. Initially, we were taken to a foster placement to be cared for by foster carers called Mary and Mike. We must have engendered feelings of pity, as they were very kind and welcoming in their words and actions. However, Mark was not able to settle well, and he continued to present them with extremely challenging behaviours because of the trauma and abuse he had suffered. He continued to have terrible temper tantrums and if Mary or Mike attempted to calm him down or restrain him for his own safety, he would lash out, kicking and biting. I instinctively knew by now that it was better to not get involved, or else I might get hurt as well. Just a few days into our stay with our new carers, he absolutely wrecked their beautiful home in a fit of rage. It was at this point when I think they knew they were not equipped to deal with such out-of-control behaviour.

Shortly after this incident, possibly as soon as the next day, our social worker, Mrs. Lincoln, visited and told us we were being moved once again. I felt somewhat sad, and I was very angry with Mark as I had wanted to stay with this very nice, kind, and gentle couple. Mary must have felt guilty about ending the foster placement, as I remember her sitting me down and trying to reassure me that I was going to be okay. She even said she would come and see me in my new home, though she never did, and I never saw either of them again. Mrs. Lincoln was a short, elderly woman who had witch like features in a way. She had an extremely wrinkled face, wispy silver hair, and a large, hooked nose. She even had a wart on her face. I think she tried to be kind in her manner, but somehow, I never felt a warm connection with her, and I was always afraid to ask her questions. Mostly, I stayed quiet and just accepted whatever she said. I have some vague memories of the journey to our 'new home.'

We travelled in a big yellow standard 1970s council bus with Mrs. Lincoln, a drive in my young mind that felt like it went on for hours. As we approached our destination, I looked in awe out the window at the lush green surroundings of Havering. I was astounded as to how different the scenery was to the grey and brown concrete surroundings of East London that I had been used to thus far. St. Leonard's Children's Home was situated in Hornchurch, Essex, and at first sight, it was very impressive and like nothing I had ever seen before. As we pulled up to the gates of St. Leonard's, the bus driver and the gatekeeper gave each other a knowing nod as if this exchange had taken place many times before. The gatekeeper opened the barrier and the bus drove through. The road on which St. Leonard's was situated was called The Drive. It was a long, winding road housing thirteen large Victorian cottages, as they were called, and each of them had its own name. The cottages were widely spaced with three to four large oak trees separating each of them. The Drive, as with most of the surrounding area, was lush and green with lots of leafy plumage; it was five to six miles long and stretched deep into the Essex countryside. Surrounding St. Leonard's were acres of orchards full of fruit trees, and rambling fields that went on forever like rolling green carpets. It truly was a beautiful and idyllic setting.

Mark and I clung to each other tightly. Fear enveloped us. We had no idea as to what to expect and all we had was each other. The bus finally stopped at a cottage named Wallis and Mrs. Lincoln, almost but not quite cheerily, said, "Come along, children, we are here." Tentatively, we approached the large oak front door which had windows leading to a wide porch area. Upon Mrs. Lincoln knocking, an old man and a younger woman opened the door with seemingly welcoming smiles. As we went into the looming house, I saw a winding wooden staircase directly in front of me. I do not have many memories of being received into the Wallis cottage. However, I do recall the old man telling us that we were to call him Uncle Bill and his much younger wife Aunt Dawn. Mrs. Lincoln informed us the couple were to be our new house 'parents,' and she seemed happy to convey they would be looking after us now. Shortly after this brief introduction, Mrs. Lincoln made a swift exit without any word of when she would be back. Once she had left, Uncle Bill showed us around the cottage and to our dormitories. He told us rather sternly that boys and girls slept in separate dormitories and that under no circumstances were to go into each other's. This was one of the many house rules I was soon to become well accustomed to.

Mark and I didn't have many belongings; in fact, I cannot remember arriving at Wallis cottage with any bags at all. We were told the next day we would be shown around St. Leonard's and that we would be taken to the stores to get some clothes. At the time, I thought they meant we would be taken out shopping for clothes. I was wrong. I felt Uncle Bill was trying to be welcoming. However, I felt something distinctly sinister about Aunt Dawn, and from the very start, I feared her. She had jet black hair, thin pursed lips, and a slit of a smile that did not quite reach her eyes. That first night, Aunt Dawn led me up the wooden stairs and coldly said, "Go to sleep." This was very different from my first entry into care, as this time, there were no words of comfort or reassurance. As I laid in my bed in the dormitory, I felt small, scared, and alone. I tiptoed to the edge of the door and called down the long landing for my brother. I loudly whispered, "Mark, Mark," but he didn't hear me. As I stood at the edge of the door and peered out into the hallway, I jolted in fear as I caught sight of

Uncle Bill. He was standing at the top of the stairs, looking intently at me with his small, beady eyes. For a long and tense moment, he just stared at me, and I was rooted to the spot, not knowing what to do. Suddenly he snapped out of his stare and said in a playfully kind manner, "Come on, you naughty little girl, it's time for you to go to sleep." I felt scared as I looked at him, causing me to run back to my bed and to cower under the covers.

Those first few weeks at St. Leonard's are memorable for many reasons. The Drive was impressive to behold, and I continued to be amazed at the beauty of the area. I appreciated the scenery even at such a young age. The setting had an Enid Blyton type of look, and initially, I was enchanted. I even began thinking life may get better after all. That was, until we were taken to meet Superintendent Alan Prescott. Overall, it was Mr. Prescott who was in charge and oversaw the running of St. Leonard's. He had his own quarters and offices at the front entrance of The Drive, and it was made abundantly clear that these were off limits and private. As part of our introduction to St. Leonard's, Mark and I were presented to Mr. Prescott for his inspection, and I remember standing in his presence, feeling intimidated, as I presume was his intention. He was a large man who exuded an air of authority and of whom Uncle Bill and Aunt Dawn appeared to simperingly grovel around. He told us we were to address him as Mr. Prescott, and that he expected us to be 'good children.' He made it clear we were to do what our house parents told us, without question, or else he would be informed of our 'bad' behaviour. The threatening undertone in his words was very clear and was not lost on me, even if it was to Mark.

Aside from Wallis cottage, the other twelve cottages were called Hawthorn, Neptune, Myrtle, Landseer, Napier, Nelson, Rose, Ivy, Laurel, Wellington, Milton, and right at the end of the long and winding drive was Forbes. Forbes stood alone, and it was rumoured to be haunted. It had the air of an old Hitchcock psycho-type looking house in that it was eerie and foreboding. However, it was when I was shown the indoor swimming pool and told that it was 'ours,' I mean actually 'ours' to use, that I thought I had died and been taken to heaven. I just could not believe we were going to live in these mansion type houses, with the beautiful tree-lined drive, set in acres of land with 'our' very own swimming pool. I was beyond amazed, and for just a very brief while, I forgot my fears.

In view of our lack of clothing, Mark and I were taken to the home stores, not out to the shops as I had initially assumed, but to a large Victorian building situated on The Drive. The stores housed everything from clothes, bedding, food, and everything that you can imagine was needed to look after the many children that came through the gates of St. Leonard's. I was provided with a selection of dresses that were made out of a gingham cheesecloth type of material. They were all the same style but in different colours. I was also given a couple of cardigans, seven pairs of knickers, some vests, and several pairs of white socks. To top off my new wardrobe, I was given a black hooded anorak type coat and a brand-new pair of shiny black shoes. These were to be my standard issue clothes for the next few years. At first, I was happy to have some new clothes. However, as I grew older and realised the uniformity of the clothing, I came to hate those gingham dresses with an absolute passion. The Drive also had its own church and a school for the 'naughty' kids, who could not be trusted to mix with the rather posh, well-to-do residents of Hornchurch. I was not considered 'naughty,' therefore I went out to a school in the community. However, such was my experience in the affluent community of Hornchurch that I began to wish I was 'naughty' so that I didn't have to face the daily trauma of going to school with children, all of whom were white, very much loved, and came from far more privileged backgrounds compared to that of my own.

More about my school days later. For now, back to Uncle Bill, Aunt Dawn, and the rest of the staff. Uncle Bill's actual name was William Starling, and even back then, he looked very old to me. He had a full head of hair that was black and heavily streaked with white and grey, and a white and black speckled stubbly beard which was tinged yellow from the No. 6 cigarettes he chain-smoked. In those days, adults smoked incessantly, with no holds barred around children or within the home. Despite my initial fears, in the early days he quickly became my favourite staff member because he took a 'special' interest and acted kindly towards me. In my innocent mind, he was what I thought of as fatherly, or should I say how I imagined 'fatherly' should be. He often cuddled me and liked me to sit on his lap, so he could tickle and make me laugh. The snag to his obvious outwardly display of affection was the effect this had upon Aunt Dawn, who took it upon herself to make it clear she was in charge, and that she did not like me. This was extremely confusing to a seven-year-old child who simply and desperately just wanted to be loved. So, sadly, I tried hard to be good so she would like me as much as Uncle Bill seemed to, but she never did.

Aunt Dawn took great delight in walking around in skin-tight, washed-out faded blue jeans, and she often liked to sashay around, titillating the older boys in the home. She was extremely flirtatious but also steely in her manner. She would flit from being giggly and flirty to stern and cruel. I mean, you just never knew where you stood with her. Her sister, who was not a member of staff, always seemed to be there, chain-smoking alongside her. Uncle Bill and Aunt Dawn had their own personal suite of rooms in Wallis, which we were not allowed to go into without their express permission. They also had a little boy, David, who was the apple of Aunt Dawn's eye, and he was spoilt rotten by the pair of them. It was made abundantly clear that 'Prince' David ruled the roost, and that we, the home kids, were unwanted peasants in comparison.

Wallis staff members included three little old ladies, whom I will call Maggie, Hyacinth, and Viv. They did all the cooking and cleaning, and while they were mostly kind and sweet in their manner and actions, they had clearly gotten used to turning a blind eye, so to speak. Then there was Haydn Davies, a senior member of staff who seemed to treat me with disdain at every opportunity he got. As I grew older, I realised this was because he was Aunt Dawn's sidekick, so who she hated, he also hated. Simple. Now, looking back, I can see they deliberately formed groups of allegiance with each other to, as the saying goes, "divide and rule," and this method of control proved very successful for a long period of time. There were others, such as Annie, a beautiful woman of dual heritage who, due to her colour, I felt I could identify with; Roy, a tall man with curly brown hair; and Gordon, who had a sinister metal hook for a right hand, very much like Captain Hook's from *Peter Pan*. While there were other staff at Wallis Cottage, some of whom I assume were sessional and others part-time, these are the ones I remember the most.

A significant memory of those early days at St. Leonard's took place on August 16, 1977. I must have only been at the home for a week or so, and I was adjusting as best as I could, when one morning I woke to what I can only describe as a collective wailing. The staff were crying, hugging, and consoling each other and amid the commotion, all I could make out was "Elvis is dead" and "Oh my God, Elvis is dead." I remember thinking to myself, "Who is Elvis?"

So, when someone asks do you remember where you were when Princess Diana, or John Lennon, or Martin Luther King passed away, I often think back to the day when I did not have an inkling that Elvis Presley even existed until the day he died. God knows how that happened, given his superstar status. Perhaps I just had too much else to worry about pre-Elvis' death.

When reflecting on the other children and my friends at St. Leonard's, it is poignant to note that I remain in touch with a fair few today, albeit mostly via Facebook. A young teenage girl, Caroline, who I met a couple of years into my stay, I remain very close with today, having met her again in a serendipitous moment that I will talk about later. Each cottage had around twenty-five, sometimes up to thirty, children in residence. Initially, I think I enjoyed those early days as I was the youngest there at the time and I think this led to some of the staff paying more interest in me, most especially Uncle Bill. I had a lovely friend, Lara, who was there with her older sister Emily, and one of our favourite pastimes was to choreograph dances to Top of the Pops. Outside in the grounds, there were radios that we could use to play Top 40 hits such as "Dance Yourself Dizzy," "Band of Gold," and "You're the One That I Want." I think we fancied ourselves to be a bit like Legs & Co., a dancing troupe who were The Pussycat Dolls of the '70s. The ethnic mixture of the children and young people accommodated within the cottages of St. Leonard's was varied and there were many black and dual heritage kids.

I think this was because of the era where black men and white women got together, had children, and found their relationships failed due to pressures of the society and their families who hated such unions. Further on, the mid-70s saw the rise of the National Front and the Skinhead movement in England. Therefore, many of the white kids assumed this identity and that of the Mod look. However, I do not remember there being any Asian children at all. I made friends with some of the kids and with a sense of solidarity, I gravitated towards the brown girls.

It seemed that I was able to settle more easily than Mark. This is likely to have been because of the earlier abuse and chronic neglect he had suffered, which was compounded by his learning difficulty. It may also have had something to do with the fact that I was again being favoured, this time by Uncle Bill. Mark and I would often squabble and at times, ferociously fight. Our fights involved the pulling of hair and biting. Such was the ferocity of our fighting that we often had to be pulled apart. We did not see our father for a long time and, to be honest, I did not even think about him for a while. I had Uncle Bill, who made me feel special, and for a while, I enjoyed the feeling of thinking that I was his favourite. One such tactic he used was to allow just me into the tuck shop, where he would give me sweets on the quiet. During these 'special' moments, he would sit me on his lap and tell me silly stories to make me laugh. I was far too young and naïve to realise this was all part of his grooming of me, and I just revelled in the moment.

Uncle Bill also protected me somewhat from the wrath of Aunt Dawn, as while she enjoyed giving me sneering dirty looks, she never intervened during our 'special' time. I was even allowed into their private sitting room to play with David. Although I think this was more to do with our being from similar age groups and their wanting or needing him to have someone to play with, rather than it being a treat for me. I could never quite make Aunt Dawn out though, as sometimes she would be okay with me being in her sitting room with David, and then at other times, she would walk in with a face like thunder and demand I leave the room. She would look at me with her steely cold eyes and point to the door, barking "OUT," and I always knew to scarper when this happened, and never needed to be told twice.

I soon came to realise that life in Wallis was a rather rule-driven and regimental kind of affair. Weekdays we would rise at 6:45 a.m. to wash in the communal bathroom. Thereafter, we would get dressed and go down for breakfast in the dining room. Breakfast often consisted of a bowl of cereal, bread and jam or marmalade, and tea or milk. The dining room had several small dining tables, with different coloured gingham tablecloths (clearly in the '70s, the gingham fabric was used in force). I mostly sat at a table with Uncle Bill and near to his fish tank, which housed his beloved Piranha fish. In the beginning, I was terrified of those fish, and I think he secretly enjoyed my fear. I hadn't even heard of Piranhas before then. I just remember every morning looking in that tank and seeing the remains of fish floating in the tank that had been mauled in the night by those little horrors. He also had a tank full of tropical fish, which was quite spectacular to a young girl who had never seen such colourful fish previously in her life. Uncle Bill loved to talk about his fish and was most amused with feeding them water fleas, which he informed me were called Daphnia. He said while this was their actual name, he preferred to call them "Dawnias" after Aunt Dawn. He would make fun of her and would encourage me to do so too. She must have hated him for this as she never gave as much as a hint of a smile when she was the butt of his jokes.

After breakfast, it was school time. Due to Mark's behaviour, he was not able to go out into the community to school with me. So, he attended The Drive school and I started at Wickham Junior. I boarded the big yellow council bus at 8:30 a.m. and he walked to school with staff. It was at my new school that I became acutely aware of my colour and of racism. Hornchurch was a mostly white and affluent area. I observed that I was the only child of colour in the school, and boy, did those kids make me know it! I was called a whole host of names from Blacky and Nigger to Golliwog and Poo Poo, and sometimes Shit Face. The kids also knew I was from the local children's home and would often taunt me by saying I was a tramp with no mum or dad. They also teased me, saying things like, "Do you know Oliver Twist?" and would roar with laughter when they meanly enquired whether he actually lived in the home with me.

Most of the kids were horrible and I hated that school. I longed to stay within the confines of St. Leonard's and go to school with the other kids in the home who at least I felt I had something in common with. I could hardly wait for the school day to finish so I could get back on the big yellow bus and go 'home.' Upon arriving 'home,' I was made to change out of my school uniform into my stores-issued gingham dress. Tea, as it was called, was at about 5 p.m. and consisted of things like fish fingers, tinned tomatoes or sausages, and baked beans or spaghetti with a piece of bread and butter. We would also have an after such as bread or rice pudding. We were allowed to watch a little TV after tea and then, as I was the youngest, my bedtime was the earliest, at 7:30 p.m. At weekends, we were allowed little treats such as swimming in 'our' pool and a cake and hot chocolate for supper. We also got pocket money on Friday nights to spend in the tuck shop. During those early days, apart from hating school, I thought life was not too bad. Not great, but at least it was bearable.

My first Christmas at St. Leonard's was a mixed experience. It was 1977, and the deep pining I felt had evolved into an overwhelming sense of sadness and longing for my absent mother, who had abandoned me on Christmas Eve a few years earlier. I am not sure how it started. Maybe it was the teasing at school, or maybe it was always going to happen. However, it was a pain that would escalate over each year that passed. Back then, I don't think I was consciously aware of the enormity of being abandoned on Christmas Eve; that came later. I just knew I felt very sad, and that I wanted my mother. To be honest, I think any mother would have done. I just knew most children had a mother who loved them, hugged them, and looked after them, and I wanted this too. Despite this, I did find myself getting caught up in the excitement of the other children and in the staff's Christmas preparations. I seem to remember singing Christmas carols, eating sweets and mince pies, and attending a Christmas party at the local Ford manufacturing plant in Dagenham, Essex. Every year, Ford Dagenham held a big Christmas party for children in care, children like us. So, despite my sadness, this was to be the best Christmas of my life so far. Mark and I even had a present under the Christmas tree with our name on it as all the children did, and there was a festive air of excitement surrounding the home.

That first Christmas morning, we went to church, which was on The Drive, and sang hymns and said prayers. Being one of Uncle Bill's favourites, I was allowed to travel in his car with David for the five-minute drive to the church, while the other kids walked. I was also chosen to sit with him for the service, while Mark sat at the back with the other kids. On this occasion, all the children from the different homes were brought together to 'worship' and give 'thanks,' especially for our carers. After the service, we all went back to our respective homes to open our presents. To my wonder and delight, I received a Ballerina Sindy doll, and Mark got an Eagle Eyes Action Man. We had never received such amazing presents in our life. I absolutely loved that doll with her beautiful golden hair, white ballet tights, and plastic pink pumps. The food we were provided with was about as close to a feast as I had ever experienced and was very different from the usual meagre fare we were used to. The day went on with fantastic TV, such as Top of the Pops and the films *National Velvet* and *The Wizard of Oz*. I think that Christmas might have been one of the best days I had experienced in my life up to that point. However, this brief feeling of joy and happiness was not to last long, as Mark and I continued to argue and fight, and he continued to display what is now termed as extremely challenging behaviour. Shortly after that first Christmas at St. Leonard's, Mark and I got into another fight, resulting in him pulling the head and legs off my precious Sindy doll. I was distraught, and even though I had sought vengeance by decapitating his Eagle Eyes Action Man, I could not be comforted. It must have been shortly after this incident, and combined with Mark's unmanageable behaviour, the decision was made to separate us.

The day they took Mark away is a day I will never forget. While we argued and fought, we really did love each other, as overall, I think we intrinsically understood we were all we had. When the staff told us they were moving Mark to Napier cottage, we panicked, and I pleaded with them not to take him away. When I realised no amount of begging was going to make them change their minds, I pulled Mark up the wooden stairs and into the girls' dormitory. I did not care that I may get into trouble for breaking the rules. My sole focus was to hide my brother so they couldn't take him away from me. In our innocence, we hid under my bed, shaking and clutching on tightly to each other. Of course, it didn't take them long to find us, and upon doing so they proceeded to drag us out from under the bed. We may have been small, but we were strongly defiant in our desperation not to be separated. In the end, they prised us apart even though we were begging, crying, kicking, and pleading. I was completely bereft that day when they took my brother away. It was another time I could not be consoled. Not even by Uncle Bill, who tried to reassure me with comforting cuddles, saying I would see Mark soon and that he was only going to be a few doors away.

It was around this time that Uncle Bill began taking me out for drives in his car around the Essex countryside. Shortly after these drives began, one day he pulled over in his car and asked me if I wanted a cuddle. I did not think much of this, as he often cuddled me, and it was something that I enjoyed as it was not as if anyone else showed me such affection. So, when he asked, I happily consented. Thereafter, he pulled me over to his seat and sat me on his lap to give me a long cuddle. However, this cuddle was very different to our usual ones, as I felt his hand wander up my dress and to my knicker area, and he put my hand over his trousers on his groin area. It felt hard and he seemed to enjoy rubbing my little hand back and forth. He didn't speak and just stared at me. I must have frozen and looked surprised, as he stopped abruptly and placed me back in the passenger seat. In silence, we drove back to the home. Upon arriving at the gates of St. Leonard's, he stopped before pulling into the drive and said, "Sweetheart, you know that you are my special girl and we won't tell anyone what we do, will we?" While slightly confused, I did instinctively know what he meant, and I nodded my agreement to collude with him in 'our' secret.

This was the beginning of Uncle Bill testing me to see if I would tell anyone about 'our' secret. When we got back, he asked me if I wanted to go to the tuck shop, which was a silly question really, as of course I did. He proceeded to give me a packet of crisps and a chocolate Mars bar whilst looking at me directly in the eye and putting his fingers to his lips in a shushing motion. I knew exactly what he meant and did as he wanted, and you know I thoroughly enjoyed that packet of crisps and Mars bar. The drives with Uncle Bill took place more or less weekly, and no one queried why he always took me out and not anyone else. Those drives always ended with an extended 'special touchy feely cuddle' and a secret trip to the tuck shop. I was not worried or afraid; I simply knew I was Uncle Bill's *special* girl and that we had our very own secret, or so I thought, anyway.

CHAPTER 6

As time went by, I again got used to being separated from Mark and just got on with my life at Wallis cottage. I did not see as much of my brother as Uncle Bill had promised, and one day, he sat me down to tell me that my brother was moving even farther away to a new boarding school. By then, I just accepted what I was told and probably realised there was little point in showing any distress. I didn't understand what was meant by a boarding school and I didn't know I would not see my brother for quite some time. My own life at school continued to be unbearable. However, I had begun to stand up for myself, which led to many fights. I mainly fought the boys, and often those fights ended with me being punished for starting trouble. Due to the awful experience of school, I actually liked going 'home' and I even liked my special outings with Uncle Bill. I had become used to the touchy feely cuddles and mostly I enjoyed—or perhaps, more aptly, craved—the attention. Rather sad, really, but true nonetheless.

Most of the staff and many of the older children in the home smoked cigarettes, and it was not long before smoking became a deep desire of mine too. So much so that shortly after my eighth birthday, I boldly asked Uncle Bill if I could have a 'fag.' To my delight, he said yes and gave me one of his Embassy No. 6s. He made sure to remind me not to tell anyone, and of course I didn't. My first taste of nicotine was not as enjoyable as I had thought it would be. However, I soon came to love having a 'sneaky fag,' which soon progressed to not being so much of a secret as I would take to smoking with the other kids at the back of the house. In those days, children were allowed to buy cigarettes, and Uncle Bill would often send me to the shop to buy his No. 6s. I never minded, as he would always give me a couple as payment.

One evening following supper, Uncle Bill came into the lounge and motioned to me that it was time for bed. I left the lounge and went up the wooden staircase with him following behind. Upon reaching the top, he pulled me into his and Aunt Dawn's private bathroom which was directly next to the girls' dormitory. I had never been in their bathroom before, so I was rather confused and took some time to look around. When I turned around to face him, he had unzipped his trousers, exposed his penis, and was touching himself. I was rooted to the spot, as I think this was the first time I had actually seen an erect penis in the flesh. He didn't do anything to me; he just rubbed himself whilst watching me watching him. After a few minutes, he zipped himself up and told me it was time for bed, and I dutifully did as I was told. As I lay in my bed that night trying to work out what had happened, I instinctively knew things were changing from the cuddles and fondles over clothes that had been taking place.

When Lara and her sister Emily came to bed, I did not say a word to them and went to sleep. Lara slept out in the dormitory with me and the other girls. However, due to her age, Emily had her very own cubicle within the dormitory. There were two cubicles in the dormitory, and these were reserved for the older girls. Later that evening when we were sleeping, the door opened, and Uncle Bill came in. At first, I thought he was coming to tell me something as he crept up to my bed. However, he looked me in my eyes and motioned a shush as he often did. Then he walked past my bed and crept into Emily's cubicle. I don't know how long he was in there. I just remember feeling somewhat jealous and thinking I was not as special as I had thought I was after all. I heard the bed creaking but no other noises. When he came out, he again looked in my direction, motioned a shush, then left the room. The next morning, nothing was said, and we all got on with our daily lives. The abuse carried on like this for a while. I was chosen to be taken for trips out, cuddles, touching now under clothes, and watching him masturbate. Emily was his late-night chosen one for 'special' visits. While I didn't like the new turn of events, I carried on colluding with the secret as I didn't really feel I had a choice, and I also liked the treats and special attention that came with it.

On one occasion, having followed Uncle Bill into his bathroom, he got my hands and put them both around his erect penis. I tried to pull them away as I didn't like the feel of it, but he just held on tightly to both of my little hands and used them to pleasure himself. When he ejaculated, I remember thinking 'yuck,' and could not wait to get away from him. By now, I did realise what we were doing was wrong; however, I felt I was just as much to blame, and I also felt guilty about taking sweets and cigarettes as payment. I know now this is exactly how he wanted me to feel. I had been groomed to believe that I was in collusion and a willing partner, as opposed to an abused child who really didn't have a choice. I was a vulnerable little girl who desperately craved love and attention, and Uncle Bill used—or should I say abused—his position of power to get me exactly where he wanted me. By now, I wasn't jealous of Emily any longer as I knew something else was happening to her and I didn't want 'IT' to happen to me, whatever 'IT' was. I did not even really like the cuddles anymore as I had begun to realise that it was not genuine affection, and I knew he would always expect something from me in return. In any case, the abuse carried on like this and I simply just got used to it.

It was the summer of 1978 when staff called us into the dayroom, as it was called, to tell us that we were all going on a holiday to Devon. We were all so excited by this news. It was my first ever holiday, and this was a big event. We were packed into a big bus with food and supplies, and we made the long trip from Hornchurch to Devon, which is in the south of England. It was a very hot summer, and the journey was long and tiring. When we arrived in Devon, we were all given jobs to do like unloading the bus, packing the food away, and helping to make the beds in the cabin we were staying in. Thereafter, we all went for a long walk in the beautiful Devonshire countryside. We were bought ice lollies, and my favourite was a Cherry Brandy as it was so sweet and tasted so good. For the most part, the holiday was great fun as Uncle Bill didn't trouble me, and the long summer days were spent swimming in a river and playing in the countryside. It was rather blissful, really. I had my friends Lara and Emily, and we loved playing a game called Cat's Cradle and seeing who could make the longest daisy chains. Oh, and of course, sneaking off to smoke cigarettes. My smoking had now become a regular habit, and not one adult ever reprimanded or attempted to stop me.

Towards the end of the holiday, we were taken to a local fairground, which had been so much fun until one of the older boys, Wayne, sat next to me on the waltzers. I was whirling around, shrieking with delight, and having the best time, until suddenly Wayne turned a greenish/yellowish colour and proceeded to vomit all over me. He did try to say sorry. However, I was not happy and felt decidedly sick myself. Wayne vomiting all over me ended our trip to the fair, and we all went back to the cabin. The other kids were angry with Wayne, and even with me for spoiling their fun. I am not sure if it was the last night or the night before the last night. Anyway, I remember staff saying to the older kids they were going to play a special game, but that we younger children were not allowed to join in. I was not happy to be excluded from the game and I did not want to go to bed. However, I didn't have any choice. We were all staying in the same cabin, so while I was not allowed to join in the 'game,' I was able to see and hear what was taking place from my bunk bed.

Prior to this night, I had never heard of a Ouija board and didn't know what it entailed; however, I was curious. The staff and the older kids all sat together in a circle and started chanting words and saying things I didn't understand. They had their hands on a glass and it seemed to be moving on the table that they were huddled around. Suddenly, and I will never know how, the glass flew into the air and smashed to the ground. This sent the kids into a panic. Some screamed, and others even started crying. In the pandemonium, one of the older kids, Andrew, who was about sixteen at the time, dropped to the floor and started having what seemed to be like an epileptic fit. He was writhing around on the ground, shaking, and mumbling strange sounds. In absolute, total fear, I was transfixed and could not help but stare at him in abject terror. When I looked at him rolling around and moaning on the floor, I saw what looked like frothing foam around his mouth, and blood (or what I thought was blood) seeping down his chin. Most of the kids were screaming, and the staff were standing over him in a panic, reciting the Lord's Prayer. Suddenly, Andrew abruptly sat up and burst out laughing. All along, he had been pretending to be taken over by an evil spirit and the supposed blood was most likely trick blood or food colouring. I was absolutely petrified and started screaming and crying. Staff tried to calm me down, saying it was just a joke, but I think I just went into some sort of hyperventilation mode. My fear and resulting behaviour just made Andrew laugh even harder, as he had achieved the desired effect of scaring the living daylights out of everyone, especially me. That was the end of the game and as if nothing had happened, they all went to bed. That night I did not, or should I say could not, sleep, and this was the start of Andrew's campaign of terror over me.

Upon discovering I was a scaredy cat, Andrew had found an outlet to satisfy his need to terrorise, and bedtimes took on a new kind of fear and anxiety for me. Not only did I have to contend with Uncle Bill's sexual demands, but I was now also terrorised by Andrew on a regular basis. One of his favourite ways to scare me was to wait until Uncle Bill had finished and had gone away. Then, as I was laying in my bed, I would hear slow, deliberate, thudding footsteps approaching my dormitory. Andrew would appear at the door with eyelids turned over, revealing just the whites. He would stare blankly ahead and stalk slowly towards my bed in a zombie type fashion. He must have known what Uncle Bill was up to and he totally ignored the rule that boys were not allowed in the dormitory. He was allowed to get away with it, and I was to find out why he was able to later on. To say I was terrified is an understatement, and Andrew knew this, as I would scream out in terror and plead with him to stop. My begging and pleading would cause him to dissolve into fits of laughter as he ran away before anyone caught him in the act. By the time staff came to see what all the racket was about, he was gone, and I was told to stop crying and go to sleep. There was no comfort for me or any reprimanding of Andrew.

I did try to tell Uncle Bill what Andrew was doing to me in the hope he would maybe protect me. However, he would also just laugh and say that Andrew was only joking and that I was not to take him so seriously. It was at this point that I began to really despise Uncle Bill as I realised he didn't really care about me, because if he did, he would have put a stop to Andrew's behaviour. As Andrew was one of the older teenagers in the home, he had his own cubicle in the boys' dormitory. One day when I was going upstairs to get something from my dormitory, I saw Haydn Davies, the senior support worker, coming out of the boys' dormitory with Andrew. They were whispering and giggling with each other. When they caught sight of me, they both looked at me slyly, and it was obvious something was going on between them. This was most likely why Andrew almost had rule of the roost. (Well, at least over us younger kids, that is.) The funny thing was, I had also seen Haydn and Aunt Dawn in similar sorts of huddles and collusions, so I was confused. I mean, what the hell was going on in this place?

It was not until a few months after Christmas 1978 that I saw my father again. One day, Uncle Bill said, "You have someone coming to see you," and when I asked who, he said, "It is a surprise." It was the weekend, so shortly after lunch, I was called into the staff office. As I walked in, I heard a familiar deep voice. It was my father sitting in the office talking with Uncle Bill. I was so pleased to see him. Even though life had been horrible when I had lived with him and I had been emotionally and physically harmed, he was my family, and I was happy and somewhat relieved that he was there. Uncle Bill said, "Your father is taking you out for a bit, but only if you want to go, that is." I am not sure why he gave me the choice, and I sensed that Uncle Bill did not like my father. In any case, I said, "Yes, Uncle Bill, it's my dad and I want to go with him. Please let me go." And with that, we walked out of the office, my small fingers clutching tightly onto my father's big hand.

My father took me to a Wimpy burger bar that was in town, and while we were eating hamburgers and fries, he asked me if I liked living at St. Leonard's. I did not tell him about Uncle Bill's sexual abuse or Andrew's reign of terror. I just said I missed Mark. I asked him where he had been and where my mother was. He sighed and said sadly that he hadn't been allowed to see me and that he didn't know where my mother was. By now, my longing for my mother's return had become an all-consuming fantasy that I often took to daydreaming about. In my fantasy, my mother told me that she loved me, that she was sorry, and that she would never ever leave me again. The more I fantasised, the surer I became that someday she would come back. When my father took me back to the 'home' a few hours later, he promised he would come back and see me soon. He also said that I might be able to visit Mark with him as well. I was happy that day because it reminded me that I did have some family and some family was better than none. Some of the children in the home didn't have any parents at all and no one ever came to visit them, so in many ways I was fortunate. When my father left, Uncle Bill called me into the office and quizzed me about my trip out with him. He asked me if I had been good. I really didn't know what he meant, but I think he was asking if I told my father about 'our' secret. I said, "Yes, Uncle Bill, I was good." He seemed satisfied with my answer and pulled me onto his lap and cuddled me and encouraged me to fondle him. By then I had become used to this and just did as he wanted. Afterwards, I received my usual treat of a Mars bar, a packet of crisps, and a couple of fags.

Following that first visit, my father came back every two weeks and he was allowed to take me out for a few hours on each occasion. On one visit, he said he was going to take me to see Mark at his boarding school soon, and I was overjoyed at the prospect of seeing my brother again. On the day of the visit, my father collected me early from St. Leonard's and we went by train to Newbury, Berkshire, to see Mark. I was so excited on the train. However, when we got there, Mark refused point-blank to see us. He ran away from the room that staff at his school had brought him to, and I was so upset as I could hardly recognise my brother.

He seemed detached and was either scared of our father or just did not want to see him. In any case, when we left the boarding school without the happy reunion I had been anticipating, I felt sad and deflated. I had been so looking forward to seeing my brother and I did not know when I would see him again. My father did not really talk to me on the journey back, preferring to sit in silence drinking a can of Special Brew, the extra strong lager that was a favourite of his for many years. He returned me to the home, said goodbye, and left, leaving me feeling sad, lonely, and once again, bereft.

Uncle Bill tried to ask me about my day out with my father. However, I did not want to talk about it. He tried to cuddle me and for once, I resisted, and I don't think he could quite believe my defiance. He didn't force the point; however, he did say he didn't think my father was a good influence upon me and that they might have to review my trips out with him, especially if I was going to be naughty when I returned. Even at the age of nine, I knew this was a thinly veiled threat, and it left me feeling scared that I would never see my father or my brother again. So, later that evening, when Uncle Bill said it was my bedtime and motioned for me to follow him into his bathroom, I did so without any resistance. He knew exactly how to control me, and he abused the power he held over me every chance he could. Little did I know, another prolonged separation from my father was about to happen anyway, and there would be nothing I could do about it.

Following the failed visit with Mark, I slipped back into my life at St. Leonard's. I started to notice that some of the young people in Wallis and the other cottages seemed to be lifeless and zombie-like in their behaviours. They had blank, dead eyes and spotty mouths, and I did not understand why for a long time. I also noticed empty crisp packets and plastic bags strewn around doorways and in places where we would go to smoke on the quiet. One such day when I sneaked off for a fag, I found out why the young people were acting so weirdly. It turned out they were glue sniffing, and I soon came to realise that many young people were being taken over by this addiction, which was rampant in the '70s and the '80s. Thankfully, I did not like the smell of the glue, and I also did not like the way it made the young people act. I had become very close to my friend Caroline that I mentioned earlier, who had come to the home after me. Caroline was a few years older than me and was also a glue sniffer. This did not faze me because I loved her. Although rather bossy, she was genuinely kind and loving towards me and often warned me about the dangers of glue sniffing. One day, some staff members sat us down to inform us that a teenage boy in another cottage had died. It was unknown whether it was an intentional act of suicide or an accident due to him being high on glue. They said he had been sniffing glue on the roof of one of the buildings on The Drive and that he had fallen off or jumped. Whatever the case, it was enough to scare me, and thankfully I never had any desire to sniff or inhale the stinking stuff myself.

Andrew continued his terror of me and not one member of staff ever attempted to stop him. Softer members of staff turned a blind eye as they did with everything else, and I think other senior members of staff such as Bill, Dawn, and Haydn got a kick out of my fear, as they would either laugh or tell me to stop being a baby. It only stopped when Caroline and another older boy in the home finally intervened to take care of me. Caroline was a loud and gobby young teenager. She was a skinhead in those days and acted as if she was full of confidence. When she was placed in St. Leonard's, she instantly took a liking to me and would spend hours combing my frizzy afro hair. My hair grew wild and was seemingly unmanageable for the staff, or they just couldn't be bothered. Caroline, however, was bothered, and prior to her taking an interest in caring for my wild head of hair, I was often taken to the home's inhouse barbers to have my hair shorn like a sheep. I hated being taken for a haircut as I always left in tears, looking like a boy. Despite their efforts to tame my hair, they never succeeded, as my hair grew thick and fast. Fortunately, Caroline's efforts and loving attention did somewhat tame my frizzy curls, so I was taken less frequently for a shearing. The children in school continued to make fun of me and would often find new names to call me, such as Hair Bear Bunch after the 1970s cartoon from Hanna-Barbera, and another favourite was Golliwog. When Caroline combed my hair, I felt like someone actually cared and that my hair was not as ugly as everyone thought it was after all. She was very caring and was always in my corner, like a much-needed older sister. Andrew could see this and while he and Caroline seemed friendly, he was wary of her.

However, it was an older boy called Paul who finally put a stop to Andrew. Paul was about Andrew's age, and they were archenemies. Paul was Mod in those days. Many young people were mods, skinheads, or rockers—well, young white people, that is. He was fastidious about his appearance and always seemed to be moody. However, with me, he was playful. He used to enjoy picking me up, tickling me, and calling me "Titch." I always enjoyed his attention as he made me laugh and it was fun. Such was the twisted pleasure Andrew got from scaring me, he simply could not stop and had taken to using every opportune moment to inflict fear upon me. He would walk past me, stop and stare, and turn his eyes inside out, and when I made a sound, froze, or begged him to stop, he would dissolve into laughter. One day, Paul and I had been playing in the innocent manner that we did when Andrew walked past us and took the opportunity when Paul's back was turned to fix his stare. As I froze in fear, Paul must have had enough, as he walked over to Andrew, told him to stop being a "fucking nonce" and knocked him clean out. Andrew was too much of a wimp to stand up to Paul, and he would not have stood a chance against him in any case. Being an amateur boxer at the time, Paul was tall, strong, and fit, the exact opposite of Andrew, who was short, puny, and spineless. He was visibly scared of Paul and retreated fast with a bloody nose and a broken spirit. I was overjoyed at my protector, and even though Paul was punished by Haydn and Dawn, he didn't care. He made sure Andrew knew not to ever come near me again, and after that, he never did.

Even though I knew Caroline and Paul were in my corner, I never said a word to either of them about Uncle Bill's abuse of me. I have often wondered why we kids did not speak between ourselves about the abuse from the staff. We just never did. It was just after Christmas 1979 when we were told we would be moving out of Wallis for two weeks and into Forbes cottage. Whereas the other cottages were evenly spaced from each other, Forbes was at the very end of The Drive and stood alone. The reason for the move was that Wallis was going to be redecorated. Forbes was rumoured to be haunted and I was not happy at the thought of having to sleep there. Due to Andrew's terrorising of me, I was very much fearful of the dark, and my fear was exacerbated through the watching of a TV series called *Armchair Thriller*. This was a popular TV show at the time, and it was often centred around scary houses and shadowy ghostlike figures. However, we had no choice. The move took place, and I could hardly sleep during that period. When the time came for us to move back to the newly redecorated Wallis, I was over the moon and very happy. The morning I left Forbes cottage for school, I could not wait for the day to end as I knew I was going back to Wallis cottage, and the fear of Forbes would be over.

That evening when the yellow bus dropped me off, I ran into Wallis through the side door, as we children were rarely allowed to use the front door unless we were with our social worker or other adults. I was eager to see to how Wallis had been redecorated, although I really do not know why I was so excited and can only conclude that as awful as the place was, it was my home. As I ran into the hallway, I was slightly disappointed to see the walls had been repainted the same magnolia colour as they had been previously, although they did look a lot brighter. I was just about to run up the stairs to have a look at our dormitory when I noticed the lace of my shoe was undone. As I bent down to tie my lace, I heard Haydn Davies's loud voice boom, "What do you think you are doing, girl?" He mostly called me girl and hardly ever called me by name. I feared Haydn, as I knew he didn't like me and he had a sinister, creepy air about him. Also, he was in Andrew's corner. In fear, I stammered, "I ... I ... am tying my laces, Haydn." We were allowed to call the other staff members by their first names. He roared, "Don't lie to me, girl!" and proceeded to slap me five or six times around my legs and once around my face. The slaps were so hard he left his large handprint with a ring indentation on my thigh. I started crying, which only enraged him further. His face turned red with anger and his eyes were bulging. In his rage, he shouted at me, saying I was ungrateful and naughty. I had no idea what he meant. Then he explained. He said, "You got what you deserved for doing handstands up the walls." So once again, I was being accused of something I didn't do and being assaulted for it.

I was so frightened of Haydn that I didn't dare challenge him. Instead, I made my way to my dormitory, the excitement I had felt earlier suitably slapped out of me. I laid down on my bed and cried my eyes out. I think it was at these times I felt my loneliest and saddest. It was times like these I would especially yearn for my mother, or any mother, to take me in her arms, soothe me, and tell me all will be okay. That soothing reassurance never came and would only ever remain a figment of my imagination. I think with Christmas rapidly approaching, I was also very aware that this was the time my mother had abandoned me, and this compounded my feelings of sadness and loneliness. Such was the force of the beating, my thigh ached, and when I woke in the morning, it was red and swollen and the ring Haydn wore had left a welt mark on my leg. I think he must have been worried as he avoided me the next morning. It could also have been because my father was due to visit to take me out for a few hours.

When my father collected me, he took me to the Wimpy burger bar restaurant as he usually did. I was so subdued, I couldn't eat, and he could see I was upset. He asked me if I was okay, and as he did, I started crying. He asked me what was wrong, but I couldn't say. Instead, I lifted my skirt and showed him my leg. He was livid and demanded to know who had hit me. Sobbing, I mumbled, "Haydn said I was doing handstands on the walls, and really I wasn't, but he didn't believe me." Having told my father, I was scared to go back. Even though my father had also been abusive when I had lived with him and Anne, this had been more out of his lack of understanding, ignorance, and poor parental capacity. The abuse I was suffering in St. Leonard's was far more sinister, as these were people entrusted to care for vulnerable children, and I was powerless to stop it. Somehow, I knew telling my father was not going to have a positive outcome and I begged him not to take me back. He didn't say why he had to take me, he just did, and he did so in a stony silence.

Upon reaching Wallis cottage, my father stormed through the front door, demanding to know where Haydn was. I pleaded with him to stop shouting as I feared the consequences. However, he was so angry, he ignored me. Uncle Bill came to see what the commotion was and said, "You need to calm down, Mr. Hylton." However, my father would not calm down and demanded to see Haydn, saying that he had hit me and marked my legs. At this point, a cowering and shameful Haydn came out to face my father. As soon as my father saw him, he stormed up to him and punched him in the face. All hell broke loose, and some staff started screaming, "Call the police! Call the police!" When the police arrived, they arrested my father. When my father tried explaining why he had hit Haydn, the police did not want to listen to him. I was distraught and once again traumatised at seeing my father being taken away in a black Mariah police van. I did not see my father again for many months after this incident.

Today, if an incident such as this occurred within a residential children's home, the child's social worker would be duty bound to visit the child and ascertain the circumstances. The staff member would most likely be suspended whilst the matter was investigated. However, Mrs. Lincoln, my social worker, did not visit me until about two weeks after my father had been arrested. By then, Haydn had admitted to a light tap to get my legs off the freshly painted walls, although this was a complete lie as I had not been doing a handstand in the first place and he had beat me with his hands so hard he had marked me. Mrs. Lincoln did not want to know why my father had punched Haydn. Instead, she told me it was not only his job to look after me but that it was also his responsibility to make sure I behaved myself. She went on and on about the newly decorated children's home and that I should respect 'my home,' not try to ruin it. Any attempts of mine to explain the truth simply fell upon her seemingly deaf ears.

Mrs. Lincoln went on to say that my father was in a lot of trouble as violent behaviour is not acceptable, and that I would not be able to see him for a while. She also said that when I did, he would not be able to take me out, because he might hurt me, and she emphasised "like he did before." I felt desolate, crushed, scared, and alone, by now all too familiar feelings. Mrs. Lincoln didn't say when I would see my father and seemed in a hurry to get away. She left me with my thoughts to go and speak with Uncle Bill and Aunt Dawn in the office. They sat huddling and talking about what they called my mad black brute of a father. Uncle Bill and Aunt Dawn fawned over Mrs. Lincoln, and she gave them far too much appreciation for the 'care they provided us poor, unfortunate children.' Upon finishing her cup of tea, she said goodbye and left. As soon as she left, Aunt Dawn and Haydn looked at me with evil dark eyes and walked off together. It was Uncle Bill who sought me out to offer his support in the usual form of cuddles, and then up the wooden stairs to his bathroom, closing the door and unzipping his trousers. By now, the abuse had progressed to me having to kiss IT, which I absolutely detested but had no power to refuse. For a while, I was sure I was never going to see my father or brother ever again.

CHAPTER 7

Sometime towards the end of 1980, my contact with my father resumed. After a while, he was again allowed to come to pick me up and take me out. By then, he was driving a transit van and he would drive up to the home and wait outside for me. He never came into the home after the 'Haydn incident,' and I don't know if this was his choice or if he was just not allowed to. I didn't ask as I was simply happy to be able to see my father again. When he arrived, staff would shout out, "Diana, your father's outside," and I would run out and get into his van. As time went by, my father was allowed to take me to his house every other weekend, and I was so happy to be able to stay away from the home.

Often during these weekends, my father would take me to his house and tell me to watch TV before leaving, saying he would be back later. He would then go out until the early hours of the morning. I never told the staff that my father often left me on my own because I was scared they would stop me from going home for weekends with him. My father also took me to see Mark on occasion, and while Mark often created a scene at having to see my father, he did want to see me, and I remember some happy occasions spent playing in the grounds of his boarding school. I had missed my brother and I was so very glad to be seeing him again. While my father was not a cuddly or demonstrative sort of man, I was happy to have a father and I was glad I could leave the home every other weekend to go to what I would fantasise about being my 'real' home. Although, my father 's house was not homely by any stretch of the imagination, and the black and white TV was disappointing, given that I had become used to the luxury of a colour TV. However, it was free from the perverted and persistent sexual demands I endured at the mercy of Uncle Bill. While I did not know it at the time, I do believe Uncle Bill must have been wary of my father and of pushing me too far. He did seem confident in the fact that I was not telling my father about our 'secret,' but he must have also been cautious just in case. While he frequently took pleasure in what he called "cuddling" and "special kissing," he did not take it any further, thank God.

It was 1982 and I was approaching twelve, when one day, I was taken by staff to a meeting which was attended by various professionals, none of whom I knew apart from Mrs. Lincoln. They all sat around a large table, and when I entered the room, I was motioned to sit next to my social worker. They proceeded to ask me questions, such as what I did when I went for home visits with my father. Did I enjoy these visits? And finally, would I be happy to go and live with my father again? To which I answered, "Yes, I want to live with my dad." Shortly after this meeting, I was visited by Mrs. Lincoln and was informed that I would soon be leaving St. Leonard's for good and going to live with my father. I could hardly believe it. I asked her about Mark, and she said he would not be joining me. She did not say why. At the time, I was happy just to know that I was leaving St. Leonard's forever, and while it did seem rather hasty, I was not going to complain. At the time, I did not know that all the staff were under scrutiny, and that St. Leonard's would officially close its doors in 1984. When the time came for me to return to my father's care, no fuss was made about my leaving. During the planning for my return to my father's care, Uncle Bill abruptly stopped his abuse of me and hardly paid any attention to me at all. I did not care, as I was happy to be leaving. The day my father collected me for the last time, I ran out of the doors with not even as much as a backward glance.

Shortly after leaving St. Leonard's, I plucked up the courage to tell my father about Bill Starling and the sexual abuse. He was so angry and demanded to know why I had not told him at the time. He did not understand that I had been scared and groomed into not telling anyone. Contrary to my wishes, he contacted Mrs. Lincoln, who was still my social worker, and insisted she come to visit. A few days later, she came to the house and my father told me to tell her what had happened. Even then, I struggled to find the right words and was painfully embarrassed, so I simply said, "Uncle Bill used to do sex things and he made me do sex things to him." To this, she sighed with deep exasperation, rolled her eyes, and said, "Diana, you must try to settle with your father and focus on your fresh start. This is what YOU wanted, after all." And that was that.

The joy I had felt at being returned home was short-lived. At the time, my father was a strict and domineering man who was then, and remains today, obsessed with his favourite pastimes, which are womanising, drinking copious amounts of alcohol, and listening to soul music. He did not know how to openly demonstrate affection, and I don't think he even realised the impact this was having upon my already significantly harmed emotional development. He demanded I take over the housework, something I did not have to do when I lived at St. Leonard's. While I detested it with a passion, saying no to my father was not an option. He also made it very clear that I was not to tell anyone about my past and was to say to anyone who queried that I had been living with an aunt. I was not, under any circumstances, allowed to say I had been in a children's home or tell anyone about the abuse. So, there began another period in my life that would be marked with secrets and an ever-increasing sense of shame and feelings of unworthiness.

Shortly after my return to my father's care, I started at Ruckholt Manor, the school I would attend for the next year. At the time, my father was reliant upon state benefits and needed financial assistance to purchase my school uniform. Suffice to say that my uniform was the cheapest and, in my view, ugly. It was not at all fashionable like the clothes of many of my peers. I also was acutely aware that most if not all of the children had a mother who loved them. If there was another motherless child in the school, I did not know of them, and this reinforced my feelings of loneliness, pain, and despair. Many a night I would cry myself to sleep, longing for my mother to come and rescue me. Although she never did, the longing did not stop, and I began to make excuses for her abandonment, such as she must be very ill, or perhaps even dead. Thinking like this made the truth just a little easier to bear. My school days at Ruckholt Manor were only slightly more bearable than they had been at Wickham. While the school was far more multicultural and racism was not as prevalent, my clothes and boyish haircut made me stand out, and again I became a target for name calling and ridicule. Due to joining the school after my peers, close friendships and clicks had already been formed. I was not popular, nor was I accepted by the 'IN' crowds who wore the desired designer brand clothes of the '80s, such as Pringle, Lyle & Scott, Sergio Tacchini, and Fila or Adidas trainers. The best trainers I managed were a pair of Zephyrs or Adidas two-stripes, as they were called, very much to the other kids' amusement.

In his strictness, my father imposed some bizarre rules, one of which was that I was not allowed to have black friends. Although he had many black male friends, he was adamant and extremely vocal that he would not date a black woman. He was also of the view that black kids would negatively influence me and lead me astray. I was far too embarrassed to ever tell anyone about my father's views for fear of even more ridicule. In my attempts to make friends, I did become close to a black girl named Gina. She really liked me and wanted us to be best friends. As I had not told her about my father's incomprehensible views, she could not understand why I would act in such a panic when walking home from school with her. The reason for my fear was in case he saw me walking with her. One day my fears were realised, and he did see me walking with Gina. He went mental, ordering me away from her and scolding me for my disobedience. Upon discovering my father's perplexing racist attitude, a strain was put on my friendship with Gina as she was understandably offended and confused. I could not explain his reasoning as I did not understand it either. Thereafter, I began to find it easier to be a loner and not attempt to build friendships. However, this only served to further increase my feelings of depression, loneliness, and low self-esteem. I was becoming tired of the seemingly never-ending battle of life.

My father, in his passion for womanising, would religiously scour the lonely-hearts columns, as they were referred to, in the weekly local newspapers of the early '80s such as *Loot* and *Yellow Advertiser*. Before the internet and social media dating sites such as Tinder and Plenty of Fish, this was the way singles met. He would also frequent single parent organised get togethers, often dragging me along. He had a constant stream of woman friends. Some I liked, and some I loathed. If I ever got close to any of the women he dated, he would invariably end up cheating on them, resulting in them dumping him. It was 1983, and he was dating a lovely woman named Deirdre. For a while, it felt like I had a female in my life whom I could trust, who liked me and wanted to look after me. She was kind and caring and really seemed to love my father. We would spend weekends at her home in Dagenham, Essex, and I would look forward to these days. She had children who were older than me, and she was motherly in her approach. However, this brief but warm and fuzzy time did not last long.

One Friday evening, my father and I caught the 148 bus to go to Deirdre's house. In those days, his fashion sense had not quite left the '70s (much to my embarrassment), and he liked to wear a Stetson (cowboy) hat and flared trousers that were called Jumbo Boeing 747s, after the aeroplane's wide wings. He did not care that he stood out a mile away in his non-inconspicuous outfits. The Stetson hat was fairly outlandish for a black man in East London in the early '80s. It was on this bus journey to Dagenham that three skinhead youths got on. As soon as they spotted my father, they shouted to one another, "Look, there's J.R. gone down a coal mine," and with that they roared with laughter at their own wit. This was in reference to J.R. Ewing, a major character from the popular '80s US soap *Dallas*. It was an extremely cringeworthy moment, making him angry and making me want the ground to open and swallow me whole. Just as I thought it couldn't get any worse, when we got to Deirdre's, she told him it was over and that he was not welcome in her home anymore. I don't know the exact details of his infidelity; I just know she had enough of him and ended it with him on her doorstep, with me forlornly in tow. She did not even say sorry to me or even consider how I felt at being scorned alongside him. However, on reflection, she was not my mother, so why should she feel sorry for me? The journey back to Leytonstone was sombre, and I vowed I would never get close to any of his 'floozies' again.

Not having a positive and loving female influence in my life profoundly impacted my adolescence in many ways. It was difficult not having a woman to talk to about female issues, and this became even more apparent on the day I started my period. The subject of menstruation had been briefly touched upon in school, and although I was naive around the subject, I instinctively knew it was something to do with developing into a woman. When my first period came, I was too embarrassed to tell my father. So, I went across the road to a neighbour who my father was friendly with and told her that I thought I might have started my period. She was very kind, gave me some sanitary towels, and then took me back over to my father's house and told him. He didn't say anything kind or nurturing, just that I had to now make sure all my underwear was washed by hand as 'dirty knickers' could never be put in the washing machine. This was most confusing, as if only clean underwear was allowed.

During my adolescence, my pleasure and passions were found in reading and music. My father, being a keen music lover, had bought me a radio/tape recorder on which I was able to record the Top 40. Every Sunday, I would sit alone in my bedroom making tapes of songs from my favourite groups such as Wham!, Soft Cell, and The Human League. Music, alongside reading, was my saviour. I found I could lose myself in both. I was an avid fan of Judy Blume and James Hadley Chase books and would often spend my weekends in Leytonstone Library. In the '80s, the British education system operated a four-tier level of state general education. After infant and junior school, children went to a middle school and then finally, a senior school. Therefore, I was only at Ruckholt for just over a year when I moved up to Leyton Senior High for Girls. I was thirteen years old and had given up on the notion of attending school to learn. I had never fit in, and I continued to feel alienated from my peers. With puberty in full swing, I also became increasingly depressed about my life thus far, especially as I now had to contend with my father's overbearing strictness. He would demand I come straight home from school and clean the house. If I was late, he would go into a frenzy, shouting that I had to show respect and adhere to his rules. This meant he would get angry if I was only just slightly later than the perceived time he thought it should take me to walk the less-than-a-mile journey home. Other kids would have money to spend in the local shop and were allowed to hang out for a while before going home. I always had to make up excuses as to why I couldn't stay behind, why I never had any money for the shop, why I couldn't go to other kids' houses, and why I didn't have a mother. I was forever cleaning, had no nice clothes or belongings, and I hated my life because it sucked.

At the end of the school day, it was not always easy to just walk away from the other kids, and sometimes they would offer to buy me sweets at the shop. On one occasion, I decided to risk being late and my father's wrath to hang about after school. I thought, as long as I was not too late, the shouting would be worth it. Anyway, I must have lost myself in the mucking around because I suddenly realised that I was two hours late. Knowing my father would go mad, I hastily said goodbye to the kids I was hanging about with, and I ran home as fast as I could. When I burst into the house, it was clear my father was angered by my deliberate defiance, so without thinking, I said it wasn't my fault and proceeded to say the first thing that came into my head. I told my father I had been scared, as an old man had pulled me into some bushes and flashed his 'thing' at me. I said I had managed to get away from him, but had been scared to walk home in case he found me, so I hid in some other bushes for a while until I was sure that he had gone. It was the only thing I could think of as a diversion from what I had really been doing, which was simply playing with the other kids. Anyway, it worked, as my father's anger quickly dissipated as he quizzed me about what had happened. He called the police, who came to the house to take a statement from me. I thought back to Bill Starling's abuse and did not feel bad about lying, as I had done it to save myself. I mean, it wasn't as if anyone was going to get into trouble. What I didn't realise was that years later, I would be forced to admit that I had in fact lied about this incident. However, for now I was just relieved that I had escaped from being in trouble with my father.

Shortly afterwards, I took to regularly truanting from school. I had no interest in learning and I could not see the point of going. I preferred to spend my days bunking off (as it was called) with my new friend Sally. I had become friends with Sally through our shared experience of not having a mother present in our lives. She did see her mother, but their relationship was strained due to her mother having left her and her brothers with their father to live with another man. Sally and I also took to shoplifting, and we found it easy to stock up on things such as books, magazines, chocolate, and stationery—the things that previously, neither of us could afford. My life at home was much more bearable with my beloved books and chocolate. After a fun day of bunking off school, I would stay up late into the night, reading Judy Blume and Sweet Valley High books. This provided a much-needed escape into another world alongside the pleasure dopamine that the soothing chocolate provided, and it is no exaggeration to say I ate copious amounts of it. However, the fun was soon put to a stop when my father received a letter inviting him to my school to discuss my persistent nonattendance and lack of progress. He was livid and demanded to know what I had been doing, where, and with whom. In my fear, I just cried and babbled that I didn't know. On the day of the meeting, I was petrified, as I knew my father was about to find out that lately I almost never went to school, and I feared what my punishment would be for lying. Oddly, he didn't really do anything aside from shouting, which I was used to anyway, and said that I would not be allowed to walk myself to and from school anymore. Despite this new and embarrassing regime, he could not always collect me, and on these days, I would be firmly warned that I was to go straight home. After a few weeks, he stopped collecting me and I happily went back to bunking off school.

My friendship with Sally continued and we became rather brazen with our shoplifting sprees. For a while it was so easy, as one of us would be lookout while the other stuffed items up our jumpers and inside our bags. We took it in turns and would hide our loot behind community bins, then go back to stock up on our much-needed goodies. Of course, our luck ran out. One day as we were leaving the local branch of Woolworths, laughing, joking, and feeling rich with our stash, we felt a firm pair of hands on each of our shoulders, pulling us back inside the shop. We tried to get away, but the burly security guard was having none of it and he was assisted in his detainment of us by another of the store workers. Upon his suspicions being confirmed that we had been shoplifting from the store for some time, he promptly called the police and thereafter, our fathers were called to collect us. My father was enraged with the shame that he perceived I was bringing upon him. As soon as we got home, he dropped the bombshell that I would not be allowed to hang around with Sally anymore, as she was also a bad influence now in his view. So alongside being prohibited from having black friends, I was now being told I was not allowed to keep the best friend I had ever had. Well, I was most certainly not going to let this happen and planned to get away from my miserable existence with my father as soon as I could. Throughout that night, I worked on my plan of escape and how I would persuade Sally to come with me. Over the next few days, we went to school because at least we could talk to each other there, and we continued to hatch a plan to run away from our fathers.

On the day of our 'escape,' Sally and I met at the school gates and made a run for it. I mean, at that time in the morning, no one was expecting us to run away, so there was no need to physically run, but run we did. In our naivety, we had decided we would try to get as far away as we could, find jobs, and get a place to live. I mean, at our age this was unrealistic, but it was our plan, and we were determined to follow through. I had managed to steal £30 from my father and Sally had also stolen some money from hers. We were rich, free, and happy. We wanted to get as far away as possible and thought that hitchhiking would provide us with the means to get out of London. We thought nothing of the risk to our safety, took a bus to Gants Hill and the A12 on the Eastern Avenue, and proceeded to stick our thumbs out in anticipation of our adventure. It was not long before a lorry pulled over and the male driver leaned out of the passenger window and beckoned us to get in. We were not scared at all, as we were pleased that our great escape was going to plan.

Upon climbing into the cab of the lorry, the man said, "Hello, girls. I'm Jim. What are your names and where are you going?" We had no idea how old he was. However, he looked friendly and was warm and approachable in his manner. We told him our names and said we were leaving London, that we would go where he was going and see where it took us. In those days, the exploitation of children and young people was not talked about as it is today. So, when Jim asked how old we were and we told him sixteen, we did not even think to question whether he believed us, which of course he didn't. When he asked if we had other clothes to put on beside our school uniforms, in unison we said, "Of course," and with that he told us to get in the back of his cab and get changed. His cab was large and roomy enough for us to get out of our uniforms and we did so, giggling and marvelling at how easy our escape was turning out to be. Jim was funny and he showed us how to use his CB radio. Thereafter, we spent the following hours making up our own CB names or handles, as they were called, and talking to other truckers. As evening approached, Jim asked if we were hungry. Upon us nodding, he stopped at a motorway café and bought us each a burger, chips, and a can of coke. No one in the café batted an eye at this older man with two young girls in tow. It was getting late when we got back on the road, and I have no idea where we were when Jim said he needed to lay down in his cab for a rest. He asked if we were okay with him having a sleep, and then early in the morning, we would get on the move again. We didn't really have a choice, so we nodded in agreement with his plan.

Jim had a bed in the back of his cab and curtains separating the cab from the driving area. He got into the back, pulled the curtains across, and left us in the front. After a while, he said, "Which one of you lovely girls would like to come and give me a cuddle?" Sally was more apprehensive than me and said, "No." I didn't say anything. To this, Jim said that he was tired, lonely, and just needed a nice cuddle, so I eventually agreed. I clambered into the back of the cab and laid next to him on the bed. For a while he just hugged me, and this was, in many ways, something I had been used to: an old man asking for and giving me affection. After a while, he kissed me on the mouth and then he took my hand and placed it on his erect penis. A familiar feeling washed over me as I instinctively knew what he wanted, and to my shame, with his guidance, I fondled him. He didn't attempt to take it further and appeared happy with my co-operation. Sally stayed in the front of the cab, not saying a word. Thereafter, we laid in the bed, him cuddling me and me hoping he wasn't going to want anything more. When he went to sleep, I got back in the front with Sally, and we sat huddled together, waiting for the dawn to break.

Early the next morning, he woke and said cheerily, "Girls, it's time for us to be on the move," and with that, he pulled his clothes on and jumped into the driving seat. We had no idea where we were going, and he obviously knew we did not have any plans other than escaping. So, when he said we would stop for some breakfast before moving on with 'our' journey, we just went along with him. Many miles later and as the next night drew in, Jim asked if we both wanted to sleep in his cab with him. Sally and I looked at each other and he must have sensed our now growing wariness as he said, "Well, if you want to have a wash and sleep in a bed, I could get us all a nice room. What do you think?" I think we must have been relieved and in unison, we said, "Yes, please." When we stopped at a bed and breakfast that Jim decided we would stay at, he turned and said, "Girls, I am going to book us a room and will come and let you know when you can come in." We thought nothing of this and agreed to wait for him in his truck. When he came back, he said the room was ready and we were to go straight up.

As we walked into the bed and breakfast, we saw the proprietor looking at us in a quizzical manner. As Jim ushered us up the stairs and into the room, we started to get really scared and vowed to each other that we would sleep on the chairs and not get into the bed with him. Fortunately, the decision was taken out of our hands as we had been in the room less than an hour when there was a loud banging on the door. We heard, "It's the police. Open up!" Jim looked very shocked and appeared to be even more scared than we were. Realising he had no choice, he opened the door and two male police officers walked into the room. They asked our names, and we didn't hesitate to tell them. We were rather relieved to have been spared from what only God knows would have happened had they not turned up. When we told the police our real ages, Jim lied and tried to protest his innocence, saying we had told him we were seventeen. In any case, the police took us out of the room and ushered us into their waiting car. After that, it was established we were runaways and that we had both been reported missing by our fathers.

We were taken to a local police station, which we were told was in Liverpool, over two hundred miles away from Leytonstone. Although they were kind to us, the police sternly warned us of the dangers of young girls hitchhiking and the position we had found ourselves in. We were very lucky, as the lady who owned the bed and breakfast had thought it odd that an older man with two young girls was booking into her bed and breakfast. We spent a few hours at the police station and then we were taken to what may have been a youth club or a similar kind of venue. We were left in the care of some nice women, and we fell asleep, as we were exhausted from our travels. When we woke up, we were told that our fathers had been informed of our whereabouts and were on their way to collect us. Those hours waiting for my father were among the longest hours of my then short life. I thought he was going to go crazy, shout, and perhaps even hit me. Whatever the police told him, he never discussed me being found in a room in Liverpool with a strange man and the endless possibilities that could have occurred. He simply took me to the train station and sat in stony silence all the way back to East London, with his usual accompaniment, a can of Special Brew. Whatever happened to Jim, I never knew.

CHAPTER 8

With me seemingly going off the rails, my father made the decision to send me to America to stay with his sister for six weeks. I think he thought it may stop me from getting into more trouble. It was a positive experience, of which I had not had many until this point, although travelling alone on the plane was a rather sad and lonely affair. When the time came for me to return, I was excited to get back to London as my brother, now age fifteen, had returned (although very much against his wishes), to my father's care and was at home. Rather selfishly, I was pleased to have someone else to share the brunt of my father's strictness, and at times, bizarre ways. Following my return to England, I was no longer allowed to speak to Sally, as both our fathers thought we were bad influences on each other. When I went back to school following the summer break, I had hoped she would be there and that we could at least talk about our experiences following the summer's separation. However, her father clearly thought better of it, and she never did return to Leyton Senior High for Girls, and I never saw her again. I did, however, have my brother back, and while he was an emotional mess and struggled to settle, we found comfort in each other, and we became allies against 'the tyrant,' which is what we liked to call our father back then.

I tried to settle back into school, although I had little interest in my education as I simply had too much on my mind, and it was not long before I took to bunking off again. This time I did not have to go too far, as across the road from my father's house was an Irish woman named Celine and her two children, Sarah and Stephen. Through their love of drinking hard liquor, my father became friends with Celine, and I became friends with Sarah. Celine would allow me stay in her flat and did not let on to my father about my truanting. She allowed me to smoke, often giving me her cigarettes, and I could watch TV all day. By now, the education authorities had given up and had stopped reporting my absences. Sarah and I became firm friends, and we would talk for hours on end about our early lives. She and her brother had been through significant trauma, so we became a comfort for each other. We found ourselves to be kindred spirits. However, Sarah was three and a half years younger than me, and while she was very mature as I was, we were at different stages of our adolescence, and I often looked out for her and looked after her.

My father became even more strict the older I became. I think he feared me getting pregnant or making some other big 'mistake,' so he thought being strict, not allowing me out, making me clean the house, and not allowing me to have black friends would keep me out of trouble. Little did he know I could not wait to escape him, and this time I vowed to make sure it was for good. As sad as I was to leave Mark behind, I knew I couldn't take living under my father's roof for much longer. By now, he had become involved with a woman named Pam who he seemed to like a lot. Pam moved in with my father very quickly. However, I did not like her at the time, and she did not like me. We often argued, and once we even had a physical fight, which to be fair, I probably started. She would often gloat that she was with my father now and that I had better get used to it. Nothing I said or did seemed to deter her, and she acted like she had won some sort of lottery prize. So, at the age of fifteen and a half, when I received my National Insurance number, I made the decision that I was going to leave school for good and get a job. So, I left without gaining any qualifications, without any prospects, and I really didn't care. I just wanted to get away from it all.

My first ever job was in Walthamstow McDonald's. I lied on the application, which was easy to do in those days, and said I was sixteen instead of fifteen. In my mind, it didn't matter, as I turned sixteen shortly after getting the job. Upon turning sixteen, I decided the time had come for me to leave home. For this, I sought and found refuge with a local youth housing service. I was placed in an all-girls hostel in Walthamstow, and for the first time in my life, I thought I was going to be happy and, more importantly, free. My father was very angry with me for leaving, but there was little he could do about it. Sadly, Mark also turned on me for a while. I think this was more to do with the fact that I had left him on his own. During this period at work, I met my first love, David. He was twenty years old, from Scotland, had a Ford Capri car, and I thought he was absolutely amazing. I fell in love hard and fast and took to staying out of the hostel and with him in his bedsit. For a short while, I had the best time that I had ever had in all my life, and for the first time ever, I felt someone loved me. Due to not adhering to the hostel rules, I was asked to leave. So, upon my eviction, I moved in with David and we set up 'home' together.

David and I went to house parties and enjoyed dancing to the music of the times and had a blast. During this period, I discovered alcohol and cannabis and quickly took to the enjoyable feelings of escape both provided. David took me to meet his mother in Scotland, and for a while, I thought we would last forever. This was not meant to be as a few months into our relationship, I fell pregnant. I had been attempting to use contraception; however, I was inconsistent in taking it. I was just sixteen and of course, not in any position to care for a baby. David did not want a baby and we began to fight and argue. When he asked me to leave his bedsit, the pain of rejection and abandonment flooded back. Coupled with my pregnancy hormones, I think I lost the plot somewhat. I took an overdose of painkillers, although this was more of a classic cry for help than a serious attempt to kill myself. Nonetheless, I was taken to hospital and had the awful experience of my stomach being pumped. Following David's dumping of me, and my overdose, I had no choice but to call my father and ask him for help. To my surprise, he allowed me back home and he also took me to the doctor, where it was arranged that I would have an abortion. At that time, I did not feel guilty about aborting my baby as I had been so stressed and had no idea how I would cope with a child. It was easy to arrange, and I was put under general anaesthetic. Therefore, I did not have to deal with the enormity of aborting a baby. When I left the hospital, I didn't even think twice about it, which now does cause me some shame. However, at the time all I felt was pure relief.

I returned to my father's house, and in thinking about a future for myself, I started a YTS (Youth Training Scheme). I attended a secretarial college to learn typing and word processing skills and was paid £27.30 per week, of which my father took £15 for my keep. Having to pay my father £15 left me with little money for myself, and I was most resentful of this. I soon took to planning my 'escape' again. Shortly after returning to my father's, David contacted me to say how sorry he was for leaving me to deal with it all on my own. However, due to the lingering pain of his abandonment and rejection, I simply did not love him as I had previously. He was still keen to help me escape my father's house and he invited me to live with him again. Such was my desire to get away, I jumped at the chance. Life in that house at that time with my father, Pam, and even Mark was unbearable, and I hated it.

My father was livid at my leaving again and said I was a fool. He also said I would never be allowed back into his home again and that now I was on my own. At the time, I did not care as I was happy that I was being offered a way of escaping again and felt that I was on my own anyway. I took whatever belongings I had and moved back into David's bedsit. This time, I treated him very badly as I had lost all respect for him, even though he tried so hard to win back my affection. He bought me lots of clothes and even took me to see Madonna in concert at Wembley. I was a huge Madonna fan at the time and was in my element, as this was the first concert I had ever been to. None of his sincere efforts were enough and I would go out to parties with my friends, leaving him waiting at home alone for my return. For a while, I was having a blast and I did not care that I was hurting David. After all, in my mind, he had hurt me first and he was now getting what he deserved. Upon completing my secretarial course, I obtained a well-paid job as an audio typist for an insurance company in the city of London. I was earning £6 an hour, which in 1987, was a lot of money for someone of my age. I thought my life was on the up. I continued to live with David, but I did not want to be with him and would often go out with my new work friends. It was during this time that I met Damien and fell in love for the second time in my life.

Damien was training to become an accountant and he worked at the same insurance company as me. He was a year older and lived at home with his mother. He was a lot of fun, and I would often not bother to go home to David, preferring to stay with Damien at his house. In the beginning, his mother did not seem to mind and was even welcoming of me to a point. Although a typical white Essex boy, Damien was an avid hip hop and soul fan, as was I at the time. He had a lot of friends, both black and white, and we enjoyed going to parties and clubs to dance the night away. David soon got the message and told me it was over. The fun times, however, were not to last, as around four months into my relationship with Damien, I fell pregnant again. I was seventeen years old. Initially, Damien and I both agreed we were too young for a baby and that an abortion would be the best thing for both of us. Damien booked a private clinic, and we went together for the consultation. On the day of consultation, I think the enormity of having an abortion hit us both, as we left without making any arrangements, planning on keeping our baby.

Damien's mother went crazy when she found out I was pregnant. She screamed at him and me, saying his life and future career would be ruined if we kept the baby and attempted to bring him or her up together. She ranted it was utter madness on both our parts. Her previously warm attitude turned cold and nasty. She told Damien he couldn't even be sure if he was the father, due to my previous relationship with David. I knew my baby was Damien's. However, he was a mummy's boy and he listened to her. So, when she demanded we rebook the clinic, he gave me the money for an abortion but left all the arrangements to me. I was extremely hurt by their treatment of me and at the time I didn't really want to have another abortion. So, I lied and said I had booked it, when in fact I had not. When Damien and his mother found out I had not booked an abortion, they demanded I leave their house and again I found myself alone and pregnant. I was seventeen and devastated at being abandoned again. I took this rejection even harder than my previous one. I had nowhere to live, and I was extremely scared. Due to the situation, I also lost my job due to my persistent nonattendance and poor punctuality. By now it was too late, or so I thought, to have an abortion, and in my desolation and fear, I shamefully thought about trying to get rid of my baby myself. One day, I spent hours trying to summon the courage to run in front of a car; however, I was not brave enough and chickened out.

Following two days of rough sleeping and in desperation, I had no choice but to go back to my fathers with my tail between my legs. At this point, I had become determined to give my baby up for adoption. My father was surprisingly supportive and allowed me back into his house despite his previous words. He was, however, extremely vocal in his clear disapproval of my intention to have my baby adopted. He reminded me of my mother's abandonment, and said if I gave my baby away, I was no better than her. I mean, my plan was not quite the same as leaving your vulnerable young children on their own on Christmas Eve, never to be seen again type of abandonment. Still, I think it was his clumsy way of trying to make me think of the consequences of giving my baby away. Upon my return to my father's, I did have some contact with Damien, and he came to see me without his mother's knowledge. Initially, he said he would support me but that he couldn't be in a relationship with me. I was so hurt and told him if he didn't want to be in a relationship with me, then I would not be having the baby anyway, and told him of my adoption plans.

I had gone as far as to contact social services and had requested help to go forward with the adoption. I was advised that I would be afforded a period after the birth to allow for a change of mind. I was sure this would not happen, as how on earth was I going to be able to look after a baby? I could barely look after myself. I was five months pregnant when I turned eighteen years old. It was a miserable coming of age birthday with no fuss or celebration. Just me and my thoughts of how I was going to get through this next stage of my life. I was rapidly feeling worn out by life and I was only just reaching adulthood.

It must have been the stress of the pregnancy, as following an antenatal check at thirty-four weeks and upon leaving the hospital, my water broke. I had no idea at the time what this meant, but I instinctively knew something was wrong. I headed back to the hospital and told the midwives I thought I had wet myself. They checked me over and informed me my water had broken. I was quickly admitted and told if my baby didn't come naturally after twenty-four hours, I would need to be induced as there would be a high risk of infection. Nursing staff asked if I wanted anyone to come to the hospital, so I asked them to call my father and Pam. As I have said, I had not liked Pam, as I thought she was a very foolish woman who seemed to think my father was the be-all and end-all. I thought she was clueless and often told her so. However, they were the only people I could think of who would come and help me, and to their credit, they did. The following day, my labour was induced.

CHAPTER 9

On August 3, 1988, I gave birth to my baby son. Being premature, he was whisked away to the special care baby unit. I was exhausted after the birth and fell straight asleep without even holding him. When I awoke the following morning, I was asked if I wanted to see my baby. While the nursing staff were aware of my plan to have him adopted, they still asked anyway. Initially, I said no, and reminded them of my intention. However, as the morning progressed, I became more curious to see the little life I had just given birth to. I was taken to the special care baby unit and shown to the incubator in which my tiny baby son was taking his first breaths of life. It is an understatement to say I was overcome with emotion the first time I laid eyes on my baby. Although he weighed five pounds, four ounces, which was a good size considering his prematurity, he looked like a tiny, scrawny little bird. Even so, my little baby boy was the most beautiful thing I had ever seen. He had creamy olive skin, pretty red lips, and big hazel eyes, and I fell instantly in love with him. He was mine, and I knew in that very moment that I was not going to give him up. I stared at him in wonderment and awe, holding his tiny little fingers in mine. With tears rolling down my face, I made a most sincere and heartfelt promise to love and look after him always. I vowed to never let him come to harm, and I meant every single word.

My father was pleased at my change of heart, and he tried to be supportive in the only way he knew how. Following informing social services, there was a brief meeting to confirm my decision, and thereafter I was left alone to care for my baby. He remained in the special care baby unit for five days, and during this time, Damien came to visit. He said he could not let his mother know of his visit and promised he would try and support me. I did not believe him, and I was right not to. However, this did not dampen my newfound strength and motivation to ensure my baby would know that he was very much loved and equally wanted. The force of my love for my son was powerful and all-consuming. I named him Reace. I continued to live at my father's house and Pam was helpful. I appreciated their help very much, and through the birth of my son, our relationships began to improve. My love for my baby deepened every day and before long, it was hard to even imagine that I had not wanted him. He was a sweet-natured and happy baby, which did make the monumental task of mothering without having been mothered somewhat easier. Fortunately, my maternal instincts developed quickly, and I did not struggle with the practical tasks of looking after my baby.

I also had the support of my father's close friends, Derek and Sharon. They were an interracial couple who had managed to stay together and raise their children very well. Derek and Sharon gave me a lot of baby things and offered to babysit whenever I needed. I chose Derek and Sharon to be Reace's godparents alongside Deena, a girl I had become good friends with. Deena had attended Leyton Senior High for Girls and although we had been friendly in school, it was not until we left school and had met again on the same YTS scheme that we became close. Deena was supportive when I had Reace. She loved him and liked to pretend he was her baby whenever we went out with him. My dear friend Sarah was also getting older and proving to be a strong source of emotional support.

It was not long before I had applied for my own council housing and the time came for me to go it alone with my son. This time I hoped it would be in a more stable manner. During the late '80s, the housing crisis was yet to hit the UK, and a young single mother like myself was considered in priority need. Reace was almost six months old when I was given my first council flat. It was a three-bedroom flat on an East London council housing estate called Cathall Road. It was a maze of concrete flats interlinked by many shadowy walkways, often smelling of urine and connected by a series of podiums. It was actually possible to cross the whole estate over the podiums without having to go to the ground level. Cathall Road was a typical British sink estate, characterised by high levels of crime and social and economic deprivation. Urban tales were rife within the local community and many people would refuse or be too scared to enter the estate, such was its negative reputation. Despite this, I was overjoyed to be finally given my own home, and I did not let fear stand in my way or dampen my enthusiasm.

It was early 1989, and coincidently, Sarah, her mother Celine, and brother Stephen had moved to a flat just opposite to the estate. Due to her mother's escalating alcoholism, Sarah was unhappy living at home, so she spent much of her time with me, helping to look after Reace. On the day I collected my keys to 300 Hollydown Way (Cathall Road), Sarah was with me when I first set eyes on my new home. The flat was extremely spacious; however, Sarah and I were both daunted when we realised it would require a lot of work before it could even remotely be considered homely. The living room had been painted black with gloss paint, with Star of Davids' dotted throughout the rooms. If I had been older, I may have been apprehensive and have pondered on the significance of this and the previous tenants. However, such was my naivety, I did not. With the grant I was given to redecorate and furnish, singlehandedly Sarah and I set about making it a home. Within a few weeks, we had repainted the whole flat a fresh magnolia colour and I even had enough money left from the grant to purchase carpets and furniture. The day I finally moved in with Reace was an immense achievement. It might have been a grotty council estate, but inside, Sarah and I had transformed it into a home. It was the first home I could call mine, and even though it had become quickly apparent that Damien was not interested in his son, I felt that maybe, just maybe, life would be okay—and possibly even good.

I was not lonely in my new home as Sarah and Deena often visited, as did my brother, who enjoyed the welcome escape from my father's house. And of course, I had my beautiful son to care for. Those first few months were exciting; however, I soon came to realise estate life came with its own set of rules, some of which I had been totally unprepared for. I had not grown up around estate life, and once again, I found myself struggling to fit in. The estate was used to house the influx of single mothers that arose during the '80s. However, I did not know any of the people on the estate and most appeared to have their own clique of friends. I would often find myself being snubbed and although guys would say hello to me, in my shyness and embarrassment, I would appear aloof. It got to the point where I started being accused of being 'stush,' urban speak for someone who thinks they are better than others. Of course, this was not how I felt; I just didn't know how to mix with the locals, so I kept to myself in those early days.

CHAPTER 10

While I had been focusing on my baby, my new home, and new life, I was not aware that for some time, my father had been planning a 'reunion' with my mother for Mark and me. One day, not long after I had moved to my flat, my father came to visit and told me that for a long time, Mark had been pestering him to find our mother. He said he had always known that she continued to live in the East End area of Mile End and said he had recently been to visit her. I was stunned to find out that not only had he known where she lived, but that he had also been to see her. Despite this, I was intrigued and excited. I asked my father why, if he had known where she lived, had he not gone to see her sooner. I had so many questions for my father, but he just could not answer them. Instead, he told me that my mother had agreed to visit us the following week. I could hardly breathe with the anticipation, and my head spun with the numerous questions that I had longed for many years to be answered, such as, Why had she left us? Where had she been? Did she even love us? What I had not known is that my father had, on several occasions, attempted to get our mother to re-enter our lives, but I was soon to find out that she had always refused. She had also gone on to have another child (a daughter), and this child she kept, and was mothering her in a way that Mark and

I had never known. Soon after moving to my new home, and some fifteen years after she had walked away from us without a backward glance, the ill-fated reunion took place.

Mark and I waited nervously but also excitedly with my father in my flat for my mother to visit. My mother came with her daughter, who was then about twelve years old. It is hard to describe the shock I felt at seeing my mother again after all those years. I simply could not believe she was alive and caring for her daughter, whilst Mark and I had been abandoned and forgotten. I was also shocked to my core by her appearance. All these years, I had longed for my mother to come back and had placed her on a pedestal. The reality was that my mother looked hideous and nothing like my fantasy. The intervening years had not been kind, and it showed on every crevice of her wrinkled and ashen looking face. Her hair was long, greasy, and grey. Her teeth were awful and protruded out her mouth in a grotesque manner. I was stunned and surely thought this pathetic creature of a woman was not my mother. I could also intuitively sense my mother was not fully aware of the enormity of her abandonment of her children. She was slow and slurred her speech, seemingly suffering with an array of mental health difficulties, as she was incoherent and vague in her explanations.

I hit my mother with a barrage of questions. "Why did you leave us? Where have you been? Do you have any idea what happened to us when you left?" My mother was obviously not able to cope with my incessant questions and tried to deflect them by saying it was not her fault, that my father had left her, and she just could not cope. This was not a good enough explanation for me, as not only was my mother physically hideous, she was also full of self-pity. She could not answer my questions and could not say why she had kept her daughter but had not even attempted to see if Mark and I were even alive. To me, this was unforgiveable, and in that moment, my longing for my mother dissolved into feelings of hatred at her apparent lack of love or care. Her daughter, my half-sister, had no idea what was happening, and in her innocence, she tried to make awkward conversation. She appeared rather slow, like Mark, but I did not stop to consider that she may have a learning difficulty and, to be honest, at that time I simply did not care. The visit ended disastrously with my mother crying and me telling her to get out of my house. She could not cope with my rage and questioning, so the visit ended with her scurrying out of my flat, with her daughter following forlornly in tow. I did not see her again for many years and I still was yet to discover she had even more skeletons in her cupboard.

We did not get any of the answers we desperately needed, and certainly no closure or promises of a new start with a mother who was sorry for her actions and who loved us. Following this disastrous visit, I began to develop strong feelings of anger and disgust for her. Now I was a mother myself and although I had struggled during my pregnancy, once my son had been born, I knew I would never ever abandon him. I knew whatever it took, I would fight to ensure he was kept safe, something our mother had not been able—or even worse—had not wanted to do. I hardened my heart towards her after that visit and I refused to speak of her with Mark or my father. This hurt my brother, as he continued to mourn the loss of our mother and he felt I had treated her badly and even suggested I had driven her away. At the time, I did not care. I resolved to get on with my life and forget I ever had a mother, although this was easier said than done, as I would come to realise over the following years.

CHAPTER 11

Damien had been a brief visitor during the first few months of my moving to my new home. He came to visit Reace twice and, on both occasions, he gave me some money, telling me he would continue to see our child without his mother knowing. However, this was a lie, and following a few broken promises to visit, I told him not to bother visiting anymore if he had no intention of keeping his word. This must have been what he had been hoping to hear, as I did not hear from him again, and my pride stopped me from contacting him. Simply, I was not going to beg the father of my son to be in his life if he did not love and care about him as deeply as I did. I was not to know at the time that sadly for Reace, Damien would never even attempt to see his son again.

Reace was about nine months old when I met Cain, who was two years older than me and lived locally in Leyton with his mother. He was acceptable to my father as he fit his two main prerequisites, which were that he was white, and that he had a job. Soon into our relationship, Cain professed his undying love for me and took on a fatherly role with Reace. He promised to care for us forever. His family was kind and his mother helped to look after Reace. It was the summer of 1989. I was with Cain and getting on with life when my generation and I entered what is now nostalgically and affectionately referred to as "The Second Summer of Love." Pirate radio stations such as Centreforce and Sunrise were springing up all over the place and the music of the era was moving from the genre of hip hop and acid house to house and hardcore rave music. My friend Deena was a frequent visitor to my flat and she was full of the joys of life, as most carefree teenagers were. She was beautiful, funny, and a very high-spirited young woman. We were the same age but had very different life experiences. She was very much loved by her parents and had had an idyllic childhood growing up in Leytonstone. It helped our friendship that she was aware of how fortunate she had been as a child and that she was caring and sympathetic about what she knew of my life up to that point. While I did not tell her everything that had happened to me, she was aware that my mother had abandoned me and that I had been in 'care.'

Sadly, Deena's father had died a few months before Reace's birth, and this alongside me becoming a mother brought us closer together. Deena, without the same responsibilities as me, had been discovering the new music scene and literally raved about it every time she came to see me. She excitedly told me about a new underground club she had been going to called Dungeons, which was in Lea Bridge Road, Leyton. She was buzzing with excitement as she told me how the people danced all night, the music was amazing, and everyone was so happy and friendly. It was not long before my curiosity was awakened, and I wanted to go to Dungeons with her. Up until that time, I smoked cannabis daily but had not taken any other drugs. Deena said when she went out, she would take this new drug, a pill called ecstasy, and she raved about it. She said you could dance for hours and hours on it and that it felt amazing. It all sounded extremely exciting, and I wanted some of it. Cain was not as outgoing as myself and tried to put me off. He was anxious and worried, and he was adamant that he did not want to try ecstasy. I did not listen, or to be fair, even care about his reservations. All I knew is that I wanted some of the fun. So, one Friday night, I made arrangements for Reace to stay with Derek and Sharon for the weekend, and I headed off with Deena to Dungeons in great anticipation.

Upon entering the club, I was stopped in my tracks in total awe. I had not been to an underground club like this before, and I was so excited. The partygoers were smiling widely and dancing with wild abandon, the music was pumping, and laser lights added to the high-octane ambience. It did not take long before I agreed to take one of the pills Deena handed me along with a bottle of water. Following her lead, I popped the little pill into my mouth and swallowed it whole with a swig of water. Within about thirty minutes, I felt a rush of euphoria sweep through me and then I danced and danced like I had never danced before. The music was the best I had ever heard, including tunes that are now classics, such as Frankie Knuckles' "Your Love," "Tears," and "Break 4 Love" by Raze. I felt the best I had ever felt. That night was one of the best I had ever had until that point, and it was like a whole new world had just been opened. We danced nonstop until 8 a.m. the next morning.

Little did I know this new scene was about to take off in the most phenomenal of ways. But one thing was for sure: I was not going to be left out. After that first weekend, I took to going out most weekends with Deena and I began to live for the weekend. I would look after Reace all week, and come Friday, I would take him to Derek and Sharon's or to Pam's, and thereafter I would head off for a weekend of wild partying. Soon after, the now famous M25 raves massively took off. I can still recall the heady excitement of meeting fellow ravers at service stations such as South Mimms, to be informed of the secret location of the rave. Only if you were in the know, were you in the know. We were a secret—I would say now, almost an elite crowd—and I loved every single second of it.

Cain and I began to drift apart as he was not going to be persuaded to go raving. I was having the best days of my life, and I was most certainly not prepared to give it up for him. I think the relationship was also impacted by the churned-up feelings the awkward and failed meeting with my mother had stirred within me. I just could not believe Cain loved me and I refused to let my guard down and trust in the relationship. I had also become a very angry and volatile young person. I took all my feelings of abandonment and despair out on him, and I would say very hurtful things. While Cain professed his love for me and wanted to take care of Reace, I simply did not feel the same about him. When, in the end, he couldn't take any more and left me, my feelings of low self-worth raged once more and with even more force than ever before. Reace was about two years old, and once again, it was just me and him against the world. I continued to party with Deena and also with Sarah. For a while, I felt that I had a new family, my party family. Each week, I went to different raves like Raindance, Fantazia, and Elevation, to name just a few, and with this brought new faces. For that evening, I would dance the whole night long, and in this I was completely in my element. For a brief while, I was able to forget my worries.

As the relationship with Cain had ended, I think I became more noticeable on the estate, particularly by the men (or maybe I just became aware that I was being noticed). In my naivety, I attempted to make friends as I didn't want to be an outsider anymore and I wanted to fit into my surroundings. There was a guy who would follow me on the estate. There was something quite creepy about him, and something inside told me to keep my distance. However, he was persistent. I did not know his real name at the time as he went by the street name of Shabba. He was a tall, skinny black man with a sinister air about him. One evening, I was at home alone with Reace. It was about 11 p.m. when I heard a loud bang. I ran up the stairs of my flat to find that my front door had been kicked wide open. To say I was terrified would be an understatement. We did not have mobile phones in those days. Fortunately, however, I did have a house phone, and in what seemed like a blind panic, I grabbed Reace out of his bed, ran into the living room and rang 999, crying down the phone for help.

The police must have been patrolling the estate, as it didn't even feel like ten minutes had passed before two uniformed police officers stormed into my flat to find me cowering in a corner with my small son. They asked what happened and all I could do was blubber that my door had been kicked in and that I had no idea why. They left and ran back out of the flat to look for the culprit. Within minutes, they were back at my door, calling, "Miss Hylton, please come to the top of the stairs." As I cautiously peeped around the corner and up the stairs, I was stunned to see the police had apprehended Shabba. He was standing with an officer by each side, with a smirk on his face. When the police asked if I knew him, I told them that he was not my friend but that I knew of him, and that he had been following me around the estate for the last few months. He denied kicking my door in, but the police hauled him away anyway. I was so upset as I could not understand why Shabba would be so cruel to frighten me like that. I was so scared I called my father and asked if he would come and take us to his house. I was scared to return home, as I felt vulnerable in the flat alone with Reace and by myself.

A few days later, I was informed by the police that no charges were to be brought against Shabba due to lack of evidence, and that me simply believing he was the culprit was not evidence. It was at this point that anger set in and I decided I would seek Shabba out and find out for myself why he had kicked my front door in. I knew he frequented Leytonstone High Road and that he hung around the local betting shops. So, leaving Reace with my father and Pam, I ventured out to find him, which did not take long. True to form, I spotted him sauntering between a pub called the Thatched House and the Cathall Road estate. In my anger, I forgot about my fear and stormed up to him. In an accusatory manner I cried, "Why did you do it? What have I ever done to you?" I should have known better, or at least exercised some caution. I mean, I did not know him at all and certainly did not know what he was capable of. He turned on me angrily, calling me a "fucking stupid bitch," telling me to move away from him. He must have seen some fear in my eyes, as he then decided he was going to be the aggressor, and I was not getting away from him after I had publicly embarrassed him in the street.

Realising the stupidity of my actions, I tried to get away. However, Shabba was not going to let that happen, so he backed me into a corner and began to taunt me. He towered over me in a menacing manner. He was over six feet tall, possibly more, to my mere five feet, two inches, and he was clearly enjoying exerting his power over me. He painfully jabbed my shoulders and poked me in my face, asking me who I thought I was to confront him in public and in front of "his people." He would not let me get away and shouted obscenities and profanities at me. Smelling my fear, he continued to follow me, making threats culminating in him warning me that this was not the end and that he was going to get some of the Reid gang girls to throw acid in my face. The Reids were a large family of drug-dealing criminals in the area, and they were well-known for their ruthlessness. I was petrified and I really believed Shabba would get the Reid girls to avenge him for me having ever dared to confront him.

By the time I had made it back to my father's house, I was in a rambling state, sobbing. I had to leave Leytonstone as Reace and I were never going to be safe. My father tried to persuade me to go to the police; however, I was too scared of the repercussions of what would be construed as grassing on Shabba. So, the next day I packed a small bag, and I took Reace to go and stay with my cousin Paul, who had a flat near Elephant and Castle in South London. Paul had continued to be a confidant of mine and I was able to seek support and advice from him. I stayed with him for about two weeks, and with his encouragement, I realised I had to pluck up the courage to return to my home. I was dreading going back to Cathall, but in the end, having no choice, I made my way back to my flat. I locked myself in and pondered how I was going to survive. I had been back in Leytonstone less than two weeks when I realised I had to pull myself together and go back to work, which at the time was in a local bakery. I summoned my courage and tried to move on. However, I was terrified that Shabba, or even worse, the Reid girls, were lying in wait and biding their time to get me.

It was my first day back at work when another local guy called Mikey approached me for a chat. Mikey and I had been on friendly terms; however, I did not know him well and by now I was wary of becoming too close to the locals. He was a skinny black guy with dreadlocks, and in all the time I had lived on the estate, we always nodded hello and sometimes I had stopped for a chat. He would often walk and talk with me, and he knew where I lived. We both liked the same music and I had seen him a few times out raving. However, when Mikey saw me on my way home from work and ran up to me to strike up conversation, I was having none of it. Walking quickly away, I said to Mikey, "Please just leave me alone. I don't want anything to do with you or any of your lot." He was perplexed and asked me what was wrong. I rambled out the whole story about Shabba, which made him laugh, and he said, "Don't be silly, Diana! He can't do nothing to you." I did not believe him, and crying, I relayed the threat of acid being thrown in my face by the Reid girls. He simply said, "Leave it to me. Go home. I will come to your house later." When he knocked at my door later and said that it was sorted and that I had nothing to worry about, I didn't believe him. He said I was to meet him the next day at the off-licence on the estate and I would see that it had been sorted. While I didn't believe him, I had nothing to lose, so I agreed to meet him after I had finished work.

The following day, as I walked solemnly towards the off-licence, I stopped dead in my tracks as I saw Mikey chatting with Shabba. I couldn't believe it and thought Mikey may have been trying to set me up. In a blind panic, I turned on my heels and tried to escape before either of them had seen me. But it was too late. As I turned, I heard Mikey shout my name. "Diana, Diana, come back! Shabba's got something to say to you." Thinking I had little choice but to humour Mikey until I was able to safely escape, I turned around and fearfully walked towards them. Upon approaching Shabba, I saw that he was looking rather sheepish. He said, "Sorry if I scared you, you know I was only joking. No one's gonna hurt you." Mikey looked at him and asked him why he had kicked my door in and threatened to get the Reid girls to throw acid in my face. Shabba made a sucking sound with his teeth, also known as kissing teeth, and said, "Mikey, the girl is foolish. You know, I never even been to her house, and she set police on me." He followed this up by saying, "The girl tried to show me up in the street, so I joked about the girls throwing acid in her face." Mikey ended the conversation warning him to leave me alone, which Shabba rather meekly agreed to. This was the start of mine and Mikey's doomed relationship.

At first, I was relieved that Mikey had put an end to Shabba, and I tentatively allowed him into my home. We would talk, not deeply, but about life in general, and listen to music. In the beginning, while he wasn't the brightest, I did find myself having a laugh with him. Mikey also sold cannabis, which was handy, and he had a lot of friends who were also into the rave scene. We went raving together to Energy, Astoria, and Camden Palace, and for a few months, we had fun. He was kind to Reace. Not fatherly in any way, but funny and kind nonetheless. However, the good times did not last long. A few months into the relationship, I became pregnant again. At that point, I was sure there was no way I was going to have a baby with Mikey, and so I had my second abortion. The abortion was uneventful and over before I even had a chance to be sorrowful or contemplate the enormity of a second abortion by the age of twenty.

Mikey was not welcomed by my father or my brother. Neither of them liked him, and both made their feelings clear. My father could not stand him as he was probably the worst man he could imagine I would ever take up with. A black man with dreadlocks, no job, and who sold drugs. I could not have taken up with anyone worse in his eyes. My brother said he didn't trust him but couldn't say why. He just stopped visiting as often. I did not listen to either of them. However, following the second abortion, Mikey and I started to argue, and quite ferociously too. Although not a great looking guy, he did seem to have a lot of friends who were girls, with whom he loved to flirt. Even though I didn't love Mikey, I struggled with feelings of intense jealousy. Our arguments were explosive and soon turned violent. I think I may have hit him first, and he was not the sort of guy to accept a woman hitting him, so he hit me back.

Shamefully, I must admit that many of the fights took place when Reace was there, and as a toddler, he must have been very scared. I had been contemplating ending the relationship when, to my horror, just six months on from my second abortion, I found myself pregnant again. I was devastated. I had been using contraception, but most likely not consistently. I was so young and so ill-equipped for life and relationships. I was not making good choices for me or Reace, but I just couldn't see it. This time I felt terrible and did not think of having another abortion as it just didn't seem right. I felt I had no choice but to go through with having a baby with Mikey. He was happy as at twenty-five, he thought the time was right for him to become a father.

However, from the moment I decided to keep the baby, the relationship deteriorated even further. Mikey was not prepared to change his ways, and his behaviour towards me became even more appalling. He would go missing for days on end and would lie through his teeth about his whereabouts. He also took to trying to make me feel like I was crazy and irrational, and this increased my feelings of jealousy. He would also taunt me about my father and brother, and the fact that I had no mother. He knew what hurt me and how to press my buttons, and he seemed to take great pleasure in doing so. For a while, I thought I was going crazy, but deep inside, I knew that I had made a big mistake.

My father was disgusted with my decision to have a baby with Mikey and told me that I had made my bed;

therefore, I had to lie in it, so to speak. Mikey had taken to hitting me more frequently and I felt trapped and alone. It was mid-December 1991, and the dreaded Christmas Eve was approaching. I was around eighteen weeks pregnant, alone, and becoming increasingly depressed. I could not see any way out. I knew I had to keep going for Reace, but I was terrified at what the future held. Mikey was becoming more abusive, and in order to protect myself and Reace, I had stopped challenging and arguing with him. I knew something was terribly wrong with Mikey, I just didn't know what it was. One evening a few days before Christmas Eve, I was alone in the flat with Reace when there was a knock at the door. Thinking it might be Mikey, who I had not seen for a few days, I opened the door, ready to ask where he had been. It was not Mikey but his cousin, Leon. Leon was a very nice guy who had often told me I was far too good for Mikey and queried why I was with him in the first place. I couldn't even answer Leon as it was something I struggled to answer even to myself. Leon could see I was in distress, and he was kind. When I broke down in tears at my predicament, he took pity on me and decided to tell me the truth about Mikey and where he actually was.

I was stunned when Leon said Mikey was not only seeing another woman and was with her as we spoke, but that even worse, they were smoking crack together. While prior to my pregnancy, I had smoked weed, loved raving, and had taken ecstasy, I had never been tempted by crack and was absolutely stunned to find out that Mikey had been on it all the time throughout our relationship. Crack was rife in London during the '80s and '90s and was fast becoming an epidemic. Thankfully, I had been scared off the stuff from films such as *New Jack City*, which showed how a person's life could be torn apart from smoking the evil stuff, and stories that prevailed about how just by smoking once you could become hooked. I was devastated and felt so stupid. How did I allow myself to become involved in a relationship with a crack-smoking waster? Besides feeling stupid, I was also terrified at the prospect of having a child with him.

It was at this point that I think I realised my life was spiralling out of control. I was almost five months pregnant, and I could see no way out. As Christmas approached, my depression worsened. I had kept my newfound knowledge away from Mikey as I tried to work out a way out of the mess I had found myself in. Somehow, I went through the motions of Christmas 1991. The day came and went without event, and I was only pleased that I had managed to make it enjoyable for Reace. We spent it alone in our flat, and I was pleased as I had not wanted Mikey around me or my son. I knew I would have to face up to the situation and confront Mikey and get him out of our life; I just didn't know how.

Knowing that Mikey was likely to lose his temper when challenged, I arranged for Reace to stay at Derek and Sharon's as I planned how I was going to confront him. I contacted a friend of Mikey's and told him it was an emergency and if he knew where Mikey was, he was to tell him it was urgent. Nervously, I waited alone in my flat. It was a few days after Christmas, and he had been missing for days. It was not the fact he was with another woman that bothered me, as I didn't want to be with a crackhead anyway. It was the fact that I was trapped and pregnant with his baby. While I was scared to confront him, I knew I had no choice as I simply could not just accept the situation.

I had refused to give Mikey a key to my home. However, I always knew it was him at the door by the way he rapped on the letter box. So, when I heard that all too familiar knock, I tentatively opened the door and let him in. As he walked down the stairs and followed me into the front room, looking around, he queried in a rather unconvincingly interested manner where Reace was. Stupidly, I screamed at him, "What has it got to do with you? You don't care about him or me, you dirty fucking crackhead!" Momentarily, Mikey was shocked into silence, as he foolishly must have thought I would never find out. At first, he tried to deny it, and tried to deflect my accusations away by calling me an idiot and inferring I was insanely jealous and mad, and it was because of this that he stayed away. However, when I told him that Leon had told me all of the truth about his crack habit and the name of his crack-smoking girlfriend, he realised his game was up. Initially, he was angrier at being betrayed by his so-called "brethren," and he still attempted to lie to my face. He said it was Leon who was the liar and was seething at the fact that I had let his cousin into my home when he wasn't there.

I could not believe it! There I was, almost five months pregnant with his baby, and he was insinuating I was being disloyal by letting his own cousin into my house when he wasn't there. Tearfully, I told him our relationship was over and that I wanted him out of my life for good. I couldn't help but shout that I did not want a crackhead near me or my child, and that his crack whore could have him as I surely did not want him. Big mistake and poor judgement on my part for thinking I could challenge Mikey about what he called his 'business' on my own, and with such vehement force. My words and my decision enraged him. He grabbed me by my shoulders and spat his disgusting phlegm with full force into my face. With his eyes bulging, he screamed, "You are going nowhere with my kid, and if you think you are leaving me, you had better think again, bitch!"

Although I was scared of his reaction, I stood up to him and said there was no way he was going to be involved in this child's life. With that, he pushed me to the floor and kicked me hard in my back and about my body. I was terrified and in pain, and realised I had been stupid to try and confront him on my own. I cowered in the corner of my living room and pleaded with him not to hurt me any further. I even attempted to lie and say that maybe we could work things out, but that I needed time. He was having none of it. As unintelligent as he was, he must have known deep inside that I was not going to suffer this situation, him, or his abuse any longer. So, coupled with the knowledge I was ending the relationship, alongside his crack comedown, he lost the plot and continued to kick me while I curled up in a ball, trying to protect myself.

The beating went on for what seemed like an eternity. Mikey knew he had messed up big time. He kept saying over and over, "Look what you made me do. I am so sorry, Diana. You know I love you, don't you?" He tried to cradle me in his arms. However, I refused to let him touch me. Bloodied and in excruciating pain, I pulled myself onto my feet and summoned all my courage to demand he leave my flat immediately. In his own fear, he did as I asked, saying he would come back to see me tomorrow. As I heard the door slam, I dropped back onto the floor in shock. I sobbed and sobbed. I was traumatised and I had no idea what I was going to do. In my despair, I got on my hands and knees and prayed. I had never asked God for help before, and while I was not religious, I was spiritual. Deep in my heart and soul, I believed God existed, and if he could not help me, then no one on earth would be able to. I sobbed my sorrowful apology for allowing myself to get into this desperate and dangerous situation. I was twenty-one, and it felt like my life was ending. I prayed long and hard for a way out and for protection for myself and Reace. I was in so much pain, but was too traumatised to do anything but fall into an exhausted yet fretful sleep.

The following morning when I awoke, my back was killing me and I was bruised all over my face and body. A small voice inside me told me to call for help. I called a good friend of mine, Jimmy, who I had met through my relationship with Cain and had remained friends with. He was a good support to me and Reace, and I knew in my heart he would help me. He, like many others, could not understand why I had even entertained a relationship with Mikey, and within a couple of hours, he came to my aid. I sobbed that I could not go on any longer and he said he would get Reace and look after him at his house while I reported Mikey to the police. The police were sympathetic to my plight, and they informed me they would put a warrant out for his arrest. I was also advised to seek medical treatment, get a solicitor, and apply for an injunction.

Still in shock, the same day, I went to my GP. When I broke down in tears in front of the receptionist, I was advised that my GP would see me for an emergency appointment. Inside the surgery, I fell apart. Sobbing, I poured out the whole story to my doctor, telling her about Mikey's crack habit, his abuse towards me, and my fear of having another baby on my own. I said I did not think I could cope and had thoughts about ending my life, but had not as I had my son to look after. After examining me, she asked if I had any bleeding. Tearfully, I said no, although in my heart, I wished I did. She then said if my decision was not to continue with the pregnancy, I would need to act fast. Thinking there were no other options, I asked what she meant. She explained that I was within the legal limits for a termination if continuing the pregnancy was a risk to my physical or mental health. However, I was warned it would be a difficult and traumatic process. Stunned by the fact I may have a way out of having the baby, at that point my feelings of tentative relief outweighed the enormity of the grave decision I was about to make.

The next few days passed in a whirlwind of solicitor and medical appointments. I was advised I would need to attend court to apply for an injunction, and in the meantime, if Mikey tried to make contact, I was to call the police immediately. Mikey must have known his time was up, as he made no attempt to contact me, which I was relieved about. My GP arranged for the termination to take place at Newham General Hospital. During the initial consultation, the doctors informed me of the procedure and warned it would not be quick or painless. I was told the abortion was being authorised on the grounds of the risk to my mental health should I continue. While I was devastated at my taking such drastic action, I truly felt I had no choice. The day of the termination arrived, and this was before the court date for the injunction. It was January 16, 1992. I was twenty-one years old and twenty-one weeks pregnant. Jimmy once again came to my aid and looked after Reace while I took myself to Newham Hospital. I had no idea as to what exactly was going to happen, and if I had, I do not think I would have gone through with it. While I felt deeply guilty, I knew I could not go through with having Mikey's child. I would be forever at his mercy, and not only would the child's life be hell, but so would Reace's, the child that I did already have and whom I needed to keep safe.

The nurses were not sympathetic to my plight at all, and it was evident I was being harshly judged for my decision. I was ordered to get undressed and advised that medication would be inserted into my cervix to induce my labour. Then I was left alone with a silver medical dish, which I was told I should push my dead baby into. I was terrified; however, there was no going back once the medication had been inserted. I was left alone with my thoughts, and the beginnings of what would come to be a burdening guilt. I prayed to God and to my baby for forgiveness. The pain over the next ten hours was even worse than my previous labour. I am told this was because the baby was undeveloped and could not help itself along the birth canal. The midwives were curt and cruel, telling me to grow up and asking me what I had expected. I cried like I had never cried before. Finally, my dead baby slipped into the cold, silver metal tray, and I stared at the lifeless tiny body in shock. While not properly formed, it was clear to see he was a baby boy, and in that moment, I could not have hated myself any more if I tried. I was devasted and overwhelmed with shame at killing my baby. Despite all I had been through in my life up until that point, this was the worst day.

Upon giving birth to my dead baby, I was given an injection and had to wait with his tiny body in the steel bowl until my placenta was delivered. While I take full responsibility for my actions, I cannot help but reflect on the cruel decision of the midwives to leave me for that period, alone and in a traumatised state of shock. Following the delivery of the placenta, the midwives must have felt some sense of sympathy, as when they took the bowl away, they started to speak a little kindlier towards me. I just wanted to get out of the hospital as soon as possible, so against the midwives' advice, I discharged myself. I was given a plethora of tablets and was instructed that if I had any excessive bleeding or temperature, I was to come back straight away. I cannot think of what a sad, desperate, and desolate soul I must have looked as I limped out of that hospital. I sat in a stunned silence in the minicab all the way home. In those days, the restrictions around smoking were not as strict. I did not even ask the cab driver if I could smoke in his cab, and this was not out of rudeness, I just think I was not really with it. The cab driver must have seen how dazed I was and did not even question it when I lit a cigarette in the back of his car.

Jimmy was waiting with Reace at my flat. Upon opening the door, my little boy, who was just three at the time, came running to greet me, saying, "Mummy, Mummy! I missed you!" It took all my emotional strength not to break down crying on him. I bent down and scooped him into my arms and held on tightly to him until he wriggled to escape. Jimmy wanted to stay with me to help, but I felt so bad I just wanted to be alone, just me and my son. I thanked him for his help and said I would call the next day. He agreed to leave only when I had promised to call the police if Mikey came to the house. Upon my promising, he reluctantly left. I took my little boy into my arms once more. That night, we snuggled together watching TV (or at least he was). I did not want to let him go. When Reace fell asleep, for the second time in my life, I got to my hands and knees and prayed. I prayed to God for forgiveness, and I made a solemn promise to turn my life around. I promised to focus on my son and our future, and once more I asked for help, as who else could really help in this horrendous situation? I was exhausted and terrified, as while I had ended the relationship and had no intention of ever speaking to Mikey again, he still had to be informed that the baby was no more. I knew if he found out I had aborted his child, he might possibly kill me.

The next morning, my friend Deena, who was aware of the situation, came around and offered to take Reace out for the day. I was grateful, as I was in turmoil with grief and in fear of what might happen should Mikey ever find out. I called Mikey's cousin Leon and asked tearfully if he could come around, as I had something I needed to tell him. He didn't ask on the phone what it was and came to my flat within the hour. When he knocked, I jumped out of my skin in fear. Looking through the keyhole, I asked if Mikey was with him. When he reassured me he wasn't, I tentatively let him in. Once in the living room, I broke down and told him I had lost the baby. Having no choice but to lie, I said as a result of the beating I had suffered, the baby had died. Leon was shocked but sympathetic. He called Mikey a whole host of names and said I was not to worry; he would tell him what he had done. I felt guilty at lying, but I knew for my own safety, it was the only way.

I told Leon I was getting an injunction and that he needed to tell Mikey that if he troubled me, I would have no hesitation but to call the police. Leon said he understood, gave me a friendly hug, and left. Shortly after the death of my baby, of which I caused, I obtained the injunction. Leon was helpful during this period as he visited me a few times to inform me that Mikey was shattered by the death of our baby and that he knew the relationship was over. Leon told me Mikey was sorry for the pain he had caused me. While I was relieved it was over, I continued to suffer crippling feelings of guilt and shame at my actions. Despite my fears of bumping into Mikey, I did not see him again for some time after that fateful and traumatic event. When I finally did see him in the local area, I think out of shame he knew not to approach me, and he never did. Of course, I felt guilty letting him believe he had caused the miscarriage, but really, I still believed I did not have any other choice.

CHAPTER 12

As the months passed, slowly I pulled myself together. I had a son who needed me, and I had promised God I would focus on Reace, and that is exactly what I did. I also knew that the time had come to try and make something of my life for both of our sakes. Having left school without any qualifications, it dawned on me during this period that without an education, I was likely to be doomed to a life of hardship and struggle. It was at this point that I decided to go to college. By this time, I had met two lovely young women, Wendy and Donna, who were to become very dear friends of mine, and we became inseparable. They both had young daughters and were single mothers like myself, and I was able to share some of my story with them. They accepted me completely with sincere compassion, understanding, and support. We talked for hours on end about our life experiences and hopes for the future. They also persuaded me to find forgiveness for myself and live a little. We shared a common desire to make something of ourselves, and together we decided we would apply for college in September of 1992.

Having no qualifications, I started at the bottom. During the period of my leaving school, the British examination system had changed from O Levels and CSEs to GCSEs. So, I began studying for English, Sociology, and Psychology GCSEs. The day we started at Waltham Forest College was a joyous and proud day for us all. The college was situated next to Waltham Forest Town Hall and, in my eyes, was rather grand in its appearance at the time. There were stairs leading up to the doors, and we pretended we were joining the *Fame* school (a popular US TV programme in the '80s) and laughed and danced our ways into the doors. I felt that maybe, just maybe, I had a chance at a decent future for Reace and myself. I threw myself into my studies and before long, found I had quite an aptitude for learning. When I received my first round of coursework results and got As, I could not have been any prouder. Although still traumatised from the late termination and guilt-ridden over my actions, I tried hard to put the trauma behind me. Although this was easier said than done, I tried nonetheless. I also got myself a part-time job in Ladbrokes, a local bookmaker, and began to feel that my life was finally on the up. I focused hard on caring for my son, my studies, and my job.

However, despite my sincere efforts, I continued to find that I would become depressed and melancholy as the months approached towards Christmas Eve. I think as I got older and was a mother myself, the trauma of being abandoned by my own mother on this day was never far from my thoughts. Little did I know that over the following years, I would begin a cycle of dreading the looming months to Christmas Eve, then go through the process of getting over it before the next Christmas approached.

It was so hard, and although I could confide in my dear friends, I did not feel able to share my story with anyone I did not feel I could trust. Trust and loss were major issues I would struggle with as the years went on, as if you cannot trust and rely on your own mother, who can you trust? I did not realise the profound effect of her abandonment upon me until this time.

Prior to and during my first year of study, I had no interest in relationships. I had been deeply scarred by the trauma of Mikey and the death of our baby, of which I took full responsibility for, so the time was right to focus only on my future. When I took my exams in the summer of 1993 and passed with two As and a B, I took this to mean I should go on to study further. I knew I had an interest in the social sciences and instinctively knew this was where my future lay. So, upon achieving success with my GCSEs, I enrolled to study for an Access to Social Science with a glimmer of hope of attending university if I passed. Reace was five years old, and he was a darling child. He gave me hope and determination to fight on for both of us. He was a child with a sunny disposition, was exceptionally cute, as I was often informed, and had a funny sense of humour. He truly made my life worth living, despite the trauma.

By the summer of 1993, I was starting to heal somewhat. While still sad and bruised by my previous experiences, I was moving on. I celebrated my achievements with my friends. We were like family, and I am forever grateful for their support. In September of the same year, I started my Access course and Reace started going to school. In those days, despite the hardships suffered by many, there was a lot of support for young single parent mothers who wanted to access education. I received funding for Reace to start a local After School and Community Club that was attached to the estate, called Holly Cats. Holly Cats was run by a kind, caring, and inspirational woman called Olivia, who was very community orientated and supportive. I was in a good place with sincere people. Reace was happy and life was looking up. I loved studying and I really enjoyed my course. It was a real eye-opener and set the path for the learning experiences I would go on to in the future. I studied sociological and psychological theories and models, and I found myself thoroughly consumed with my learning. The tutor of the course, Adam, was an interesting and dynamic teacher and he made learning most enjoyable.

One day, Adam gave a lecture on John Bowlby's theories of Attachment, Loss, and Maternal Deprivation. Up until that point, I had not heard of such theories, and I found myself becoming uncontrollably emotional during the class. I had no idea that scholars had studied the cases of motherless children like myself, and the impact of such a loss. I became so emotional that I ran out of the class with tears streaming down my face. Adam compassionately left the class to find me. He instinctively knew the psychological subject had stirred my emotions, and I found myself telling him a snippet of my life story. He was kind and sensitive and said he could sense there was a profound story within me. He said I had what it took to do well in the course and in higher education. He gave me lots of encouragement to continue, and continue I did. Again, I achieved high grades in my assignments, and this gave me the confidence to feel better about myself. I still struggled at Christmas with all the feelings it churned up in me, but something deep inside told me to carry on, as life was going to get better.

The New Year's Eve of 1993, going into 1994, I was twenty-three and had started going out raving again, mostly with Sarah. The scene was still in full force and the music was a mixture of hardcore and a new genre that was called jungle. Like hardcore, jungle was electronic music characterised with rapid break beats, heavy bass lines, and fantastic MCs to accompany. Raves were held in massive warehouses and venues, and the culture was like nothing else. If you were not part of it, then you were missing out big time. Sarah and I were as close as sisters, perhaps even closer due to our shared experiences of childhood trauma. We loved getting dressed up to go out and party, and as I tentatively began to forgive myself, I found myself once again in the highs of raving—and boy, I loved it! I also enjoyed the wonderful, reciprocal, close, and supportive relationships I had with my other friends, Wendy, Donna, and Deena, and I would often go out with them. We were a force to be reckoned with. How I managed to fit in parenting, studying, working, and raving, I don't know; however, I did. I was able to compartmentalise my life and make sure I focused on all. It was around this time I began to truly feel I was turning a corner and that life was on the up.

Reace was a happy little six-year-old. Everyone loved him, such was his endearing and sweet personality. He was settled in school with lots of friends, and I was continuing to make great progress in my further education. I felt the best I had ever felt in my life till now. I loved learning and felt that at last, I was achieving something good in my life and that I was going somewhere, not being clueless anymore. I also made three new friends at college, Angela, Annette, and Lorraine. These young women were extremely supportive and caring, and it was a joy for me to be in their company. Such was our camaraderie at college that we took to calling ourselves the four musketeers. We supported each other in our parenting and education, and we also loved a good time partying as well.

One day early into the new year, Angela said she was going to a World Dance rave, which was frequently held in an aircraft hangar at Lydd Airport in Kent. She said that she was going with a couple of her friends, whom I did not know. She asked if I wanted to go with her. She said she would like me to meet one of her friends, as she knew we would get along very well. She left it at that, and I did not think much more of it. I had been to World Dance raves at Lydd Airport before and had always had an amazing time; therefore, I was very much up for it. I said if I could arrange for Reace to be looked after for the weekend, I would love to go. Little did I know this would be a most significant and wonderful turning point, and that my life was about to take an entirely different course, one that I had not expected or had ever known possible.

CHAPTER 13

It was an early Saturday evening during February 1994. Reace was at Derek and Sharon's for the weekend, and I was dressed in my favourite raving outfit, consisting of Daisy Duke jean shorts, a black sparkly midriff top, Nike trainers, and a black satin jacket. Even if I do say so myself, I looked fabulous, and I was very much looking forward to the night ahead. Over the years, I had truly blossomed. My hair was a mass of long, thick, beautiful black curls, which were now easily managed, thanks to the wide range of black hair products that had flooded the market from the USA. I was very slim, fit, and toned, and I was more confident in my looks, much more than I had ever been during my younger years. Angela had informed me we would meet her friends at a nearby petrol station, and from there we would travel with them to World Dance. I was in high spirits as I walked the short walk from my flat to her house, and from there, we took a cab to a petrol station that was just off the A12. During this short trip, we excitedly chattered about the night ahead and of the fun we knew for sure we were going to have.

As the cab drove into the petrol station, Angela waved excitedly to two guys parked in a blue Honda Prelude sports car. She introduced her friends as Keith and Matthew. They made it obvious they were very happy to be taking us to World Dance, and both were full of humour throughout the drive to Lydd Airport in Kent. As I did not know either of them, I did not say too much and did not need to. However, I could see through the driver's rear mirror that Keith, who was driving, could not take his eyes off me. Every so often, I felt him trying to make eye contact and smiling broadly at me whenever we did.

Throughout that night, we partied wildly. It was clear we both enjoyed the same music and the rave scene. The music was buzzing, as were we. The laser lights were spectacular, and we had a fabulous time. In comparison to me, Keith appeared tall. He was a strong, muscular, cheeky-looking chappie, with twinkly hazel eyes and a crew cut hairstyle. He was twenty-seven and was obviously totally and completely enamoured with me. He made it clear from the minute we met that he really liked me and wanted to get to know me. While I was attracted to him, I did not want to rush into anything, and following the weekend of partying, I went home alone, leaving him with my number but hoping he would call. He did soon after, and from the very start, he was so funny and charming in his approach. We spent hours talking on the phone, which were home phone landlines in those days. I told him all about Reace and I was very happy to discover he was genuinely interested. He told me that he had a son who was a year younger than Reace, and we shared some of our relationship histories with each other. He enjoyed talking about his boy and it was clear he very much enjoyed being a father. It was not long before we had a date on our own.

On our first date, Keith brought me a massive bunch of flowers and a kettle, as I had previously casually mentioned during one of our chats that my kettle was broken. While I had not been expecting him to buy me a kettle, I was secretly chuffed that he had cared enough to do so. Over the next few months, I revelled in being treated like a princess. We fell totally in love and for the first time in my life, I was completely and utterly adored. Upon their first meeting, Reace and Keith took to each other instantly, and this made me fall in love with him even more. He was kind, loving, and boisterously playful with Reace, who responded as eagerly to the sincere and genuine affection Keith abundantly gave. My father and brother were equally happy that I had found such a caring man, who was clearly nothing but focused on looking after Reace and me. Keith was especially kind to Mark, and while during those early days, I hadn't shared with him a lot about my past, he intuitively knew that my brother was very important to me and did all he could to help him and make him feel part of our life.

Being of similar ages, Keith's son and Reace got on like a house on fire, and we loved spending family days out and evenings together. On my twenty-fourth birthday, Keith took me to see *Grease The Musical* at the Dominion, a West End theatre. It was the best birthday I had ever had, and by then, I was as smitten with him as he was with me. Keith was also loved by my friends and their children, as he was a lot of fun, very helpful, and always had something exciting planned. It was also very reassuring to be welcomed by

Keith's mother, two brothers, and sister. Matthew, the other guy on the day I met Keith, was in a relationship with Keith's sister and they had three daughters, who also got on very well with Reace.

As the joyous months rolled by, our relationship became firmly established and Keith moved into my flat. He proved to be very handy around the home, was keen to redecorate, and spent all his spare money transforming my flat. Much to Reace's delight, Keith decorated his bedroom with his favourite cartoon characters, the Teenage Mutant Ninja Turtles and Bart Simpson, and he set about making vast improvements to the other rooms. Simply put, Keith would do anything for me and to make me happy. I was able to drive but didn't have a car, so he bought me a little Honda to match his and he supported me in all that I did. He loved to sing to me, and one of his favourite songs to sing was *Endless Love* by Lionel Richie and Diana Ross. He told me from the start he would love me forever, and he truly meant it. I was the happiest I had ever been in my entire life.

During the summer of 1994, we took our first family holiday together to Herne Bay in Kent. For two blissful weeks, we rented a caravan in a holiday park in a coastal resort called Reculver. Reculver is a beautiful, peaceful, quaint, and idyllic spot nestled on the south coast about three miles east of Herne Bay. It is steeped in history, as it was once a twelfth century Roman fort, and the remains of the two towers and castle continue standing today, right on the cliffs of Reculver. The towers and fort are protected as part of the English Heritage, which cares for over four hundred historic places in the United Kingdom. Reace celebrated his seventh birthday on this holiday, and we also took my friend Wendy's daughter, Carrie Ann, as she often spent time with us. We spent days picnicking on the beach, swimming in the sea, crabbing, and riding bikes. In the evenings, we went to Dreamland, a big static funfair in Margate, and had more fun on the rides and in the arcades. We enjoyed taking long walks around the Reculver Towers, which Reace and Carrie Ann loved climbing all over, as all the kids did.

The only blight was that Keith's son was not there, even though we would have loved to have had him with us too. At the time, he was living with his maternal grandparents. Sadly, for a while, due to family disagreements, they stopped him from seeing his father and from spending time with us. This broke Keith's heart somewhat. However, he never gave up on him. It would be many months before his son could spend time with us again, and the matter turned into a long, bitter, costly, and drawn-out court battle for contact. It was granted in time, but was stressful and hurtful for Keith, as he loved his son dearly and I think he felt slightly guilty that he was fathering Reace and not his own son. However, he did not let the situation affect his feelings for either Reace or me, and determinedly ensured we had the best of times. Keith, being somewhat of a speed freak, loved cars and was an avid motorbike fan. For his birthday, he bought Reace his first little motorbike with a number seven on it. To say that Reace was ecstatic would be an understatement.

As our holiday was nearing the end, we knew we had found a place where we wanted to spend more family time together. We really didn't want to leave, so we resolved to buy our own caravan, and on the last day of our holiday, this is exactly what we did. Our first caravan was a cosy six-berth home away from home. From then on, every chance we got, we would jump in the car and head off to Reculver and to our lovely caravan by the sea. It was a wholly welcome relief from the concrete jungle of Cathall Road estate and London. Reace could freely and safely roam on his BMX bike. My friend Wendy's daughter, Carrie Ann, often came with us, and we considered each other to be auntie and niece. She and Reace made many friends at Reculver caravan park, and for the rest of that year, we spent as much time as possible there until the season ended and we had to pack up for the winter months. We were not sad, though, as we knew we would be back on the first day of spring of the following year and the next season.

As my relationship with Keith deepened, he tried to be emotionally supportive about my past, but somehow, I was never able to fully open up to him. If I tried, he would well up with tears and I knew from early on that he was not able to bear my pain. So, I mostly spared him the details. However, he knew Mark and I had been abandoned by our mother on Christmas Eve, and he knew at some level that I had experienced sexual abuse and other traumas. We just never spoke about it in any depth. He would do his utmost best to make Christmas magical, and once I had got over the dreaded Christmas Eve, I would find myself having some of the best Christmases I had ever had. Reace was insanely spoiled, and I loved this, as nothing made me happier than to see my child happy and excited, which he totally and utterly was. I always made sure Christmas was fun for him. Thereafter, on New Year's Eve, Keith and I would head out to rave and party into the New Year.

During this period, the local council had decided that Cathall Road was to be regenerated. This involved bulldozing the whole estate and building brand-new houses to replace the grey and decaying blocks of flats. We enjoyed watching this process as it meant we would soon be moving. Early in 1995, I was informed that I would be given a brand-new three-bedroom house. We were all very excited to say the least, and loved spending hours talking about our soon-to-be new home. When Reculver caravan park closed for the winter season, Keith would take Reace out on his motorbike, fishing, or swimming on weekends, and it was not long before Reace was calling him Dad. As Reace did not have his own father and Keith was missing his own son, their relationship turned out to be easy and mutually loving. Keith made it clear he was not replacing his son, and we knew he was doing whatever he could to get him back in his and our lives. However, he sincerely loved Reace as a father should, and therefore it felt like a natural process. I knew that in Keith, I had found a true love, and that he would continue to do his best for us.

That same year I passed my Access course with flying colours and applied to attend university in September. I thought long and hard about what to study. Many of my fellow students went on to apply for social work degrees. However, at the time, I continued to have no faith in social workers and a system that had failed my brother and I so catastrophically; therefore, this was not an option for me. I knew my future career would involve supporting children who had suffered trauma and abuse, and therefore my educational interests were in the social sciences. When I applied and was accepted into a BA honours degree in Psychosocial Studies with Professional Studies, I could not have been prouder. This was a four-year degree owing to the professional studies, and was at the University of East London.

As I was in education myself, I had school holidays off with Reace. Therefore, we would often head off to Reculver, where he could be free to play in nature and not be encumbered with the stress and tribulations of growing up in London on a council estate. Keith would work all week, then join us as soon as he finished work on the Friday evening. Weekends and holidays were full of fun. We would have barbeques with my friends, who loved to visit and spend warm, balmy nights by the sea. I felt like I was experiencing a little piece of heaven. Many times, my brother would also come with us to Reculver, and on occasion, he too found some peace at this beautiful, peaceful place that we had found. However, Mark was in a very different place to me and was not faring as well.

He continued to be distressed and depressed over his past traumas and found it impossible to forget his past. As I loved my brother dearly, along with Keith, we did whatever we could to make his life as bearable as we could.

Although still sometimes contentious, mostly due to our differing yet equally strong personalities, my relationship with my father had also vastly improved. Having Reace and giving him a grandson whom he was very proud of and making progress in my life helped us bond. While he still held some strange views and continued to focus his life on his passions, I found I was more able to tolerate him and felt in my heart that he had done the best that he could with the circumstances that we had. However, Mark did not feel the same way and continued to blame our father for his childhood traumas and poor mental health. During this period, my dear brother attempted to take his life. This led to one further disastrous meeting with my mother to try to persuade her to help him. I had not seen her since our first meeting back in 1989, and suffice to say this meeting did not fare any better.

Due to Mark's mild learning and mental health difficulties, he was allocated a social worker and a wonderful psychiatrist called Dr. Abanda. He was a kind, compassionate, and insightful man, and later I found out that he was an eminent leader in his specialised field. Following several consultations, Dr. Abanda demonstrated that he very much understood the difficulties Mark was troubled with. He was also very encouraging and most impressed with my own efforts to succeed in life. He was clear that we both most likely suffered with complex PTSD, and he ensured that Mark was referred for specialised psychotherapy, which did help somewhat.

I became resolute in my decision to not allow my mother or my past to stop me from achieving my goals. In my mind, I would never see her again. I became even more determined to make good of my life and a good life for my family. I threw myself into my studies and was happy, as I had my son and Keith, who continued to show me the love I had so desperately yearned for but had never received as a child. Mark was getting some support from community mental health and social services, and I felt somewhat reassured that he also knew he could at least depend on me.

CHAPTER 14

University was so inspiring, and I loved developing my knowledge of psychological and sociological theories. Before I knew it, it was June 1996, and I had completed my first year of higher education with flying colours. My self-esteem was improving by the day, and I was, dare I say it, becoming proud of myself. This year was also momentous for another reason. The regeneration of Cathall Road estate was in full swing. The grey, dingy concrete jungle maze was bulldozed and replaced with houses and low-level flats. Just as I finished my last exams, I was handed the keys to my new home. Even though it was still an estate, it was the best house I had ever had, and while owned by the council, it was my home. It was a brand spanking new, three-bedroom, three-storeyed town house with a garden, situated in the middle of a small cul-de-sac. Keith and I had saved money to furnish our new home and it was beautiful. We could not have been any happier. Such was our happiness that we would often sing the '80s Madness hit, "Our house, in the middle of our street" in sheer delight. Having moved into our new home and upon finishing my first year of university, we spent the summer holidays at our second home, our caravan at Reculver. I had a loving partner, a wonderful son, a lovely new house, and a holiday home. Life was getting better and better by the day, and I was as content as I could be. We had the best summer ever, and that September, I returned to university for my second year.

During the half-term holiday of my second year, we decided that instead of going to our caravan, we would visit some of Keith's family who lived in Newcastle. We took Wendy's daughter Carrie Ann along, as she and Reace were more like cousins and as such, we often took her away with us. We stayed with Keith's aunt and uncle, and we had some lovely days out to Durham Castle and bike rides around the stunning Northumberland countryside. One day during our trip, I found myself feeling extremely tired and simply could not find the energy to ride the bike and had to keep stopping. This was very unlike me, as I was very fit and always had energy. I started to think something else might be wrong. Then it dawned on me: I had not had a period for at least six weeks, possibly more. I was still taking contraception and I think with all the busyness of life, it had not occurred to me that I may be pregnant. That evening, I voiced my worry with Keith and shared that I thought I might be pregnant. Although I was not concerned about his reaction as I knew he loved me deeply and would be there for me, I was worried about the impact having a baby would have upon my studies and our life. However, for the first time ever, I was excited, and something inside told me this would be very different to any of my previous pregnancies. I did know for sure that if I was pregnant, I would be keeping our baby.

Keith was ecstatic and told me he hoped I was pregnant and that he could not wait to find out. The next morning, he went to a local pharmacy and purchased a pregnancy testing kit. When we saw the two blue lines which confirmed that I was indeed pregnant, we were completely overjoyed. For the first time in my life, I was feeling secure in the knowledge that my baby was dearly loved and wanted by his or her father. In my heart, I didn't care about the gender of our baby, but secretly I began to long for a little girl. Keith's son was back in our life, and he was having regular contact with him, so initially we shared our news with the children. They were incredibly happy and clearly excited at the prospect of becoming big brothers. Our baby, even before being born, was already bringing us even closer as a family. My father, Pam, and Mark also shared in our happiness, as did all my friends. My pregnancy was a total joyful experience. Keith tenderly cared for me, and nothing was too much for him. He would caress my growing bump and sing songs to our baby, and I loved every minute of it. He came to all my scans and most of my appointments. When halfway through my pregnancy, we found out we were expecting a baby girl, we could not have been happier.

Despite my initial concerns about my studies, when I spoke to my university tutor, I was reassured that this happened to many women, especially mature students, and that I would be able to defer my course at an appropriate point. My expected delivery date was May 2, 1997, a couple of weeks before my twenty-seventh birthday. Therefore, I decided I would complete the first semester of my second year and then take a year off to have my baby. When it was confirmed that I would be able to restart my course for the last semester of year two in January 1998, I was able to relax and felt less worried about how having my baby would impede upon the education that I had fought so hard to achieve.

As happy as I was at that time, there remained an underlying feeling of sadness and incompleteness. Back then I was unable to articulate my feelings as well as I can now, and upon reflection, I think it always felt like there were ghosts chasing me from my past, and a deep fear within that someday they would catch me. I tried hard to express my feelings to Keith, and although he was caring, he was not able to empathise and simply did not have the words I needed. This was not his fault and I told myself I could not expect to have it all within our relationship, and I was grateful for what I did have.

During my pregnancy, I focused hard on my studies, and as a result, I continued to achieve excellent grades. Upon successfully completing my first semester, the time was right to place my studies on hold. As a pre-baby treat, Keith booked a romantic trip to the Isle of Wight for the two of us. I have such fond memories of this period in my life as I was so happy and was completely cherished. I spent the last weeks of my pregnancy preparing for our baby, nesting in our lovely home, and being a stay-at-home mother to Reace. In my mind, life was as idyllic as it could and would ever be.

On April 26, 1997, a few days short of my due date, I went into labour. As with most, mine was exceptionally painful, but this time I had Keith by my side, lovingly supporting and encouraging me throughout. Early Sunday morning on April 27, 1997, my beautiful baby girl entered the world. Weighing six pounds and twelve ounces, she had a bright red scrunched-up little face and a shock of jet-black hair. She looked like a baby Cherokee Indian at birth, and it would be a complete understatement to say that I fell in love with my little girl instantly. Keith and I named our baby daughter Jessica, and we were beyond proud of her. Of course, most mothers think their children are beautiful, but I am not exaggerating when I say my Jess was the most exquisite-looking baby, and very much doll like. She had gorgeous creamy olive skin, jet-black shiny curls, wide and bright hazel eyes, and a pink rosebud mouth.

Reace was also enamoured with his little sister, as was Keith's son. Everyone adored her and she was the light of our lives. I was so happy, I thought I might burst. Keith cherished his little girl, and nothing was too much for him. He loved to cuddle her and sing in her little ears the Guns N' Roses classic, "Sweet Child O' Mine," and I was fiercely protective of my baby. While I loved and protected Reace with equal passion and determination, it felt different being the mother of a daughter. Being motherless, I knew I was never ever going to let my daughter suffer like I had. On my twenty-seventh birthday, when Jessica was two weeks old, Keith proposed to me, and of course I said yes. I felt loved and safe, and at the time, I did not think anything could upset our beautiful family unit.

In July of that year, we all headed off to our caravan for our first family holiday with our new addition, Jessica, who was three months old. By then we had upgraded our caravan, and we simply loved the life. We had a wonderful summer with the usual visitors. I stayed with Reace and Jessica for the whole six-week summer holiday, and as Keith was working, he came every Friday for the weekend. He also enjoyed a two-week break with us in August. Keith's son came for one of these weeks and in between this, I had my brother stay for a week and my friends Sarah, Wendy, and Donna also came and stayed with us. They all loved Reculver as much as we did, and we loved to share the happy times with them all.

As much as I loved my little baby, Jessica was extremely hard work and what some might say a difficult baby, as she was a crier. She would hardly ever let me put her down, and this was something I had not been used to. Reace had been such an easy baby and I do not think I was prepared for how hard a demanding baby would be. My love for her was all-consuming, so I coped and hoped it would get better as she got older. I will never forget that trip to the caravan, as this was the summer that Princess Diana died. It was August 31, 1997, a beautiful, sunny Sunday morning, and it was just me, Keith, and the kids at the caravan. I got up early with Jessica, leaving Keith to sleep in. As I switched on the television, the newsreader solemnly announced Diana was dead. At first, I thought he meant Diana Ross. Then when it dawned on me that it was Princess Diana who had died, I was totally shocked along with the whole world.

I woke Keith up to tell him and then we continued to watch as the whole tragedy unfolded. While clearly it was an immense tragedy for Princess Diana's children and family, it was also a very sad day for the UK. We had all come to love the brave princess who wore her heart on her sleeve, cared for the underdog, and who had been treated, in my view, appallingly in the years leading up to her death. The rest of the day there was an eerie silence across the whole caravan park, which I believe continued around the country and possibly across the world. It was a momentous time in our history and a period I will never forget. When we returned to London after our summer break, the whole of the UK was in mourning for the late great Princess Diana.

Upon our return to London, our happy family life continued. However, I was in for another soul-churning period in that following the birth of Jessica, I was not prepared for how I was going to view Christmas. As I have said previously, Christmas had always been a difficult period for me. In the lead up to it, I found I was always focused on and then relieved to get Christmas Eve out of the way. The feelings of dread as I recalled that fateful

Christmas Eve when my mother abandoned my brother and I threatened to consume me. It felt like I was stuck in a kind of Groundhog Day, having to relive the trauma and all that subsequently followed. I just could not help it, and while initially Keith did not say anything, he began to feel frustrated with my feelings of depression and sadness. He felt I needed to get over my trauma, as I should have been content that I had him and the children. If only life were as simple as this, I might have been able to.

I think it was because I had a daughter that it now pained me even more deeply to remember what had happened to me. The feelings that resulted from not being protected, loved, or cared for as a child seemed to overwhelm me. The pain of loss and the trauma I had suffered had never been addressed and continued to be unrelentingly unresolved. While I tried my best to bury my feelings, this strategy was completely unsuccessful. I took to not showing my feelings to Keith, and this was the start of my pulling away from him. I did not know this at the time, and I would never have believed it even if I had been told. As Christmas Eve passed, I seemed to be able to move forward and was able to put my energies into making Christmas Day a lovely day for my children, Keith, and Mark. Mark always spent Christmas with me as I could never bear to leave him on his own, and Keith did understand and support me in this. I also had the support of my dear friends.

It is fair to say that my relationship with my father at this time was variable, in that it was up and down. Sometimes

I was able to see that he had tried, even if he had failed. In this, I was able to acknowledge that he had done the best he could in view of his own emotional limitations. However, I could also swing between these feelings to that of anger, and would passionately blame him for the trauma Mark and I had suffered. In his defence, he did take on board my outpourings of anger and would say sorry for some of his actions. He was and remains the only individual from my childhood who did acknowledge his failings or wrongdoings. Even so, sometimes it only took him saying something out of turn, which he did often, for me to become fiercely angry with him. Periodically, I would cut him off and go for months without talking to him. He did love my children and wanted to be in our lives, so he would take my anger and would attempt to build bridges if I let him. Pam proved to be a significant support with my children. She was not my mother, as I have never had a mother and I could never call anyone mum, but she was my children's grandmother, and I was and still am very grateful for her support.

As Christmas 1997 passed and the New Year rolled in, it was soon time to return to university. It was January 1998 and Jessica was nine months old by now. While I knew it was going to be difficult studying with a baby and a young child, I knew I had to return before I lost the momentum and all that I had worked so hard to achieve. I was not prepared to let go of my education.

CHAPTER 15

Upon returning to university, I settled into a routine with the children. In view of my competing responsibilities, if I was to successfully complete my studies, I had to be focused and well prepared, such as ensuring I had access to journals and literature reviews at home. Even then, studying at home could only begin once I had cleaned the house and made sure the children's needs had been taken care of. Mostly, I would find myself studying in the early hours of the morning, as this would be the only time I could be sure of having to myself without any interruption. It was far from easy and at times, I was beyond exhausted. I didn't realise it at the time, but Keith had started to become resentful of the time I was devoting to my studies. He felt I was neglecting him as opposed to feeling that what I was doing was for the good of our family.

During my first week back to university, in a departure from the normal routine, all the student names were called during a roll call in one of the large lecture halls. I heard a name that I was deeply familiar with, which at the time I shrugged off, as how was I to know what would happen next? Following that lecture, as all the students spilled out into the communal halls, I noticed a beautiful, tall, and voluptuous blonde woman approaching me. She had quizzically penetrating light blue eyes and was direct in her approach as she asked, "Have you got a twenty pence piece for the phone?" She offered a handful of change meant for the exchange for a coin. This was just before mobile phones were about to explode, and although they were not as prevalent as they are now, I did have one.

As I scrambled through my purse, I debated on whether I should just offer her my mobile to use. Just as I was about to make the offer, she said, "I think we know each other. Is your name Diana Hylton?" As I looked up into her eyes, a feeling of recognition swept over me as I tentatively answered yes. It was then that she said, "Diana, is it really you?" Tears welled up in her eyes and threatened to spill down her lovely face. She went on. "Diana, it's me, Caroline … Caroline from St. Leonard's." In that moment you could have knocked me down with a feather, as I realised that standing before me was my dear friend from St. Leonard's. I mean, what were the chances of finding myself in the same university course and in the same year, all these years later? It was even more surprising, having taken a year out previously to have my baby girl. To say I was astounded does not even come close, and I certainly do not believe this was a coincidence.

Caroline and I were equally delighted and shocked as we hugged each other tightly. It felt like coming face to face with a dear family member that you thought you might never see again. We spent the next few hours in the university café catching up on the intervening years that had followed our departure from that hell hole. Caroline said she had been desperate to find me and that she had never forgotten me over all the years that had passed. She told me she was happy that I had made it this far, and I was equally eager to hear all about her life. We found we could be completely honest with each other. This was a refreshing feeling, as I was still quite guarded when expressing my innermost thoughts and feelings. This was another defence mechanism to protect myself from predators and untrustworthy people. Caroline was open in that she told me she had continued to struggle with addiction problems, mainly to opioids, which to look at her you would never know as she carried herself so beautifully. However, having started university and in her own experiences of motherhood, she told me she was hopeful as she felt she was gaining some control over her life and over her demons.

During our first meeting, we chatted for hours and shared our stories about our relationships and our children. As a result, I was late to pick up Jessica. This angered Keith and caused some friction, especially as I had neglected to call him. When it all tumbled out about my meeting with Caroline, he tried to pretend to be happy for me, but deep down, the feelings of jealousy and inadequacy that would soon consume him had started to develop. However, initially he tried to be supportive, and I think he was even a little intrigued. I mean, how could you not be?

Caroline and I took to meeting regularly after lectures and study groups. It was during one of these meetings that she asked if I was in touch with any of the others from St. Leonard's. When I told her that I hadn't seen anyone since the day I had left, she said she had, and that she had been told some children had been sexually abused by the staff. It was then I spilled out that it was true, that it had happened to me. I told her I had known of one other girl that had suffered the same fate, and that I had been a kind of behind closed doors witness to it. I recounted the times Uncle Bill had crept into Emily's cubicle, having satisfied some of his perverted feelings with me. Caroline was stunned that she had not been aware of it at the time, and we were perplexed as to why we had never said anything to each other, especially as we had been so close. Caroline told me of the times staff had encouraged her to watch pornographic films with them, and of how they turned a blind eye to her glue sniffing. She realised that this was part of their grooming of her to feel like an adult, instead of supporting the deeply troubled teenager that she was.

Caroline and I shared a deep sense of responsibility and felt we could not and should not let those monsters get away with it. We felt compelled to report the abuse to the police. Due to the historic nature of the abuse, we were not sure who to report it to, so in the end we decided to contact a police station within Tower Hamlets. Caroline, being a bossy and forceful character, took the lead. Initially, we called the Bow Police Station and gave a brief account of the abuse, specific names, dates, and our own personal details. The police officer on the phone was kind and said he would pass the information to the team that dealt with such offences. He advised us that someone would contact us shortly.

The case was allocated to a DI Channing, who arranged to visit my home to take a comprehensive statement. Keith and my friends had been blown away by my reunion with Caroline, as was I, and it was clear after we had shared our experiences that there had to be a deeper reason or purpose. In his defence, I will say that Keith did try to be supportive for a while. I was beyond nervous the day DI Channing came to my home. While I had disclosed some of the abuse to Caroline, I had never had to recount it in the way I had to in the making of this initial statement. I had buried my feelings so deep that it was stressful and anxiety-provoking to relive the memories of the sexual abuse. I was embarrassed and ashamed, and I think this was the beginning of my becoming re-traumatised. A can of worms was opened that I was going to struggle for many years to come to grips with. DI Channing was sensitive and kind in his questioning, and at the end of our first meeting, I believe he was sincere in telling me that he thought I was brave. On leaving my home, he said he was not clear as to what the next steps would be. However, he reassured me that he would make contact as soon as possible with an update. It must have been due to speaking out loud for the first time that I was so emotional after that first meeting, and I cried myself to sleep that night.

A few weeks later, DI Channing contacted me to say that while he had believed what I had told him, the CPS had decided that at that time, there was little that could be done due to the lack of evidence and the time that had passed. However, I was informed that the case was not being closed and that I would be contacted at a later date. I was devastated, as I had hoped some action would be taken and was not confident that any would be at any date in the future. It felt just like the time I told my social worker of the abuse, and she told me to focus on my new life. I was crushed and angry, and so was Caroline, but there was little we could do. All we could do was wait for a decision to be made by the police, which we both concluded was not going to happen anytime soon.

I tried to move on and attempted to re-bury the trauma, but found this was difficult, as the floodgates had now been opened and I did not have the psychological skills to close them. I pulled away from Keith and he, not knowing how to deal with even his own feelings, let alone mine, became even more frustrated and angry with me. He told me on many occasions that I should not spend so much time with Caroline and that I should concentrate on my children and on him. He would say things like, "Caroline is not good for you," or "She is making things worse for you," and "You are being selfish. Your children need you and I need you." So, overwhelmed with feelings of guilt, I really did try to put the trauma out of my head. I found the only way to cope was to immerse myself in my studies. How I passed my second year of study, I will never know. However, during that summer, I spent my usual break at Reculver with my children, and for a brief period, I did find some peace. The Christmas of 1998 was immensely difficult, and try as I might, my feelings of anger and depression snowballed and my relationship with Keith rapidly deteriorated.

It was early February 1999 when I was stunned to learn that my dear old friend Deena, who had been such a support when I had Reace and lived on Cathall Road estate, had been stricken down with a most cruel and debilitating terminal illness. Having lost touch with Deena over the last few years, I was to learn that she had contracted what was then cruelly known and referred to as mad cow disease, the correct term being human BSE or new variant CJD. Back then, little was known about BSE, but as time went on, it became known that the disease was a progressive fatal neurological disorder of cattle, caused by the greedy and unscrupulous farming industry that had thought it appropriate to feed cows contaminated bovine parts of other cows infected with BSE. Tragically, Deena was the first person in Waltham Forest to contract the disease.

Deena and her family had been kind to me in the past and I was sad that we had not kept in touch. No one or anything specific was to blame; we had just drifted apart, as people often do. I contacted Deena's mother and I visited the next day and then every day till she tragically took her last breath, which sadly, was just two weeks later. She was only twenty-eight years old and a broken little bird who could not talk, walk, eat, or even swallow in her final hours. Never in my life had I seen such a beautiful and vivacious spirit wiped away so quickly. I think at this time, the trauma of losing Deena and the months that followed her funeral took over some of my dark thoughts as I focused on trying to be supportive to her mother. I was under enormous pressure to be a mother, a partner, a friend, and not least, myself.

Somehow, I managed to get through my studies and progress to my third year. In the spring term of 1999, I started a hundred-day student placement, which was an integral part of my degree, with a domestic abuse charity called NAADV (Newham Action Against Domestic Violence). My placement with NAADV was positive, as I was able to focus on the future. It helped me to develop my natural caring skills and qualities, which were to form the foundation of my future professional career. I was a project worker and trained to support women and children who were suffering domestic abuse. Due to my own childhood and early adult experiences, I found I had a natural empathy and a deep understanding for the women and children I supported. This shone through in my words and actions, in that I was sincere and passionate, and I always went the extra mile. This was particularly true when I began working with a young woman, who at the time was just seventeen and a mother of a daughter aged two. She had suffered significant childhood and adolescent trauma, and I very much saw myself within her. Unfortunately, she was experiencing serious domestic abuse, and I knew I just had to help her as she was very much alone in the world, without any kind of family support. I did go well beyond my role, against the advice of Keith and my friends. However, I did not regret it and we have gone on to become lifelong friends. Our daughters are the same age, and they have enjoyed a close relationship throughout their childhoods. Keith and I even became her daughter's godparents, and I love her as my niece.

I found solace and inspiration in my work with NAADV, and my motivation and passion did not go unnoticed. I finished this placement with top grades and was kept on as a part-time volunteer, which I was happy to do, as not only did I enjoy my work, but I also knew it was going to assist me in terms of my future career. While I had absolutely no intention of becoming a statutory social worker, I did know my future lay in the social care field. With my professional placement complete, I progressed on to the fourth and final year of my degree. I also obtained a part-time post as a mental health support worker. With my work with NAADV and upon completing my degree, I hoped this would provide me with the further experience I needed for my future career endeavours. Once again, I found that my innate caring skills helped me in my work with troubled people with mental health difficulties, and they found me sincere and supportive. Just as I started to feel I was making some progress, I received a call that would again turn everything on its head.

CHAPTER 16

As the last year of the decade and the millennium approached, deep inside I felt a foreboding feeling of dread that my life was going to fall apart. It was the end of the summer of 1999 when I was contacted by the Metropolitan Police's Serious Crime unit. The police officer at the other end of the line introduced herself and advised that she would like to visit me as soon as possible to discuss my statement that I had made the previous year. I agreed for the visit to take place that same week, and having discussed with Caroline, I found she had also been contacted and that she was due to meet with the same officers the day after my meeting. I was so anxious waiting for that first meeting, but when I opened the door to DI Karen Sinclair and DI Amy Collins, I was struck by their warmth and kindly dispositions. Both immediately asked me to call them by their first names, and it was on this note that my first interview with them proceeded.

I was informed that due to numerous other complaints of sexual abuse, it was decided the matter required a formal investigation, and this was called Operation Mapperton. I was informed that one young person who had also been at St. Leonard's, Liam Carroll, had recently tragically taken his own life. I had known of Liam and his siblings, but I had not known he had been sexually abused or that he had made a complaint to the police just as I had. I was also informed that sadly, there had been more past residents of St. Leonard's who had committed suicide, and that many of those had also disclosed horrific abuse at the hands of the former staff members. Karen and Amy were sensitive in their work with me and at all times made it clear that they recognised how difficult and traumatic it must be for me to have to recount my experiences to complete strangers. This helped, as I had to provide my full statement over the course of the next few weeks and go over my previous statement that I had made to DI Channing.

Late into the autumn of 1999, William Starling was arrested and charged with the sexual abuse of many children who had been placed in his care. I learned there were eleven known victims, including myself, who would all testify against him. I was advised that a criminal trial would take place at the Old Bailey in January 2001. The news hit me like a ton of bricks. While I was relieved he had finally been charged, I had no idea of the magnitude of the abuse and of how far and wide it had reached. I felt a deep feeling of apprehension of what was to come. I was informed that the delay in Starling being charged and the actual trial was due to the complexity of the case and the number of witnesses that would be giving evidence.

The next few years proved to be turbulent and a time of unravelling. Upon reflection, I now understand that at this point, everything became just too much for me to cope with. The combination of having to relive and confront the past, Starling's arrest, Deena's untimely and most tragic death, and the realisation that I was approaching the twenty-fifth anniversary of when my mother abandoned us on Christmas Eve. It just became psychologically and emotionally too much to handle. Try as I might, I was anxious beyond belief. I could not sleep or eat, I struggled to maintain focus on my studies and work, and I was often tearful and depressed. Keith was at a loss as to how to help, and he became increasingly frustrated and impatient.

During a welfare call from Karen, it all came tumbling out, and I told her that I was not coping. She asked for my GP's contact details, said to me she would make an emergency appointment for the next day, and that she and Amy would accompany me. I had no idea where to start with my GP, but fortunately Karen took the lead. She explained about the abuse, the investigation, and that a trial at the Old Bailey would take place, of which I was to be an integral witness. She requested I be referred for psychotherapy at the Tavistock. At the time, I was unaware that the Tavistock was world-renowned for its therapeutic treatment and training. I did, however, trust Karen and Amy, and instinctively I felt they had my best interests at the fore.

My GP also prescribed Prozac, and this was the first time in my life I had ever taken any kind of antidepressant. It was not something I wanted, but in desperation, I knew I didn't have much choice. Over the course of my life, I had briefly attempted therapy, particularly during my most desperate times. I had found that it was either not the right therapy or I had never found a therapist with whom I felt a connection. Or with whom I felt understood my innermost thoughts and feelings. It had always felt like I was telling some story with no point. With these previous experiences in mind, I did not have any confidence that therapy at the Tavistock would be any different. But I did not have any choice but to try it, as it was that or lose my mind.

When I attended that first appointment, I was extremely guarded. I felt mentally and emotionally drained. I made the decision that I was not going to go through the pain of reliving my trauma to yet another stranger. Therefore, ahead of my first appointment, I decided I would write a summary of my life and ask whoever the therapist was to read it prior to talking with me. Upon entering the therapy room, I was struck by how glamourous the therapist looked. She was stunning, tall, had silky blonde hair, and was dressed impeccably. I felt small and shabby in comparison. She introduced herself as Amelia and asked me to tell her a little bit about myself. Immediately my defences rose, and I pulled out my pieces of A4 paper on which I had attempted to write the details of some of the traumas that I had suffered. Initially, Amelia was resistant, as she firmly yet gently tried to explain that it would not be helpful to either myself or her for our therapeutic relationship to begin in this manner. However, I was adamant that if she would not read it, I could not even begin the arduous task of reliving my life. It was a battle of wills. However, in the end, she agreed and began to read while I sat tentatively like a small bird in a chair that felt like it could swallow me whole.

Amelia read with slow deliberateness. When finished, she stared at me thoughtfully before saying, "Diana, I can see how very difficult it has been for you to come here and that it will be hard for you to commit to this process, although I hope you do. She continued by saying I hope you do come back to see me next week." She then nodded that it was time for our first session to end. I was surprised and somewhat annoyed, as in my mind I had not even started, let alone finished. However, this was my first introduction to the fifty-minute therapeutic hour, and I would come to understand the signal for our session to end very well over the next few years. Amelia was firm but kind in letting me know that this was how our sessions would take place. Even so, I left that room in a flood of tears.

It was these initial sessions that helped me get through the exceptionally difficult period leading up to Christmas Eve of 1999. It seemed this time was more painful in view of all that was happening. I felt exceptionally weighed down, anxious, and above all, deeply sad. Keith was unable to cope with my sadness and he left it to my friends to comfort me. Sadly, as the months passed, Keith became more critical in his actions and words, and more unfeeling in his approach towards me. His lack of compassion and subsequent cruel and uncaring behaviours manifested in many ways. It was becoming starkly clear that intrinsically, we were very different people, that there was a deep divide in our core beliefs, and this deeply unsettled me. I was becoming more spiritually aware and was growing in depth. I had always been a deep-thinking and spiritual person. Keith was not. In our early years, I thought of it as differing views and assured myself that this was normal and was okay. The realisation of our major differences engulfed me, and it was in this context that I began to withdraw and pull away from Keith. There was only so much of him saying things like "pull yourself together" and "stop crying" I could bear.

The Christmas of 1999 passed, and a week later, it was Millennium Eve. During a family friend's party, Keith accused me of flirting with a dear friend. I was absolutely stunned and incredibly hurt by his wild accusations. I could not believe he was speaking to me the way he was, and his jealousy was totally unfounded and untrue. I had a deep and sinking feeling that if I did not get away from the situation and Keith and his cruel behaviours, I would, without a doubt, have a breakdown. I felt an overwhelming urge to run away from it all. I felt a deep need to be by the sea, and to be near the place I had derived so much comfort and joy from over the years, so I went to Herne Bay. I cried the whole journey, and upon booking into a small bed and breakfast on the seafront, I took myself to bed and cried some more. It is no exaggeration to say I cried for four days almost nonstop. I cried like I had never cried in my entire life. I cried for the abused and abandoned little girl within me, for the loss of my mother. I was also mourning the breaking down of the only relationship I had that had been supportive and loving, and I feared what was to come.

On day three of my emotional breakdown, in tears, I plucked up the courage to call Keith. I had left him with Reace and Jessica; therefore, I knew I had no choice but to let him know where I was. While he tried to apologise for his actions, I could tell by his voice that he was not being sincere but was saying what he felt I wanted to hear. However, when he asked me where I was, I could not lie, so I gave him the name of the bed and breakfast, but not before pleading with him to allow me some time to pull myself together. Time was not something Keith felt he could give, and on day four, amid another bout of tears, I heard a knock on my door. The proprietor had been very kind, and he could sense my deep distress, so he had left me alone during my short stay. When I opened the door, he looked embarrassed to have disturbed me but said I had a visitor and enquired whether I wanted to come down to the waiting area to meet him. Of course, I knew it was Keith. As soon as he saw me, he drew me into his arms and hugged me. He said the children were with his mother and that he had felt unable to leave me alone.

Once alone in the room, Keith tried to explain how he felt and why he had acted in the way that he had. He tried to make me believe that he had not meant to make such wild accusations, but that it was my fault for not giving him the attention he needed. I was forced to accept that it was my fault and that I had made him act in the way that he had. So, amid the guilt that was forced upon me, I agreed to go home. Having returned home with Keith, I tried to give him the attention he craved. However, something inside of me had broken. I had been devastated by his lack of compassion, and try as I might, I was not able to get over it.

CHAPTER 17

I attempted to continue my work as a mental health support worker and to finish my studies. However, by now the Prozac was fully in my system and my feelings were being stunted. It was like I had almost stopped feeling anything. I continued to attend my therapy sessions with Amelia, who, thankfully, was proving to be an enormous support. She instinctively knew when to say something, to explore something more deeply, and she also knew when to say nothing. In times of silence, I really struggled, and while I did not know it at the time, this is an essential part of the psychotherapeutic process. I would often ask Amelia why she was not saying anything, to which she would indicate she understood my discomfort and smiled reassuringly. I talked about my mother, Keith, and my kids, but steered away from the elephant in the room: the abuse I had suffered in the home. She never asked me to talk about anything I was not comfortable talking about, and for this, I was grateful. On many occasions when she gently nodded to the clock that our session had ended, I would run like the wind to get away, with tears streaming down my face.

While initially I did not talk of the abuse, I did talk about how the prospect of facing Starling at the impending trial was causing me deep anxiety, distress, and flashbacks. In

April of 2000, during another visit from Karen and Amy, I was required again to go over the explicit details and what I knew about the abuse of others. I think the more I spoke of the abuse, the more traumatised I became. All my relationships were suffering. My brother tried to be supportive in his own way, but I know he felt somewhat aggrieved, as my abuser was being taken to task, and this was something he would never experience. He was not jealous as he loved me deeply and wanted the best for me; however, I do think he felt left out and overlooked. I tried to keep my feelings from him as I knew how fragile he was. My father also did not know how to communicate with me, and I sensed he could not bear to talk about the abuse I had suffered. I think he was resentful with what he considered as me dragging the past back out into the open. Sadly, even my poor children did not have the present mother they needed. I don't know if it was because of the Prozac, the posttraumatic stress I was clearly suffering, the breaking down of my relationship, or a consequence of it all; I just know I was a deep emotional and psychological mess.

Due to my unravelling, I had no choice but to request another deferment from university. I had tried so hard to avoid this. However, in the end, I simply could not give my studies the dedicated time and required attention. It was during this period, May 2000, that I turned thirty years old. There was no big celebration and no fuss, and during this period I became close to a work colleague for emotional support. Confused and distressed, I felt I had no choice but to end my relationship with Keith. He found it impossible to accept that our relationship was over. As a result, he acted uncharacteristically out of control, and because of this, our relationship completely broke down. In addition to this, the trial was looming and heavily weighed upon me.

In the lead-up to Christmas that year and the trial, which had been set for January 15, 2001, I was well supported by my friends, my family, Amelia, Karen, and Amy. I was taken to the Old Bailey to be shown around the court and the waiting room, where I would sit between giving evidence. The idea was to try and make it less intimidating when the trial started. However, with the best will in the world, I don't think anything, or anyone, could have prepared me for what would prove to be a significantly traumatic process. I was aware the Old Bailey was the central criminal court and the most well-known British court. During the pre-trial visit, I was met by my assigned witness support worker, who was kind and friendly in a matronly kind of way. She took her time to explain the process, although I have to say I did not take much of this in and have little recollection of what was said.

The Old Bailey is an imposing yet also magnificent building, with the words "Defend the Children of the Poor and Punish the Wrongdoer" aptly etched into the stone wall above the entrance. At the very least, I felt rather overwhelmed and insignificant as I was shown around. It felt like I was on a sinister tour that I was spectator to. With the imminent trial approaching, my anxiety spiralled out of control and my GP increased my medication. I was also prescribed Stelazine to help me cope. Stelazine, which in the past was used to treat anxiety disorders such as the kind I was suffering, is in fact an antipsychotic medication used to primarily treat schizophrenia. At the time, I had no idea. If I had, I would probably never have taken it. However, in my desperation to ensure I coped, I didn't even query it. I do believe the combination of Prozac and Stelazine had a deeply profound impact upon my mental state, and while they did help me to feel less anxious about the trial, I am also acutely aware that they significantly stunted my feelings in every area. I also experienced what I can only describe as glitches in my feelings, like a flickering, weak internet connection or light switch.

On January 15, 2001, I was informed of when I was scheduled to give evidence during the trial. Sadly, Caroline, who had suffered a relapse, was in a rehabilitation facility in Plymouth and was not able to support me at this time. On the first day of my evidence, my close friend Donna, who was a tower of support, travelled with me by underground train to St. Paul's in Central London in silence. I felt ill as I tried to quell the daunting feelings that threatened to consume me. While some preparation had been attempted, after twenty years, how could I have been prepared to face the sinister, cruel, and perverted monster who had exerted such power over me as a child? I felt extremely self-conscious on the train, as if everyone could tell what had happened and what I was about to do. I don't know if this was paranoia because of the medication, or if this was another effect of the re-traumatisation I was going through. However, to say I was nervous at the prospect of challenging Starling does not even come close, as I had never testified against anyone before, much less at the Old Bailey.

When we got to the court, I was met by a witness support officer, who tried her best to put me at ease. After being ushered into the assigned waiting area, I was thankful that Donna was allowed to stay with me. I was advised that the prosecution and defence barristers wanted to meet me prior to my evidence. The prosecution barrister, Ms. Sally Howes, sensitively tried to put me at ease whilst explaining her role and how she would take me through my evidence. Thereafter, I was informed that I would be cross-examined by Starling's defence barrister, and at that point, I did sincerely trust her kind and professional demeanour.

As I tentatively entered the courtroom and was ushered to the witness stand, I felt a wave of determination course through me as I raised my eyes to confront Starling. I was shocked to see that he had not changed significantly since I had last seen him. I mean, by now he was seventy-four years old, and he did look old, but then he had always looked old to me. I noticed his previously black and white streaked hair was now white and silver and was becoming sparse, but apart from this, he pretty much looked the same. He met my eyes with a steely ice-cold stare. I felt instinctively that he was attempting to intimidate me, and in that moment, I knew this was my chance, and that whatever he attempted to do, this was my moment of justice. The judge who presided over the trial seemed wise and kindly as he advised me to direct my answers to him. I was also aware of the twelve male and female jurors, all of whom stared intently at me. The atmosphere was thick and tense.

Ms. Howes, gently but painstakingly took me step by step through my evidence. She asked me to go into detail as to how I had been groomed and how the sexual abuse had impacted me as a child and as an adult. It was excruciatingly embarrassing to have to relay the particulars of the abuse and be questioned on this. Though I had been a small, vulnerable child and had been powerless, I was still ashamed. I was ashamed to admit that I had been bribed with sweets, cigarettes, and money in return for sexual favours and my silence; however, I had to tell the truth. I was also questioned about the abuse I had been aware of regarding the others. Throughout the whole of my testimony, I could feel Starling's eyes penetratingly boring into and through me. I felt like he was trying to will me into silence again. This was never going to happen. My testimony took the whole day and by the end, I was mentally exhausted but relieved to have gotten through it. I wanted to get off the witness stand and get out of the courtroom. So much so, that when I was excused for the day, in my haste to get away, I stumbled down the steps of the witness box. Mortified, I ran out of the courtroom.

While I had been advised the cross-examination would be very difficult and stressful, I had never given evidence before and I was completely unprepared for what it entailed. As I have said, I had been somewhat reassured by Starling's defence barrister. However, when on the stand, I felt she was cold and calculated in her cross-examination as she took me back over my evidence. While the following is not a verbatim account of her questioning, she outright accused me on several occasions that in her opinion, I was lying. I felt she tried to make Starling look like some sort of fatherly benefactor who had only had my best interests at heart. She inferred that I was confused and that I had gravely mistaken his kindness for evilness. She brought up details of my mother's abandonment and my father's actions, and I felt she was trying to say that I was lying to make Starling pay for the trauma I had suffered. All of which was, of course, ludicrous, and I resolutely stood my ground. I found my courage and was bolstered in this by Starling's smirking at me from the dock where he sat.

She argued that I was not a reliable witness to testify about the abuse I had reported that Emily had suffered. In a harsh and accusatory manner, she asked questions along the lines of, "How could YOU possibly know that Mr. Starling, in your words, was sexually abusing your co-resident Emily, when WE all know that it is not possible to see through the doors? How can YOU be sure that Mr. Starling was not actually talking or comforting her?" She queried, if we as children had not spoken about the abuse to each other, then how could I be sure this had happened to her? When she realised I was adamant in my testimony of the abuse that Starling had perpetrated and would not be moved, she tried another tactic, which shocked me to my core. While I accept that any person accused of an offence has the right to a defence, particularly such a horrible crime as the sexual abuse of children, I am still taken aback by the extent some barristers will go to prove their client's alleged innocence.

In her cross-examination, Starling's barrister said it was important to discuss what had happened in my life once I had left St. Leonard's. She even made some sort of remark implying that if I had such a good memory, I should not have any difficulties with this. She started to talk about my life when I had been returned to my father's care. She asked me if I had been happy. I was honest and said, "I was not happy, but I was happier to be with my father than I had been in the children's home." I really had no idea where she was going with her line of questioning when she said something like, "Miss Hylton, would it be fair to say that YOU have never been happy in your father's care, and that this is not the first time you have lied about such matters?" I had no idea what she was talking about and said as much. She said, "Okay, let me refresh your memory and take you back to 1983." She went on, "Miss Hylton, did you or did you not make a statement to the police that a man, a stranger, had ambushed you and that he had been sexually indecent towards you?"

Momentarily stunned, I did not answer. I knew what she meant, but I was not sure why she was bringing this up. So, after a long period of silence, I tentatively answered, "Erm, yes." She then went on to say, "Can you please tell the court about this ALLEGED incident?" It was then that I knew exactly where she was going with her line of questioning. Sensing my hesitancy, she said something similar like, "Miss Hylton, I will assist you by reading out the statement YOU made to the police about the 'alleged attack.'" She read out my statement about the incident in which I had lied to my father and to the police on the day I had been home late from school in 1983. She said, "Miss Hylton, is this an accurate statement of what you said happened to you on this date in question?" Quietly, I said, "I did make that statement to the police, but it did not happen." To this, she seized the opportunity to say something along the lines of, "Miss Hylton, are you telling me and the court that YOU lied about a man ambushing you and being sexually indecent towards you?" It was at this point that I looked at the judge and the jury in earnest and tearfully admitted that I had lied in order to escape my father's wrath. I told them that I had not known my father would call the police and subsequently, I had no choice but to continue with the lie once he had done so.

She went on, "So you admit you lied about a man pulling you into some bushes and being sexually indecent, so how can you expect the court to believe you are telling the truth about Mr. Starling?" At this point, I gathered my strength to look her squarely and purposefully in her eyes and said, "I honestly believe if I had not been sexually abused by Bill Starling, I would not have thought of that as a reason for me getting home from school late." I went on to say, "It is because of the abuse that I had these thoughts in my mind." With that, I looked directly at Starling and willed him to look away. He must have felt my determination, as he lowered his eyes, unable to keep staring at me. I also sensed that she had exhausted her questioning of me as she rather dismissively turned away from me and said to the judge, "No further questions, your honour."

Thereafter, I was excused, and while I was exhausted from my two days on the stand, I was relieved that it was over. I felt resigned, and that whatever would be, would be. This time, while leaving the stand, I did not run, as I knew I had done my best and that I had been honest. On my exit from the courtroom, I gave one more glance Starling's way; he did not look up. I felt small but somewhat triumphant that I had at least faced him, and he could not look at me.

Upon the trial concluding, I was advised by the police that the jury would take time to deliberate their verdict, and that this could possibly take weeks. However, the evidence was overwhelming, and we did not have to wait very long before the verdict was announced. Starling was found guilty of nineteen offences, including indecent assaults, rape, and buggery over a period of twenty years. Amid all the stress, this was a time to be briefly jubilant in the victory. I was relieved it was over and that some justice was going to be served. Starling was remanded into custody while he awaited his sentencing. Due to the complexity of the case, the sentencing was delayed until April of 2001. I was informed by the police that I would be able to attend the sentencing and that other victims would also be invited, and now, since the trial was over, we would be allowed to meet with each other.

During this period, the police informed me that Alan Prescott, the former superintendent of St. Leonard's, and Haydn Davies, had also been charged with the sexual abuse of many children at St. Leonard's. Throughout the years, I had known about Emily and of course what had happened to me, but I had no idea of the scale of the abuse and over how many years this took place. I was deeply shocked. However, I was also relieved that I had escaped, was alive to tell the tale, and able to at least see some justice being served. I was also surprised to learn that Alan Prescott had been so revered and respected within the community that he had gone on to become the assistant director of social services in Tower Hamlets, a labour councillor, and a local magistrate. Further, when St. Leonard's had finally closed in a shroud of secrecy in 1984, the Grade II listed buildings had been converted into luxury houses for the more affluent residents of Hornchurch. Gallingly, Prescott even had a road named after him on The Drive in his honour, to commemorate the good work he had undertaken with the poor, unwanted, and abandoned children who had been placed in his care. I was sickened to learn this. I was further informed that while charges had been brought, this was suspected to be the tip of the iceberg. It was believed there were likely more than seventy victims of abuse during the period from 1965–1984, and the investigation would continue.

Starling was sentenced on April 14, 2001. I felt nervous as I entered the Old Bailey, but I was feeling stronger than I had felt for a while. I was ushered into the public gallery for the sentencing, and I came face to face with some of the other victims for the first time in twenty years. I recognised a couple of my former house children and I smiled and nodded. I was sad to see Emily was not there. The police advised that some simply did not have the strength to face the ordeal. I understood this. I looked—or perhaps, more likely glared—triumphantly at Starling, who this time looked like a shadow of himself. The months between the verdict and the sentencing had clearly had an impact. He looked like exactly what he was: a wizened, old, broken, deviant man.

When the judge read out the sentence, he began by commending us all for our courage in standing up and speaking out. He said it was an appalling failure on the part of The London Borough of Tower Hamlets, and it was clear they had failed in their duty of care. He said something like, Starling was beyond evil, as he had been employed to look after some of the most vulnerable children in the country, and that he had not only abused us, but he had also abused his power and position. He was sentenced to serve fourteen years. While some may say this is not enough, I felt it was at least some justice. Starling could not get away with this, and I hoped he would spend the rest of his days in prison. He looked forlorn as he was led away in handcuffs to start his sentence. We cheered, for this was a victory not just for us, but for all his victims who had suffered abuse at his hands.

After the sentencing, the jurors requested to meet us, and it was very comforting and reassuring to hear their words of compassion, encouragement, and respect. I thank all of them for their diligent and conscientious work, and can sincerely say that the process helped a great deal towards my healing, even if at that time, I was not there yet. Following the sentencing, I met with the other survivors for the first time. However, it was a bittersweet and awkward meeting, as we were an eclectic bunch of troubled and damaged adults.

Some months later, I was advised that Alan Prescott had pleaded guilty to some lesser charges of sexual abuse and was sentenced to two years imprisonment. The fact that he had pleaded guilty was taken into consideration. The trial against Haydn Davies was stayed due to contamination of evidence. Therefore, neither deviant has received the punishment they deserve. Even more unbelievable, I discovered that Haydn had served time in prison many years prior to his employment at St. Leonard's for the sexual abuse of a minor. While I believe this would and could not happen today, I remain incredulous that it could even happen in the'70s and '80s. This is appalling, as the lives of many children and subsequent adults have been ruined by these men. A number of these children are dead, and their blood is on the hands of their abusers. There is, however, some small consolation. Following Prescott's conviction, the road named in his honour was changed, but not before a survivor campaigned to get this done.

CHAPTER 18

It was an anti-climax following Starling's sentencing, and the months passed by in a blur. So much had happened prior to and during this period that I had mountains to climb if I was ever to achieve any of my dreams, and I was right at the bottom. I was glad the trial was finally over, although my life was a mess. I had attempted a relationship with my dear friend that had led to the end of my relationship with Keith. While my friend was an exceptionally caring, kind, and supportive man, he was not right for me, nor me for him. During the turbulence, I married him. However, it broke down quickly, and regrettably, I hurt him very deeply. Knowing how he had also been hurt by Keith, I felt incredibly guilty about the trauma I knew I had caused my friend. Despite the tremendous upset, I felt I could not continue the relationship.

Thereafter continued a period of deep distress, the only security I had ever had in tatters, my family broken. Furthermore, I had no employment, and I still had the final year of my degree to complete. I remained on antidepressants and the Stelazine too, scared to give them up in case I really fell apart. I had two small children who were depending on me for everything. I had to find the strength somehow to pull myself together, and I still had so much to do if this was going to happen. Thankfully, I still had Amelia, who unfailingly did her best to help me make some sense of it all.

I was aware that I was to receive financial compensation for the abuse I had suffered, but again, I was ill-prepared for the process of the numerous soul-bearing, soul-destroying sessions I was required to undergo with solicitors and psychologists. They were kind people, experts in their own fields, and whom I believe tried their best to be sensitive and sympathetic. However, I did not want sympathy, and it was impossible for these professionals to show empathy, as true empathy requires a person to have had a similar sort of experience. Upon reflection, I find it distasteful and rather cruel that it was not sufficient for it to be accepted that we had been abused and neglected by the people employed by the same system meant to keep us safe and cared for. We had to again quantify how much we had been damaged, and how does anyone do this?

During this same period, I was advised that I was able to read my social care records, and at the time, I thought this might help me to fill in some of the gaps and perhaps even be cathartic in some way. I was very wrong, and in hindsight, it was not the right time (if there was ever going to be one). However, curiosity won over sensibility, and I went to Tower Hamlets social services offices in Globe Road, Bethnal Green, East London. I went alone, as I was informed that due to the confidential nature of the records, I would not be allowed to have anyone attend with me. The journey by public transport was sombre, as I had to pass so many sad places of my past, including Priestman Point, the tower block where I had lived with my parents, the squat where my mother had abandoned my brother and I, and Bow Road Police Station. A melancholic trip down memory lane that, upon reflection, I could have done without. When I arrived at the social services offices, I was met by a grey-haired, wrinkled old lady (a social worker, I presume) who, rather unfortunately for me, given her role, seemed to distinctly lack sensitivity, compassion, and tact.

It was a daunting task preparing to read about my early years and my social care history, and I was not prepared for the barriers that would be put in my way. The social worker said there were conditions and rules she had to go through with me before I would be able to read my files. She coldly informed me that much had been redacted due to data protection. She explained that I would not be able to read the third-party information, as this would be without their consent and would contravene data protection legislation. This included some of my brother's information and that of my mother. In the '70s and'80s, siblings' files were often combined, so it was not possible to redact it all. Even so, I was somewhat shocked to be given a bundle of paper files with lots of information blacked out. I was also perturbed and unsettled by the fact that the social worker insisted she had to sit next to me while I read my files. This was in case there was anything that needed to be further withheld. The whole experience enraged me. I was rather curt with her as I felt she was trying to protect the system that had hurt me, as opposed to what she should have been doing, which was supporting me.

I read about that fateful Christmas Eve when my mother abandoned us and in between the blacked-out lines, I gleaned that it had been suspected Mark and possibly myself had been sexually abused whilst in her care. I don't have any recollection of being sexually abused prior to going to St. Leonard's, and I do not think that it happened to me. It was clear that on Boxing Day, when Mark was placed in Langley House, it was strongly suspected that he had been sexually abused in the preceding hours. Mark had already disclosed this many years previous anyway. With tears streaming down my cheeks, incredibly, I read that Starling and the others were able to write things like, "Diana is a very pretty child who is well behaved," and "Mark is uncontrollable and is mentally retarded. He is not suitable for care at St. Leonard's." I mean, what the hell did they mean by this? I suspect it was a way of staff formally recording to suit their own evil gains. Still, it didn't make it any easier to process the stark information.

I was shocked to my core to see how even my own social worker, Mrs. Lincoln, had recorded the event that led to my father punching Haydn Davies following his physical and emotional abuse of me. My father was described as "an angry, violent man, like many men of West Indian background." It was recorded that my father had violently attacked Davies for simply attempting to discipline me. Suffice to say I was outraged and extremely distressed.

The social worker was not skilled to deal with the kind of trauma it was reawakening within me. I was not able to stand any more of the lies, and therefore I told her in no uncertain terms to stick it where the sun doesn't shine. Having read enough, I ran from that office in a flood of tears. I never ever did go back to read any more of my files; the pain of it was too much to bear. I knew deep within that there was nothing to gain and that it was not going to help me.

However, Amelia, my wonderful therapist, was appropriately skilled, and she supported me throughout this period. I never told her this, but when I look back, I can now see I had begun to view her as a kind of psychological mother. She was strong and caring, wise, and intuitive. She validated my experiences, and it was this kind of treatment that I needed, and which I very much responded to. She also helped me to think about my own father's position and how difficult it had been for him, especially considering his own limitations. Despite his failings, he had fought for my brother and me, and in my softening and understanding, I began to find forgiveness for him. I knew he loved my brother and me; he was the only one who had stood by us and fought for us. My father had never given up, and I dread to think what could or would have happened to us had he not persevered.

It was through the process of my therapy that I began to feel the strong desire to resume my studies. I admired Amelia and I wanted a little of what she had in terms of her academic and professional success. She also had an air of sophistication that at the time I admired and was also rather envious of, as I instinctively sensed her life was worlds away from mine. She was extremely encouraging of my plans to resume my studies, and I thank her for this, as I truly believe I may never have gained the psychological strength to return to university if it had not been for her.

Amelia was instrumental in helping me figure out my next steps. She always provided a safe space for me to ponder my life and be honest about my feelings. She encouraged me to think of my children at Christmas, and the long, slow, and arduous process of healing began. I contacted the University of East London with the support of the Mapperton police team, who wrote a mitigating letter explaining the reasons for my prolonged deferment, and I was beyond happy when it was agreed that I would resume my studies in January 2002.

I had completed most of my degree apart from my dissertation, and I wanted this to be focused on an aspect I could relate to and what I considered to be important. Therefore, I chose to research the impact and effectiveness of (at the time), the newly introduced Children (Leaving Care) Act 2000. This had been a new piece of legislation that had been passed which acknowledged comprehensive support when leaving the care system. This was an area that had been woefully neglected, thus leaving many vulnerable young people without the vital support that other young people who had parents and families benefitted from. It had become recognised that care leavers were overrepresented in the criminal justice and mental health systems, and that life chances for care leavers were overwhelmingly poor as compared to young people of the same age range who had not been in care, and that this needed to be addressed.

Prior to this, the only provisions local authorities were duty bound to provide to young people leaving care were inadequately set out in the Children Act 1989. It was not until I began my academic journey that I found out the laws in relation to when I had been in care were extremely poor and facilitated the culture of lack of accountability and duty upon local authorities. I became very much interested in legislation and law and its impact on children. As a way of coping with my personal situation, I found this to be a welcome distraction. I was sincerely committed to my research, of which the aim was to find out whether the new Act was effective in assisting young care leavers or not. In research terms, it was a qualitative study in that the focus was on human behaviour and the way people feel and think, as opposed to quantitative, which uses data, statistics, and logic to answer research questions.

I interviewed eight care leavers aged eighteen to twenty-five and explored their experiences with the support they had been provided, and their hopes and aspirations. I was encouraged to find they were enthusiastic and willing participants, and from my small sample, I gleaned a wealth of information which informed my research. I cannot lay any scientific claims due to the size of the study, and of course, this is not the purpose of an undergraduate dissertation anyway. I was, however, pleasantly surprised to find the new Act was making a small difference. The older individuals were understandably more cynical about the difference in support they were being provided, and their feelings about this ran deep. The younger individuals, while hardly full of praise for a system they mostly considered had let them down, concluded they were at least benefiting from the additional support. I finished my dissertation by the summer of 2002.

Over the course of the following months, my relationship with my father vastly improved. He was, in his own way, trying to support me and the children. While he is not an overly emotionally expressive man, the older I was becoming, the more able I was to acknowledge that life is not black and white. I began to appreciate that he had taken the more difficult route of sticking by us through thick and thin, when no one else had. I was studying, had my children to look after, and was still in therapy and on medication, but overall, I felt that I was on the other side of the trauma and that things could only get better. I had not received any compensation as yet, as this was yet another long, protracted process. However, I was reassured that it was coming. I had some debts, and so I hoped it would come soon. Even so, life was getting better by the day. Even the Christmas Eve of 2002 was not as daunting as the previous ones, as Amelia, in her therapeutic wisdom, had begun to help me to see things slightly differently. She gave me the idea of doing something fun with Jessica either on or around Christmas Eve to make it about our mother/daughter relationship, and not the painful, nonexistent relationship with my own mother and the dark memories. In turn, this led to less time and emphasis spent on brooding over the past.

Early in 2003, I received my compensation of £45,000, and around the same time, I was also informed that I had achieved a 2.1 for my degree. The latter gave me more joy than the former, and I could not have been any prouder of myself the day I graduated at the Barbican. With my compensation, I paid off my debts. Then, I crazily spoiled my children with new toys, bikes, and clothes. I took them on holidays, to concerts including Eminem, and to see shows like *Wicked* and *Mamma Mia!* They had also suffered due to my mental anguish and the breakdown of my relationship with their father, and I wanted to try to ameliorate some of their pain. I spent the money fast. I did not value it, as it came from a place of bad feelings and traumatic memories. I did, however, save some for a small deposit, as I intended to cash in on the right to buy a social housing scheme that had come into force.

Prior to my graduation, I successfully applied for a post as a leaving care support worker with the renowned Coram children's charity. I also made the decision that the time had come for me to stop taking my medication. I was acutely aware that my feelings were being stunted, and in the back of my mind, I knew it was because of the medication. After almost four years, I felt it was now or never. I did not want to have to rely on antidepressants and anxiety medication all my life, and I became determined not to. I gradually reduced the dose over a period of six weeks, and I was pleased with my strength and determination, which gave me the will to continue. For the first couple of months, I felt most strange. It was like waking up from a dream—or perhaps a nightmare—and this was going to become more apparent as the months progressed. It was around this period that my ill-fated marriage completely broke down.

I threw myself into my role of supporting young people during their transition from care to independence. Coram is England's oldest children's charity, created in 1739 by the great philanthropist Thomas Coram. I was proud to have secured this post and I was sincere in giving it my all. I was enthusiastic and motivated, and this got me noticed in positive ways. I found I had an affinity with the young people whom I was supporting, and I was very much an ardent champion of their rights. My role was to ensure they developed the skills they needed to move into independence and to also help them access training, apply for employment, and any relevant benefits they were entitled to. I wholeheartedly enjoyed supporting young people to obtain tenancies and to set up and move into their new homes. I was encouraging, motivating, and overall empathetic. I believe the young people I worked with warmed to this approach, and I felt proud.

As Christmas 2003 approached, with my newly developing strategy, I focused on making the week leading up to

Christmas Eve all about my children. Jess and I went to see *The Lion King* on London's West End stage at the Lyceum Theatre, and I took Reace to the cinema, on different days, of course. While I often took the children to various activities, it was very different in that I had never done so during the week leading up to Christmas, and it was in the making of good memories with my own children during this period that helped me to recover from the Groundhog Day that had been my experience for so many years previous. I grew stronger in this day by day. I would also say it was around this period that I started to develop my awareness of how it was possible to take control of my thoughts and to effect more positive feelings, although this was just the start of what continues to be a lifelong practice.

CHAPTER 19

In what I can only describe as my awakening, I started to feel more than deeply sad about my relationship with Keith and how it had ended. I felt very much that when the going had got tough, as it had done, I'd given up on the only relationship where I had truly felt like I had a family. I felt like I had not given it a chance. Due to the time that had passed (it was now 2004), I was in a different place both emotionally and psychologically.

We had been separated for around four years, and while I had not suffered a memory lapse about how Keith had lacked empathy and had been unsupportive, culminating in violence, I recalled that he had also been affected to the point of breakdown. I remembered the good and loving times and could not help but think he had not been violent ever before or since. I felt that we had unfinished business and that the medication had caused me to act in a more rash way than I perhaps would have normally done.

My children adored him, and he was a good father to them both. What he lacked in emotional intelligence, he made up for in other ways. He had not once, in all that had taken place, neglected Reace or made him feel any different to Jessica. I loved and appreciated him for this. Furthermore, any chance he got, he told me he still loved me and that he always would. When Keith collected the children on a Friday evening for the weekend, he seemed to sense my unhappiness and appeared open and motivated to talk with me. Over the years, he had come to understand my need to be open, to talk, and to deeply reflect.

Within the safety of my therapy sessions, I explored my feelings with Amelia. She was clearly concerned that I was going to make another monumental, disastrous decision, particularly in view of my brief failed marriage. When I voiced my feelings about Keith, I am sure she thought that I had gone and lost my mind. I had not, but I felt that after the trauma of the trial and my awakening from the medication-induced haze, I was now looking at my life with a clear head. I honestly felt like I had taken a hand grenade to the one relationship that had given me a family and security and blown it into smithereens. I missed everything about it, and I even missed my caravan.

I started to feel envious when Keith picked the children up to take them to Reculver and began to yearn to go with them. Therefore, despite the reservations of my family, friends, and Amelia, Keith and I reconciled. Strangely, Keith and I never talked about the past and all that had taken place between us. I would have been able to, and deep down I knew that the answer did not lie in burying it. However, Keith lacked the emotional intelligence to have a soul-searching discussion about what had happened. He preferred to bury the past, and his way was to focus on the future and attempt to wipe it all away as if it had never happened. So, I pushed any feelings of doubt to the side and became determined to be the best mother I could and to forge ahead and achieve a positive career in the social care field. It was also around this time that I realised I needed to end my therapy. I knew I could not stay in therapy forever, and I felt that I needed to make it on my own.

Amelia was understanding and supportive of my decision, and she made it clear that if I ever needed support, I could always contact her. I had been seeing her for five years. She had helped me enormously through the traumatic times, and she had also helped me to look at things differently. While she had naturally expressed her concern about my reconciliation with Keith, she helped me think it through. I was no longer crippled with guilt as I had been in the past, and I felt that I was through the worst. I was a much more secure and insightful person as a result. Amelia was a wonderful therapist who always helped me to see my strengths and to feel pride in my achievements. I always felt I was more than a patient for her and that she genuinely cared about me, and I am forever grateful to her. As I left the Tavistock, I felt lighter and more hopeful than I had in years.

I had been working as a leaving care support worker for less than a year when I was offered the chance to step up to a more senior role in an exciting new mentoring project, which was being developed by Coram. My manager at the time, a beautiful soul inside and out, saw a lot of potential in me and was most encouraging in terms of my professional development. She was a qualified social worker but had chosen to work for a charity within the voluntary sector instead of statutory social services. For those who may not know, the voluntary sector is the sector of services and agencies that are not government-led or funded through public taxation.

My manager showed me volumes of compassion and kindness. I found it extremely easy to be myself with her, and it was not long before we became firm friends. She was the manager of the mentoring project under the umbrella of Coram, and I was most impressed by her leadership skills and creativity. I was keen to learn as much as I could from her. She had created the project and with me as her deputy, she was able to focus upon the strategic development of the service. She was keen to show me the ropes and encouraged me to develop my professional career. I was more than eager to absorb all she imparted.

I enthusiastically and passionately believed in our work. My role was to recruit and train members of the public to work in a voluntary capacity to mentor young care leavers and teenage parents. It was through my work within the mentoring project that I have come to love and, moreover, truly believe in the concept of mentoring and coaching. We trained the volunteer mentors for six weeks, and then matched them with young people with whom we felt there would be a connection. We supported the young people and the volunteer mentors and assisted both with their self-development. My natural affinity continued to shine through, and again, this is likely to be due to my having a sincere understanding and genuine empathy for the young people's experiences and struggles.

When supporting vulnerable people, there is nothing that comes close to the benefits a volunteer mentor can offer, and I can say this with great confidence. It was clear to see the difference these people made to the young people's lives, hopes, and aspirations. The trust and bond came because the young people felt their mentors cared about them so much, they did it for free. This was immensely powerful and facilitated some amazing relationships and positive outcomes. Even when the official mentoring relationship ended, many of the mentors and mentees stayed in touch. I felt proud to be part of this process and I gave it my all and had a lot of fun along the way. During this period, Keith and I secured a mortgage on our house, so I was making solid progress in all areas. I was happier than I had been for many years, and my children were settled. Life was truly on the up.

However, as the mentoring service was run by a charity, funding—or the lack of it, I should say—invariably reared its ugly head. The issue of my manager having to fundraise for the service was difficult and a time-consuming role. While she gave it her all and did her utmost best, it was incredibly stressful. Furthermore, she wanted to start her own family, and the stress of trying to keep the service going was impacting this. It came to a head one day and we decided that we would see the last round of the mentoring relationships to conclusion, and then we would both look for different jobs. It was at this point that I began to think deeply as to where I would move onto in terms of my professional career. During this time, I applied for the role of a leaving care personal advisor, which had been implemented by the government as a statutory role. I thought this was a perfect position for me, and with deep determination, I set about going for it.

I was so pleased when I was shortlisted to attend the second stage of recruitment, which involved an interview and a series of activities. On the day, I found there were perhaps thirty other applicants. Following an individual interview, we were required to participate in group sessions, undertake role-plays, and complete a test. I was so energised and excited by the position, I really thought I was going to be offered a post. So, when I was informed that I had not, I was very disappointed, and I could not believe I had not been chosen for the role. However, what is meant to be, is meant to be. If I had secured this post, I would have been very happy to take it and it would have been a positive move, but I would not have looked for anything else at that point, and this would have changed the whole course of my professional career, subsequent vocation, and perhaps my overall purpose.

Despite the disappointment of not getting the leaving care advisor post, I did not give up and I went back to the drawing board. It was early January 2005 when looking through *The Guardian*, I came across an advertisement I simply could not ignore. It was spread over two pages, recruiting for postgraduate trainee social workers. The London Borough of Haringey was piloting a new project, which was one of the first of its kind at the time. The offer was to fund postgraduates to take a master's degree in social work, whilst training on the job. This meant all university fees would be paid alongside a salaried position. The idea behind this was for the local authority to grow their own social workers from a pool of graduates who would already have a high level of education and experience. The trade-off, if accepted onto the scheme, was the commitment to work for the local authority for at least three years post qualification.

As I have previously said, I had absolutely no intention of ever becoming a statutory social worker. I used to think that my experience of the care system had scarred me forever, and it had led me to believe that it would never be for me. However, the offer to be paid to study for a master's degree proved to be extremely alluring. I started to feel differently and considered that just because I had been let down by the system, it did not mean I had to be a let-down too. Further, it began to dawn on me that I would be able to make much more of a difference in my professional endeavours if I had a thorough understanding of both sides of the track. I began to feel more excited than I had ever been about any aspect of my education or my professional career. The prerequisites for this fantastic opportunity were a bachelor's degree of at least a 2.1 (tick), and relevant work experience (another tick). But moreover, I knew I had a wealth of life experience that I could and would bring to the role.

I began to feel very differently and passionately about the opportunity and of social work in general. At that time, I had little knowledge of Haringey Children's Services or the tragic fate of Victoria Climbié. I had an awareness of her name, but I had no idea of the scale of the abuse and torture she had suffered. Further, how she had been failed by four local authorities, two hospitals, two police child protection teams, and the NSPCC. It was my manager who expressed some caution in my applying for the post and who urged me to investigate what had happened. In my research and preparation for what was going to be the most arduous recruitment process I had ever experienced, I was horrified to learn of how little Victoria had been known to all these services, but none had been able to protect her or ultimately save her life.

I do think it is important to talk a little about Victoria and the most unimaginable trauma she suffered, as she is an integral reason for my absolute determination to train to become a social worker. Most significantly, because of the cataclysmic failure of the multi-agency working which culminated in her tragic death, the most comprehensive inquiry ever into the child protection system failures was undertaken. The findings set out in Lord Laming's report (2003) led to the major overhaul of all the UK's child protection services. Furthermore, it led to the biggest revision of legislation since the introduction of the Children Act 1989, the law that is the foundation of and which underpins all child protection practice, even today. The more aware I became of Victoria, the more important it became to understand what had happened. With the advent of the internet, it was now possible to access public inquiries online. Therefore, I read the entire 432-page report, sometimes in horror, sometimes in shock, but moreover in extreme sadness for this poor child's tragic plight.

Victoria was born on the Ivory Coast in West Africa. Her parents, while very loving, were extremely poor. Eighteen months prior to her murder, in good faith, they allowed her great aunt, Marie-Thérèse Kouao, to bring her to the UK for what they had thought would lead to a good education and subsequently a better life. Sadly, this was not to be the case, as on February 25, 2000, at the tender age of eight, she was horrifically murdered by Kouao and her boyfriend Carl Manning. At the time of her death, Victoria was found to have 128 separate injuries on her tiny scar-ravaged body. In Kouao's care, she was mercilessly tortured and beaten with bicycle chains, hammers, and wires. She had been burnt with cigarettes and tied up for hours naked in a bath, lying in her own urine and excrement. Such was the extent of the torture that she was starved before finally succumbing to a cruel, painful, and slow death of malnutrition and hypothermia. Dr. Nathaniel Cary, Home Office Pathologist, said, "All nonaccidental injuries to children are awful and difficult for everybody to deal with, but in terms of the nature and extent of the injury, and the almost systematic nature of the inflicted injury, I certainly regard this as the worst I have ever dealt with, and it is just about the worst I have ever heard of" (Laming 2003: p. 14).

The murder trial began at the Old Bailey in November 2000 and lasted over two months. The court heard that Kouao had believed Victoria was possessed by evil spirits, and she had, on many occasions, taken her to a church to be exorcised. (Batty, David: *The Guardian*: 2002). It is known that Kouao moved with Victoria between at least four London boroughs, claiming to be her mother, seeking financial and housing support and medical attention. The overall tragedy is that on none of these occasions was the alarm raised to step in and remove Victoria from this heinous woman's care. The trial opened with the prosecution making it clear that the blame lay not only with Kouao and Manning but also with the child protection authorities who had been *"blindingly incompetent"* (Batty, David: *The Guardian*: 2001). On January 12, 2001, Kouao and Manning were jailed for life.

The Crown Prosecutor for Kouao and Manning, Ms. Sally Howes, moved on to become the Crown Prosecutor of William Starling at the St. Leonard's trial on January 15, 2001, just three days after their sentencing. Of course, I did not know this, and I don't even think I was aware of the magnitude of what had happened to little Victoria at that time, as I had been so immersed in my own difficult situation. Having only recently become aware of Sally Howes now a QC, being the same prosecutor, I remain blown away by some of the synchronicities in my life. I could never have known the significance of this and how the impact of the failings of the system regarding Victoria—and lesser so, myself—would come to have upon my future professional career. When I applied for the Haringey graduate social work position, I was completely unaware of this poignant coincidence. However, it is not an understatement to say that upon reading the full Laming Inquiry, I was moved beyond belief to a position of knowing intrinsically that I would become a child protection social worker. I knew I would sincerely and emphatically do everything I could to keep children safe and that this would become my life's vocation. Similarly, what I could not have known at that stage was that some years later, I would find myself, along with many of my colleagues, in the firing line for the public vilification of the system's failing of yet another innocent child who died.

The Laming Inquiry found there had been an "inexcusable gross failure of the system," as there had been at least twelve opportunities for publicly funded statutory agencies to have intervened and to have saved Victoria's life. Laming said across the board that all the agencies were "underfunded, inadequately staffed, and poorly led." He stated, *"Even after listening to all the evidence, I remain amazed that nobody in any of the key agencies had the presence of mind to follow what are relatively straightforward procedures on how to respond to a child about whom there is concern of deliberate harm" (Laming*

2003: p. 4). He ended by stating, *"Having considered the response to Victoria from each of the agencies, I am forced to conclude that the principal failure to protect her was the result of widespread organisational malaise"* (Laming 2003: p. 4). Laming made 108 recommendations which, as I have said, subsequently led to the most comprehensive overhaul of the UK child protection system to that date.

It was amid these monumental changes, and considering my own experiences of being failed by the system, that I simply knew I had to secure a position. What I did not know was there were another seventy-five people vying for only ten places. I also did not know a further prerequisite of the social work master's degree was to have an English and Maths GCSE or equivalent. While I had obtained an English GCSE, I had not ventured into the maths area. For one, I had no interest in it whatsoever, and two, I thought I had never been any good at maths anyway. I was greatly encouraged when I found out I had been shortlisted, but was also deeply apprehensive upon being advised I would have to undergo a maths test that would be at the level of GCSE.

I was not going to be deterred, and via the internet, I set about teaching myself algebra, fractions, ratios, percentages, etc. I found that basically there are fundamental laws and formulas, including BODMAS and the mean, mode, and median, and that once these are understood, it is possible to work out mathematical questions and equations. This would have been about the time I started to become aware of the principle that if you really want something and take definitive action alongside sincere belief and gratitude, you can achieve anything you want. I had not heard of the Law of Attraction at that point, but now I know I implemented it in my quest to win my place on the graduate trainee scheme.

The maths test took place at Bruce Castle Museum, a beautiful sixteenth century Grade 1 listed manor house, which is in the North London area of Tottenham. Bruce Castle and the park is quite a contrast from the rest of the significantly deprived, disadvantaged, and run-down area of Tottenham. It is also a stone's throw away from where Victoria Climbié had died. This sombre fact was not lost on me, and I was even more motivated. It was a bright, crisp, and sunny but cold February morning in 2005 when I entered the beautiful historic building to take the test. With wracking nerves, I looked up to the sky and silently prayed, "Please, God, help me pass this test so that I can become a social worker and help to keep children safe." I truly and sincerely meant this from the bottom of my heart. While the test was somewhat difficult, I knew in my heart I had passed.

When I was informed that I had passed with 65%, I was elated. I could not believe that I, the girl who had always hated maths, had passed. Nothing was going to stop me now. With the application and maths test in the bag, I moved onto the next stages of the recruitment process, the presentation and the interview. Such was my passion and drive, my conviction shone through. I answered all the questions, and with just ten minutes to plan, I gave an inspirational presentation to the interview panel on a topic of their choice. I just knew I was going to be offered a place on the scheme, and when I got my offer letter, I was beyond elated. This was my biggest professional achievement to date. I was going to study for my master's, and I was going to train to become a child protection social worker.

The graduate trainee scheme started in April 2005. I could not have been any prouder when, on the first day of the induction, myself and nine others were informed that we were the first cohort on the programme and that we had beaten so many other applicants for the post. The head of practice learning talked about the harrowing journey the local authority of Haringey had been through, and I came to learn that it was one of the most deprived and diverse of all the London boroughs. He informed us that we were an integral part of the new start, of a new kind of social care and of a new kind of social worker, and it would be an understatement to say that I was totally inspired by him. Haringey was investing in people and wanted to make sure the terrible events that had led to Victoria Climbié being catastrophically failed would not happen again.

However, it was not lazy social work that led to the failings; it was a system that was at its knees and relying on underqualified workers with caseloads that were too high, coupled with poor information sharing systems. I felt positive that things were changing and would continue to evolve. I felt a deep sense of responsibility that I was a small part of the change. I found I really bonded with my cohort and with our lovely head of practice learning. I was able to share some of my past in a way that engendered admiration and not pity. I was bolstered in this and began to really see and believe in my strength. I had already overcome my past and I was going to make something good come of it. I was the most inspired I had ever been, and I was raring to go.

Keith and I settled into trying to find happiness again. We had moved on from the preceding turbulent years and we both accepted that mistakes had been made. He was supportive of my intention to undertake my master's and to train to become a social worker. It was not the same as in the early years, but somehow, we re-bonded and were enjoying family time once again. This included lovely holidays at the caravan, and now also abroad, around the Caribbean. I was happy that my children were happy and that they were enjoying participating in various extracurricular activities, Reace motorbiking and Jessica cheerleading. Dare I say, I felt relieved that the worst was behind us, and we were a family once again.

My relationship with my father was improving greatly year upon year. He was also supportive of my plans to become a social worker, of the children, and even of my reconciliation with Keith. I think despite everything that had happened, my father felt it was more positive for the children that they had their father, and he could see I was happier and more settled than I had been for a long time. My brother Mark was coping with his depression, and he was happy to spend weekends at our house. I was back in touch with Caroline, and I had my dear supportive friends. I really felt I was making progress and achieving, which, of course, I was.

In 2005, during the period between April to September, it was all systems go. While I had been accepted into the graduate trainee scheme, I still had to submit a university application and I had to attend another panel interview prior to being accepted into the social work master's programme at Middlesex University. We, Cohort 1, were very well supported in this by the whole practice learning team. To prepare for our practice placements, we were put into various social work teams, and I was placed in the Children in Care team for the beginning of my social work journey.

Within a short span of time, I learned so much in terms of looked after children's processes and procedures. I met lots of lovely, interesting, like-minded professionals, many of whom I remain good friends with today. One man, who was a senior social worker at the time, was designated to be my mentor for the period I was on the team. He was a massive encouragement and such a great laugh. Some years later, he became my direct line manager, and although we don't see each other much now, we have remained good friends, and I have a lot of affection for the guy. During the years we worked together, I found him to be extremely knowledgeable and I liked how he knew to strike the balance between ensuring children's safety, their needs being met, and having enough humour as not to allow oneself to be so serious to become overwhelmed or burned out. This was one of the first survival strategies I would learn during my career.

I regularly attended the Family Court which was in Highgate, North London, and I shadowed my manager. She was an expert in the court arena, and she taught me so much about the legal processes in relation to looked after children and care proceedings. I was eager to learn, as while I had a wealth of relevant life experience, as to be expected, it was completely different being on the other side as a professional. During this period, I worked with parents who suffered with addiction and mental illness, and although I had empathy for their difficulties, my focus remained firmly on the best interests of the children. I also worked with parents who were facing criminal charges for physical and/or sexual abuse, and naturally, it was more difficult to find compassion in these instances. Having had my own experiences of abuse and trauma, I found that this helped considerably in terms of differentiating between what can be described as abject and sinister abuse of children to that of parental ignorance and lack of awareness regarding physical chastisement. I also found it most interesting to study and learn the effects, both short- and long-term, and the law in relation to practice.

Other aspects of my early training within the Children in Care team included the completion of life story work for children who were adopted away from their birth families, the undertaking of statutory visits to children in care, attendance at professional meetings, and the drafting of contact plans between children and their parents. On occasions when the contact service could not meet the high demand due to lack of capacity, I was called upon to undertake supervised contact. It was on one such occasion that I experienced being attacked by a vulnerable and distressed child who struggled with the effects of foetal alcohol syndrome. I have to say this was not going to be the last time in my career that I would be assaulted by a poor child who did not have the capacity to verbally express their distress.

At this stage, it is important to note that it is not possible for me to write about specific cases that I have been involved with, not even if I changed individual's names. This is not only due to the obvious reasons in terms of data protection, but also the fact that if, for some reason, a child, a parent, or a family member recognised themselves, it would be completely unethical, possibly distressing, and could reawaken traumas, which I would never want to do. Therefore, it is fundamentally essential that I always protect the privacy of anyone who I have worked with and that I always maintain confidentiality. On this basis, moving forward, I will talk about incidents and themes, but not specific to any cases I have worked upon.

Having successfully obtained my place at Middlesex University, I set about preparing to study for my master's, a two-year course. Not all social workers complete a master's, and it is possible to become a statutory social worker with a Bachelor of Arts, although this still must be a specific social work degree. Back then, to qualify as a social worker, a trainee on a master's course was required to undertake two, one-hundred-day practice placements. As part of the graduate trainee scheme, I was fortunate in that I was given the opportunity to complete one placement in a statutory adults' team and my final placement within a statutory children and families team. The idea was to provide all graduate trainees with an experience of both services, to assist in the decision as to which area we would choose to specialise in when the time came. While there was never any doubt in my mind that I would specialise in children and families, I was more than happy to gain some experience in adults' services.

While I was making great strides in my professional development and my personal life was so much more settled, I do have to mention that it was during this period that I sadly lost my dearly loved cousin Paul. I spoke of him earlier in this book, as he had been such a loving, caring, and supportive influence in my life. As a small child, it was he who had taught me to read, and out of my extensive extended paternal family, it was only he, aside from my father, who had maintained contact whilst I was in local authority care. Further, as an adult, it was he who supported me following the attack I suffered when on the Cathall Road estate, and to put it simply, it was he who had been there for me when many others had not. Being that much older than me, I had viewed him as a kind of father figure.

Although I was heartbroken, I was also deeply relieved, as Paul's last five years on earth had been nothing short of a living hell. In his late forties, he suffered a series of strokes that had left him paralysed from the neck down and completely blind. The worst part of this most debilitating illness and disability was that he was completely aware of his situation. He maintained his sharp mind and all of his faculties, which was indescribably cruel, as he could no longer read, see, or do anything for himself. It was nothing short of a living torture, so when he passed on June 15, 2005, while deeply saddened, I was relieved that he did not have to suffer anymore. He was a strong man with deep courage, and he was dignified till the very end. Rest in peace, my dearest cousin. I will always love you!

In September of the same year, I started my course and began my first hundred-day placement in the Adults Combined Learning Disabilities team. It was a large multi-disciplinary team, with the overall purpose to assess risk and to implement services to meet the social, emotional, health, housing, and leisure needs of adults with learning disabilities and their carers. While I had thought because of my brother's mild learning difficulty that I had some experience in this area, it was hugely different to social work practice and being on placement. The range of learning disabilities between mild, moderate, and severe is vast, and my knowledge, awareness, and compassion expanded as a result. The difficulties families face in supporting their loved ones are mostly unseen and hidden from the public. As a result, most people have little idea of the significant challenges faced if they do not have any direct experience of living with a family member who has a learning disability or difficulty. I became aware of disorders such as Prader-Willi, and I supported individuals who were nonverbal or severely autistic, many with multiple impairments.

My work involved a wide range of tasks which included managing a caseload, the undertaking of comprehensive carer and continuing care assessments, placement reviews, duty cover, and convening and participating in professional and strategy meetings. I devised care plans that followed a person-centred approach which, overall, aimed to afford vulnerable people choice and autonomy, a basic human right that is often taken for granted. While I cannot say my passion is in this area, this placement greatly assisted the expansion of my knowledge, skills, and awareness. I was also supported very well by my practice assessor, whom I liked a lot and learned a great deal from about the processes and procedures within this specific area of social work. Of course, caring for my family, studying, and attending placement was difficult, but I was energised and motivated, and as a result, I continued to excel. I thoroughly enjoyed my university course and learning about law and social work theories. I sailed through my first year, achieved excellent grades, and made some friends for life along the way.

My second-year placement began in September 2006, and I chose to go to a child protection referral and assessment team. I was eager to learn all I could about frontline child protection social work, as this was where I envisioned my future career would be. I instantly connected with my practice assessor Sylvia, and I was most impressed by her down-to-earth, real, and what I considered to be an expert approach (and still do). She was the manager of the referral and assessment team (R&A), and boy, did she know her stuff! I was very happy to be under her wing, and I immersed myself in completing assessments, attending child protection conferences, court, and a wide range of both statutory and non-statutory professional meetings. I was supported by the whole team and my practice developed swiftly. I am a fast learner, and my previous life and professional experiences provided a firm foundation on which to learn from.

I really enjoyed and still do take great pride in the undertaking of child protection risk and parenting assessments. I find the process of direct work with parents and children, the gathering and analysis of information, the making of recommendations, and thereafter, the drafting of plans to address concerns and meet needs most interesting. It is an essential aspect of social work that requires significant skill, and even if I do say so myself, I have a great aptitude for it. Sylvia recognised this quality in me and was keen for me to progress further. I was afforded many learning opportunities of which I took full advantage. I liked being on duty and I was able to cope well with the fast-paced nature of it.

It requires a lot of resilience to be a child protection social worker, as it is often extremely stressful in terms of the nature of the work and the incidents that workers are exposed to. Even the most resilient of workers will be brought to tears when faced with a baby or a child who has been sexually abused or has sustained significant injuries because of abuse and neglect. Or a child who is inconsolable, as a parent has died, or even worse, been murdered by the other parent. These are tragic situations a social worker on the frontline in a deprived area is often faced with, and while it is an essential service, it is not for everyone. It takes a great deal of courage and compassion, on top of the phenomenal volume of procedural work that must be juggled alongside competing demands and priorities. This is the very nature of social work.

Sylvia was always encouraging and conveyed to me that she was confident in my natural abilities and developing skills. We got on really well and I felt we had been well matched in terms of personality, sincerity, and focus. Although she did not speak much of her previous experiences, I could tell she was a woman of depth, with most likely a significant life story of her own to tell. During my official hundred-day placement, I had no idea that she had some involvement with Victoria Climbié, although this had been in her work within a local NSPCC family centre. To be clear, she had not been involved in any direct way with the social work case, or the failings. She had, however, given evidence at the Laming Inquiry in 2003, and I did not find this out until I qualified and had successfully obtained a post within the same R&A team. I say this now, as following the tragic murder of another child that is again infamously synonymous with Haringey, and which led to even more legislative and procedural changes, I was to witness a terrible injustice against Sylvia just a couple of years later. The vilification she suffered is, even now, indescribable, and while she has been professionally vindicated, how she did not lose her mind, I will never know. I will shed further light on this in the coming pages.

As time flew by, I had no time to sit and ponder on my past, as life was moving forward swiftly. I was exceptionally busy and extremely focused. So, imagine my total surprise when, out of the blue, shortly after beginning my final placement, I received a letter from a private investigator that was going to bring me sharply back to my past in a way that I could never have known. Even now, recounting it still amazes me to this day. The letter was intriguing from the outset. It was a large, cream, expensive-looking envelope, and something told me it was going to be important before I even opened it. It was a short letter of a professional nature enquiring if I was the daughter of Patricia Daniels, also known as Patricia Hylton. If I was, I was to call the company office, as there was some important information that needed to be shared with me. It was around 7 p.m., so the office was closed. I had to wait until the next morning, and for the life of me, I could not have guessed what was going to come next.

The next morning at 9 a.m., I called and confirmed that I was indeed my mother's daughter. The private investigator introduced himself and then advised I may be shocked with what he had to tell me. Having waited the whole night, I said that I doubted anything to do with my mother could shock me. However, I could not have been more wrong. He continued, "Diana, for some time now I have been searching for your mother on behalf of my client." He went on to ask if I knew where my mother was. At this point I felt rather perturbed and was becoming suspicious. Therefore, I advised that I had a fair idea of where my mother was, but that I was not going to share any further information without him explaining who his client was and why they wanted to know where she was. He said, "Well, Diana, you have an older sister, and her name is Rosalind. She would like to speak with you, if you would be okay with this?" Still, not really grasping what he meant, he went on to say my sister had been adopted as a small baby, and that she had never had contact with our mother. He said he had obtained my details from the electoral register, but that it seemed my mother was either not registered or perhaps she now had a different name. This was said as both a statement and a question.

My first question to the private investigator was, "How old is she?" Upon his reply, I worked out that she was six years older than me and just four and a half years older than Mark. I could not have been more stunned to learn that in the years prior to meeting and marrying my father, having my brother and I, she had another child and had given her away for adoption. To call my mother an enigma would be an understatement. The private investigator was clearly wanting to ask me more questions, and he persisted in enquiring whether I was in contact with my mother, and if so, would I be prepared to share her details with him? It was at this point when I informed him that the situation between my mother and I was extremely complex, for lack of better words. I did not inform him of the whole story, but I did advise that I had not been brought up by her. I told him that she had abandoned my brother and I when I was four, and that I had been in care. I said our relationship was one that could only be described as nonexistent. I went on to say that while I had not seen her for some years, I did know her last address, and that it was highly possible that she still lived there. I did have to add, "That is, if she is still alive," as to be honest, how would I know if she was or not?

At this point, I think the private investigator realised it was an extremely sensitive situation and a conversation best left for those who were directly affected. He again enquired if I would be prepared to speak with my sister, as she was keen to speak with me. Although immensely shocked,

I have to say I was also deeply intrigued and said, "Of course, I would." He said he would speak to my sister and if possible, asked if I would be happy for a call later that day around 6 p.m. I said yes. After that call, I told Keith and my friends, who all shared my surprise. I did not call Mark or my father, as I felt I needed to speak to my sister first. For all I knew, she might not even be my mother's child. Who knew? I went to university that day, but how I focused on the work, I have no idea.

Ros, my sister, called at exactly 6 p.m. Initially, we were slightly wary of what to say to each other, but strangely enough, before five minutes were up, we found ourselves chatting away with no awkward silences as one might expect. She was keen to know what had happened to Mark and I, and she was very kind and sensitive in her manner. While she had been adopted, she sensed the enormity of what it may have been like to have been abandoned on Christmas Eve, and then to have not seen our mother for the next fifteen years. She told me that she had been adopted by a distant relative of our mother's, and in this, she had quite a bit of information about my mother's younger years (more than what I knew, anyway). She said that sadly, her adoptive mother had died when she was five, and that she had been brought up by her adoptive father. She said that she had been loved and well cared for, but had always known and felt that she was different. She was of mixed heritage and her adoptive family was white. So, like my father, my mother clearly had her own penchant for interracial romances. I cannot imagine how this even happened. I mean, for a white woman to have a relationship with a black man in those days, as I have said, was not the done thing, and usually ended in dire consequences, as it clearly did in mine and my siblings' lives.

During that first conversation, we talked for a few hours and found the conversation flowed easily with each other. I told her about the abuse I had suffered in St. Leonard's. We talked about Mark and his struggles, and we talked about her life. I sensed she was holding back something when she said that while she did not want to upset me, she did have to tell me something. She said she would understand any difficult feelings I may have, but that she had to let me know that she was a child protection social worker. To say the least, I was dumbfounded. She said she was worried to tell me this in case I had any issues with social services, as she felt it would have been understandable if so. When I told her that I was in my last year of training to become a social worker and my chosen area was child protection, she was as surprised as I was. I mean, what were the chances of my older sister being a child protection social worker, and me about to qualify?

Such was our curiosity and intrigue, Ros and I made plans to meet that weekend, and when we did, you could have knocked us down with a feather, as the likeness between us was undeniable. It was clear as day that we were sisters. We were also very alike in our manner, and of course, our chosen profession—although, I still affectionately say that she is the more sophisticated of us both. She was eager to hear everything about Mark, myself, and our story, and I was equally eager to hear about hers. She knew about my father and of his marriage to our mother from her investigations, and she even knew my mother had lost a baby in 1974. She told me the pregnancy had been twins, and that the deaths had been registered as stillborn. She knew much more than I did about our mother's early life, and informed me that she had been brought up by her grandmother following her own mother's rejection of her. It was clear our mother had suffered a very difficult childhood herself. It was not long before she broached the subject of her deep need to meet our mother. I told her about my experiences, and I warned her not to expect too much. Even though I had moved on significantly since my last meeting with my mother, I did have to say that I could not be sure that she was even still alive. I told my sister that I did remember where she had lived, and this would be where I would take her to, if this is what she wanted.

While we had had very differing childhood experiences, it was clear my sister yearned to know where she came from and in this, she needed to have some closure, if this was possible. So not long after our first meeting and before she had even met our brother Mark, we made the trip to our mother's last known home just off the Mile End Road. I tried to prepare my sister for what I considered to be the horror of our mother, but I could not have even prepared myself for the significant deterioration that had befallen her over the intervening years. What I could not have known is that a few years on from our last meeting, she had suffered a brain aneurism, and at this point, was profoundly disabled. Further, she was dependent upon the man she lived with, who had fathered her last child, and who was reportedly her husband.

Even though I had memories of living with my mother in the squat, and I had visited her current home once many years before to try to help Mark, I was not prepared to see her so profoundly disabled. I can only liken it to what looked like a head on a bed. The covers were tucked right up her neck to her head, which she could move, but she could not move the rest of her body. The man, her husband (or whoever), looked rather coldly at her and in an accusatory tone, barked, "Your daughters are here to see you." As we approached her bed, she tentatively turned to look at me, then at Ros, and then back at me. Coming to my senses, following the shock of seeing her so incapacitated, I said, "This is Rosalind, your daughter." I looked deep into her eyes and asked, "Is this YOUR daughter?" to which she rather forlornly but simply nodded. In exasperation, I said, "You are unbelievable." I could feel my old anger rising within me. She looked scared and Ros became anxious. She begged me to not say anything more, as she needed to speak to our mother and was afraid this would not be possible. I looked at my mother and disdainfully said, "Don't worry, I am leaving." Then I turned and walked out of the house, without so much as a backward glance.

Following that visit with Ros, I resolved that I would never see my mother again. It was too painful and distressing, and I did not need these feelings reawakened. I considered that I had been through enough. Ros and I focused on our sibling relationship, and she began building a relationship with Mark too. If anything, she was the most positive aspect to come from the trauma and sadness, and I felt proud to call her my elder sister. We met up when we could; however, we were both exceptionally busy, so this was not as often as perhaps we would have liked. Keith, my father, and my friends were all supportive and most intrigued by the story and of our likeness to each other, not only because of our similar looks, but also our professions.

CHAPTER 20

I grew even stronger from the experience, and with deep resolution, I focused on completing my studies and my placement. My life experiences, at the very least, held me in good stead for the resilience that is without a doubt required when working directly on the frontlines with children who have been abused and/or neglected. Back then, before the second major overhaul of Children's Services, of which I will discuss very soon, the focus of a referral and assessment team was to review all referrals which came from the police, schools, health, other agencies, and the public, to consider what information is known in regard to the child and family, and to complete an assessment to identify the level of risk and/or need. The Children Act 1989 was, and still is, clear as to the duties it places on local authorities in this regard.

The Children Act 1989, and the subsequent reformed Children Act 2004 remains the most important piece of legislation which underpins all children's social work. The fundamental principle of the Act is that the welfare of the child is paramount and that overall, children are best cared for, wherever possible, within their own families. The law requires that every effort to support this principle be undertaken. If there is a reasonable cause to suspect a child is at risk of significant harm, section 47 (s47) of the

Act requires the local authority in which the child resides to make appropriate enquiries to decide whether action is necessary to keep them safe. The s47 inquiry must be undertaken if there is cause to suspect that a child has or is likely to suffer significant harm by way of physical, sexual, or emotional abuse or neglect. The Children Act 1989 also provides for children considered to be in need under section 17 (s17). Here, the local authority is duty bound to provide services to promote and safeguard the welfare of all children assessed as in need. Further, there are many other significant pieces of legislation and procedural documents that underpin all children's social work practice. However, it is not my intention to explain all of this. I just wanted to illustrate that these sections of the Act were central within my training and continue to be the foundation of any child protection social worker's practice (The Children Act 1989).

So, back to my social work training, and my placement, which took place within the Duty s47/Core Assessment team, where, under the supervision of Sylvia, I learned the skills required to undertake core assessments (and pre-birth assessments), and I co-worked s47 investigations with the police. My practice also included presenting at strategy and various professional meetings and implementing child protection plans following child protection conferences. I provided advocacy, facilitated access to benefits and housing, referrals to support agencies, contact supervision, duty cover, and direct work with children to ascertain wishes and feelings. This was the foundation of my future social work practice. As can probably be imagined, amid my intensive training and, of course, my busy family life, I simply did not have the time to ponder at all upon my mother, her sad predicament, or my past. I just didn't, as my life was on a new trajectory—and this was even with Christmas approaching! Just before Christmas 2006, an incident occurred. It was the beginning of a tragedy which was about to ensue involving another poor, defenceless child who was at the mercy of those who were meant to care for him. The unthinkable was about to happen again, and this time, it would have a profound impact upon my social work practice, Sylvia, Haringey social workers, and social workers all over the UK (and quite possibly across the world). I would not know the enormity of what was about to take place, and I would not know the full extent of the tragedy until two years later. Another tragic child's murder was about to take place, which would lead to the second major overhaul of child protection laws and procedures. It was an early December evening, and I was working late (which is often the life of a duty child protection social worker—even that of a trainee) when I heard Sylvia and the service manager at the time having an extremely heated debate. I was not sure what it was about, but I knew Sylvia was very upset and that she was standing her ground regarding what she believed needed to take place to keep a child safe. The little baby was Peter Connelly, the poor, defenceless child who came to be widely referred to as Baby P.

Peter had been just nine months old when he had been referred to the assessment team. This had been due to what was suspected as him having suffered a nonaccidental injury. An s47 investigation was underway, and he was an inpatient at the North Middlesex hospital awaiting discharge. Sylvia was arguing that until, following the police investigation, it was clear as to how he had sustained his injuries, specifically bruises, he should not be returned to the care of his mother. This was what the heated debate with the service manager was about. Sylvia was adamant that he should be placed in a foster placement for the interim. However, in line with the main principle of the Children Act 1989 *(where possible, children should be cared for in their families)*, the service manager did not agree and considered that Peter should be placed with a family friend, where he could be monitored during the ongoing police investigation. I would not like to say that limited resources influenced this decision, but in view of the costs involved in accommodating children into care and any subsequent care proceedings that may be initiated, when in charge of a limited social care budget, who can say? What I do know is that Sylvia wanted to protect Peter as best she could, but that this was overruled.

Peter was discharged from hospital to the family friend, and sometime in the New Year of 2007, he was returned to his mother's care. Following the completion of the s47 inquiry, the concern that he was at risk of significant harm was substantiated. Peter and his siblings were placed on child protection plans. The police investigation remained ongoing and efforts to support his mother in her parenting were put into place. Due to his mother's limited parenting skills because of her own parents' poor parenting, the main area of concern at that stage was neglect. There were concerns around her supervision of the children, and it was thought that this had possibly led to him sustaining the bruises. Following the conclusion of the assessment process and an Initial Child Protection Conference having been undertaken, the case was transferred to the safeguarding team in February 2007. At this point, there was no further involvement from the duty assessment team, and I certainly did not think any more of the situation. It was not my case, and I had little knowledge of what had happened, aside from Sylvia wanting Peter to be placed into foster care that night in the office just before Christmas.

The months that followed were exceptionally demanding. I worked hard on completing my assignments and my dissertation. As with my first dissertation that looked at the impact of the Children (Leaving Care) Act 2000, I wanted my master's dissertation to look at a current social work issue. At that time, in view of the monumental legislative changes that had already taken place, I wanted to look at one of the recommendations made by Lord Laming and research the impact of its implementation. The Common Assessment Framework (CAF) was an integral aspect of these changes. The corc work of a referral and assessment team is to undertake assessments of children 'at risk' and children and families 'in need.' Therefore, the main aim of my small-scale research project was to explore how assessment social workers were experiencing the CAF in its (then) early implementation. I wanted to know if it was assisting in the undertaking of statutory assessments, and what, if any, were the anticipated difficulties? In July 2007, I passed my master's with flying colours. In view of my progress and my clear aptitude towards child protection, I was offered a full-time social work post within the team. I was more than happy to accept. I was to have a three-week break that summer, and thereafter, I would remain on the team, but now as a qualified social worker. While it was not a lifetime ago, when reflecting, I find it hard to believe that in those days, there was no newly qualified period, or what is now called an ASYE (Assessed and Supported Year in Employment) to complete. The purpose of the ASYE year, as it currently stands, is to ensure that all newly qualified social workers are protected and supported during their first-year post qualification, and that all practice throughout this year is continually assessed. When I qualified, the expectation was to hit the ground running with a full caseload. However, this was on the brink of what would be another significant and perhaps even greater shake-up of the system.

It was just prior to my summer break that our assessment team received the news that no social worker ever wants to hear, and which would shock not just the social care profession, but would in time make the grimmest international news. Sylvia called the team into an urgent meeting to advise us that little Peter was dead and that his mother had been arrested. At that time, children's services had not been aware that his mother had a boyfriend or that her boyfriend's brother had also moved into the home. We were stunned and beyond extremely saddened. Such was the shock that you could have heard a pin drop in the room, and this led to many tears of sadness. It was August 3, and Peter was just seventeen months old. Ironically, on August 2, the police had informed his mother that she would not face any charges regarding the previous concerns in December 2006 as to how Peter had sustained his bruises.

Sadly, Peter was killed very close to where Victoria Climbié was murdered just seven years ago, literally within a mile of each other. Following the post-mortem, it was found that Peter had suffered over fifty injuries which included a fractured spine, eight fractured ribs, multiple bruises to his head and body, the loss of a finger and a toenail, and even one of his little baby teeth was found in his colon. He was severely malnourished and had a gruesome fungal infection around his ear and scalp. It was simply and utterly heart-breaking. He was still subject to a child protection plan, but this had not prevented his death. It is this which caused the public furore and that had led to what can only be described as the macabre witch hunt of the director of children's services, Sharon Shoesmith;

Peter's social worker, Maria; and a few other managers and key professionals, including Sylvia. The witch hunt that ensued had immediately followed the criminal trial and was instigated in the main by a well-known and now infamous tabloid. This awful tabloid quite incredulously and insidiously influenced national and local government to scapegoat these professionals. This tabloid was not alone in this, as numerous others seized the mantle. However, the furore and drama surrounding this would not unfold until a year after Peter's death, in the autumn of 2008. I was just a year post qualified, and Haringey came under the spotlight again, in a manner that had never been seen ever before in UK children's social work.

During the year between Peter's death and the criminal trial, we (Haringey child protection social workers, that is) all did our best to focus on the task at hand, which is keeping children as safe as we could. I was responsible for at least thirty children who were at risk or in need. Even though this was higher than the recommended number for a social worker who had recently qualified, more experienced social workers often exceeded forty plus children on their caseloads, and this was the norm. Even now, caseloads are way too high and, at times, impossible to manage without cutting corners. The problem then, as it is now, is that demand far exceeds resources and capacity, and there is simply no choice but to over allocate, no matter what recommendations have been made or major overhauls of the system take place.

During the autumn of 2007, I had my graduation, which took place at Hendon. Even at this point, no one had any idea as to how the social work profession—but moreover, how Haringey social workers—were going to be vilified and demonised in the way that we were soon going to be. I was as proud as I had been at my first graduation. If anything, I was prouder, if that was possible. Following my graduation, I became a fully-fledged warrior in the trenches, a foot soldier fighting what seemed an impossible battle with little resources. Haringey was and still is one of the most challenging boroughs to practice child protection social work. There are several contributory reasons for this, including the ever-transient and fast-growing population, exceptionally high levels of deprivation, and continuously depleting and limited resources. It truly felt like a war zone at times. I often likened it to attempting to put out a raging forest fire with a watering can, or putting a plaster that had no sticky back over a deep wound, as often this is how it felt. I assessed children being abused due to their parents' and carers' perceived witchcraft, children whose parents (whom I do have to say, mostly mothers) had been murdered, parents who were suffering with acute mental illness and could not care for their children, parents who fought with each other to the point that they injured themselves and their children, children of prolific substance misusers and alcohol-related difficulties, and little children who were being subjected to physical and sexual abuse and chronic neglect. The nature of the work was relentlessly shocking, challenging, and stressful. However, I dug deep, was extremely focused, and took sincere responsibility for my work. No two days were the same, and I knew my work was most crucially important, as what can be more important than trying to keep children safe and prevent abuse? My practice developed quickly and when good outcomes happened (as they did), despite the stress, I felt a small sense of accomplishment.

Throughout this first year post qualification, I and most Haringey social workers were still completely unaware of the impending tsunami which was about to shake us beyond recognition. This was all under the dark cloud of what was taking place in terms of the first serious case review for Peter and the criminal trials of Peter's mother, Tracey Connelly, her boyfriend, Steven Barker, and his brother, Jason Owen. At the conclusion of their trials, we were aware that the news was about to be made public, and we were of course acutely aware that this was going to have a significant impact upon us all. Peter's mother did not stand full trial, as she pleaded guilty to causing or allowing his death. On November 11, 2008, Steven Barker and Jason Owen were both found guilty of the same. It was considered not possible to determine who had caused the fatal injuries; therefore, this was the conviction. Even now, as a seasoned professional, I struggle to understand why this was the conviction. I mean, Peter was killed in a most horrific manner, wasn't he? Steven Barker was also found guilty of raping a two-and-a-half-year-old child six months prior to Peter's death. He was sentenced to twelve years for causing or allowing Peter to die and a life sentence with a minimum of ten years for the rape of the child. Peter's mother, Tracey, was given what was reported as an indeterminate period of imprisonment, but would have to serve at least five years. Jason Owen, Barker's brother, was given the same indeterminant sentence, having to serve at least three years. Shocking sentences, in my opinion, for the killing of a defenceless little boy.

Immediately after the trials, in November 2008, the press first released the tragic fate of Peter. Initially, he was referred to as Baby P, and it was reported across all news mediums and channels with attention-grabbing headlines such *"Baby P, failed by the council who failed Victoria Climbié."* Almost immediately, Sharon Shoesmith, then the director of children's services, called an all-service meeting to advise workers of the situation. I remember that day very well. It was clear at that stage that while it was known the media attention was going to be tough, Sharon wanted us all to know that she considered us to be in it together, and we would come out of it together. Haringey had recently had an Ofsted inspection and it had been rated good. Therefore, the overall view at the time was that Peter's mother had been devious (which she was), cunning, and had worked with professionals in what is called within the social work profession a disguised compliant manner.

Disguised compliance is a term used for a parent or carer who works with professionals in a way to give the idea that they are doing what is needed to address the concerns. However, behind closed doors, they are often acting to the contrary. As with Tracey Connelly, she did all that was asked of her in terms of attending parenting programmes, being available for visits, and taking her children for medical appointments when needed. However, she lied extensively about having a boyfriend and that he had been living in her home. She also did not tell professionals that his brother had moved in with three of his own children and a fifteen-year-old girl who has been described as his girlfriend. Given his age, which was thirty at the time, this was a sexually exploitative and unlawful relationship. No one will ever know who assaulted Tracey Connelly's little boy and who caused his fatal injuries. What we do know is that at the very least, she was fully aware of what was going on, that she allowed his face to be smeared with chocolate to cover his bruises, and that she did nothing to save his life.

It was within days following the service meeting called by Sharon Shoesmith that she was publicly sacked on live television by Ed Balls, the children's minister at that time. He, in turn, had been pressured by the awful media campaign that hailed headlines such as *"Blood on their Hands," "Sixty missed chances to save Baby P,"* and *"Bungling social workers fail Baby P."* Haringey council and all its social workers came under intense public scrutiny. Very soon afterwards, the media riled the public with a relentless six-month campaign called *"Justice for Baby P."* With misleading, at times incorrect, and libellous claims to sell newspapers, a petition was created that led to more than 1.5 million members of the British public signing. They expressed anger, horror, and demands for Sharon Shoesmith, Maria (his social worker), Sylvia, Gillie (Maria's manager), and a GP to be held accountable for Peter's death and to be sacked. They and their families were mercilessly and relentlessly hounded in the street wherever they went. They were subjected to news helicopters circling their homes for photographs and shamelessly knocking on their doors for their accounts, which of course they would not share with tabloid papers. Political leaders of the time also seized upon this opportunity to further their own agendas.

The media and political campaigns worked, as amid the public fury, many of the named and shamed were sacked, including Sharon Shoesmith, although this was found to be unlawful in the way that it was done. She later successfully challenged her unlawful dismissal and was even publicly vilified for this. Sylvia left her job in the end since the stress became too much, as she was being libellously attributed to the failings, of which she too successfully took court action. Maria unsuccessfully challenged her sacking and subsequent social work deregistration, as it was found that she had failed to keep full records, and that she had failed to undertake the appropriate number of statutory visits to Peter. While I am in no way attempting to say mistakes were not made, I remain dismayed. It is widely known that many social workers with very high caseloads struggle to adhere to all statutory requirements, as sometimes it is just not humanly possible. At times corners must be cut, and all child protection social workers live with a kind of "There but for the grace of God go I" mentality. It often is the only way to survive in the shockingly poorly resourced and underfunded climate in which we practice. What I can say for sure is that in the time I knew and worked with Maria, she was a conscientious, caring, and skilled professional. Quite simply, she was not able to manage the competing and excessive demands of child protection social work with the tools and resources she had, alongside the scheming and deceptive individuals hell-bent on harming Peter.

I do know Maria was incredibly concerned for this little boy, and that despite seeking legal advice in the weeks prior to his death, with the aim to remove Peter and his siblings from their mother's care, she and her manager Gillie were instructed that the threshold to initiate care proceedings had not been met. This left the team with no other choice but to continue to attempt to monitor what was soon to prove an escalating and heinously abusive situation with the most tragic of outcomes. This is contrary to the view held by many that social workers often illegally take children away from their parents. Care proceedings are complex and challenging, and ensure that professionals act (quite rightly so) within the strict confines of the law. Maria had everything taken from her, as if she had killed Peter. She was subjected to death threats and even had death threats aimed at her own child. She had to move out of London and I have no idea where or how she is now, but I do hope she has recovered, is well, and is happy. She very much deserves to be.

During this period, which lasted about nine months, we could not enter or leave the Haringey council offices without having to run the gauntlet of enraged members of the public who picketed the North London Wood Green area around the offices and the Civic Centre to heckle, abuse, and hiss at us. They would shout things like, "There they are, the baby killers!" or "You should ALL be ashamed of yourselves," and, "It's your fault that Baby P is dead." Even answering the phones became a nightmare, as some of the public took to this form to abuse us, saying things like, "We hope your children die," and "You are all useless." I do believe these are people with nothing better to do than to cause hurt and pain without truly understanding the consequences of their actions, like those who viciously troll people over social media. My better sense of judgement tells me that most people do not behave in this manner, even if in that period it felt this way.

As a social worker in the early stages of my career, I was not only demoralised, but it was also extremely stressful and scary. The task of assessing parents became, dare I say, almost impossible for an exceptionally long time. Parents in Haringey and most likely nationwide, who were subject to child protection investigations, took this opportunity to attempt to deflect attention away from the concerns about their own poor parenting capacity. They would say things like, "You lot didn't even save poor Baby P, and you want to assess me?" or "You let Baby P die. Don't think you can tell me how to bring up my children." It went on and on. Social workers left Haringey in droves, and it became impossible to fill their positions even with agency staff. This, in turn, increased caseloads, and a vicious circle ensued. No one wanted to be a child protection social worker in Haringey. Even social workers in other local authorities would casually say, "I don't know how you do it," or "I couldn't work in Haringey." I am grateful for the deep well of resilience from which I had to draw from, as it can only be this that ensured I stayed the course.

As with most cases of child deaths that are known to social services, systemic failures are often the root cause, and no one single professional or agency can be attributed the total blame. In this, we must look at poorly resourced departments, which have only worsened given the last thirteen years of austerity cuts, unmanageable caseloads, lack of staff, poor IT systems, poor working conditions, and the list goes on. For example, pre-Coronavirus, local authorities forced to make cuts to essential services introduced hot desking as a means to save money. Hot desking is where workers have no specific place or space to work. All desks are shared on a first come, first served basis. In most social services offices, there were, and still are, never enough desks for all the staff. This is not conducive to the nature of the challenging work of a child protection social worker. In fact, it is not conducive for any professional dealing with complex work and having to complete a phenomenal amount of written case work. These are just a few examples of the conditions. Yet, when the case of Peter Connelly hit the headlines, even though it was deemed that all agencies involved with his care had collectively failed, it was Haringey Social Services and particularly the few named and publicly shamed professionals who bore the brunt of the relentless media attack. The police, health, Ofsted, and legal services barely got mentioned. Yet, as in this case, there were a number of failings that led to Peter ultimately not being saved even though he was the subject of a child protection plan at the time of his death (Jones, 2014).

It may seem to the general public that if a child is subject to a protection plan, they should be protected from abuse. However, a child protection plan is not infallible. It can monitor a situation, reduce the risk, and put in interventions to address the concerns. However, it cannot see through doors, or through parents' lies, and sadly, as in Peter's case, it does not always prevent deaths. It is widely known that at least one child dies per week in the UK due to physical abuse or neglect (NSPCC, 2021). While this is a shocking figure, many of these children are known to various local authorities at the time of their deaths—sad, but true. What is not widely reported is that there are thousands of children every year who are protected from harm and abuse.

The media frenzy, public furore, and vilification of Haringey Social Services and the social work profession in general has, and continues to this day, to undermine the very difficult and complex work tasked to child protection services. It also led to what has been termed the "Baby P effect," which I will talk about the impact of in the next chapter. For now, I will say that this book is not, and was never intended to be, another book about the terribly tragic fate of little Peter Connelly. Moreover, I hope I have provided a depiction of the collective experience from my standpoint as a newly qualified social worker in Haringey. An informed discussion of what took place can be found in the excellent book *The Story of Baby P: Setting the Record Straight* by the eminent social worker Professor Ray Jones. I urge anyone who is particularly interested in child protection and most specifically trainee social workers to read this book.

It was within this context that Sylvia was forced to leave Haringey and the social work profession she had dedicated more than twenty-five years to. Even though she was cleared of any malpractice or misconduct, she found it impossible to continue to practice within child protection. The day she left Haringey, I was deeply saddened, and I felt at that point that after two years of battling the public vilification, and at times, other professionals' unfair criticism, I had no choice but to seek a transfer from the duty and assessment team. I decided that I would move to the court team and continue my career in this area.

CHAPTER 21

It was 2009, and having emerged from the outcry of the Peter Connelly tragedy, my transfer to the children in care court team in Haringey was accepted. It was a very much needed, welcome breath of fresh air as I moved to the new team and a new practice area. Thankfully, my passion to keep children safe and work with parents to address safeguarding concerns with the aim of keeping families together, remained intact. My mentor during my training years within the children in care team had now been promoted to team manager, and it was his team that I joined. I had moved from the direct frontline to what I would say is the most complex area of social work. For desperate parents who find themselves in the terrifying quagmire of care proceedings, the stakes are the highest they can be, as sadly, the culmination of proceedings can see a child being permanently removed from their care.

Contrary to what is sometimes thought, most social workers believe in the fundamental human right and legal principle that children are better cared for and have better outcomes when they remain in their birth families. Care proceedings seek to establish if a child has suffered or is at risk of significant harm, and following this, what the best option is in terms of their ongoing care. Often, due to a myriad of reasons, parents, unfortunately and sadly, cannot keep their children safe or meet their needs to what is termed in social work as a good enough standard. In these instances, the task of the court is to decide the next best option. A range of assessments of the parents and other family members are undertaken to ascertain what outcome is in the best interests of the child. The task of a court social worker is, by no exaggeration, phenomenally challenging and complex. There are numerous duties to undertake, and all of these are under the watchful gaze of the court, whose role is to ensure the law is upheld and that the rights of children and their parents are not contravened.

I mentioned the Baby P effect in the previous chapter, and I will now elaborate on that. Following a review of child protection practice in 2009, Lord Laming made fifty-eight updated recommendations from those he had made in 2003 following the Victoria Climbié Inquiry, with the overall aim that all services would work effectively together to ensure the safety of children. In the case of Peter, it was found that while all services had been "well motivated to protect him," collective practice had been woefully inadequate in the main by neglecting to effectively challenge his mother's explanations as to how he had sustained his injuries. Once again, part of the problem was found in the inherent challenges of multi-agency working that had ultimately failed to save his life. Thereafter, in 2011, Eileen Munro published a government commissioned report providing fifteen recommendations aimed at assisting the reform of child protection, or what is now widely referred to as safeguarding practice. She was clear the focus must move from being what she termed "overly bureaucratic and process-driven" to being child-centred and facilitating help that works. So, once again, experts were being called upon to overhaul the child protection system, the social work profession, and overall social work practice (Munro: 2011).

The very nature of child protection social work requires an element of working with and tolerating risk; there is no escaping this. Social work, post the death of Peter Connelly, became risk-averse for a long time. Professionals now worked in a perpetual climate of fear, where few risks were prepared to be taken. This extended to other professions such as education, the police, and health. Referrals to children's services skyrocketed and, in turn, local authority applications for care orders significantly increased. CAFCASS (The Children and Family Court Advisory and Support Service) argued that children were being accommodated into care with good reason, as the local authorities were now more focused on placing the needs and safety of children before the rights of parents. In this, it was argued that social services were taking heed of Laming's advice to always "err on the side of caution" to ensure children are appropriately kept safe, whereas, in previous years, the focus had been on working towards the human rights and welfare principle that children should, where possible, always remain in their birth families. The increase in care applications led to the increase for a need for more foster carers and placements, and subsequently placed an even greater strain on the family court system, and local authority budgets and resources. In summary, this is what is known as the "Baby P effect" (Storey: 2012).

As to be expected, Haringey children's services remained under scrutiny from all areas—the media, Ofsted, and particularly the family courts. As I began my court social work career, I was initially somewhat disheartened to find that other agencies and professionals simply did not trust Haringey and seemed to hold a view that most of its social workers, or the authority as a whole, was incompetent. In my view, this most likely stemmed from individuals and agencies not wanting to fall prey to the dreaded curse that was deemed to have beset the beleaguered local authority. It became easier to take on a "it's them, not us" kind of attitude, which was divisive and not helpful at all. However, I began to take heart and draw strength from what I could clearly see as a wholly unfair attribution and scapegoating to a complicated and multifaceted problem. I knew that many Haringey social workers, managers, and heads of services were doing their best to keep children safe within a system that often undermined this very aim. I also knew that it was not Haringey alone that was struggling, as most public services were, even back then, nearing the point of collapse. It remains clear that all public services, i.e., NHS, police, and education, were and are failing due to ongoing austerity measures, lack of resources, and increased demand. It is also known, as I have previously mentioned, that at least one child per week dies at the hands of their parents or carers, many of whom are known to social services.

The focus on Haringey is due to several factors, which include the significant changes to legislation and procedures to child protection law and practice following the murder of Victoria Climbié. An informed individual will be aware that what happened was a result of multi-agency failure, not because of the failure of a single local authority. Thereafter, following the murder of Peter Connelly, the frenzy that followed was mainly due to the media, whose sole aim was to sell newspapers and make millions to line their pockets, the unscrupulous conservative politicians whose aim was to topple the labour party, and finally, it satisfied society's need to proportion blame when faced with the horror of a child's death in this manner. Therefore, Haringey, due to the significant changes to legislation, policy, and practice, will always be considered newsworthy, even if the same did, and sadly, still does occur nationwide. As I say, the issue is extremely complex and cannot be attributed to a particular local authority or any one director, head of service, or social worker (Jones: 2014).

It was in the context of the Baby P effect that I developed my court social work experience. When I look back, I am grateful for the support and solidarity of my Haringey social work and legal colleagues, as we constantly battled to keep children safe, uphold the law, and tried to make a difference alongside public and professional mistrust and, at times, in my view, unfair treatment. My work continued to involve assessing parents, as well as ensuring all children who had been removed from their parents' care had their needs met by the local authority who was now their corporate parent. Alongside this, we endeavoured to ensure that all parents had every opportunity, with support, to address the concerns in order for the welfare principle to be adhered to—no easy feat, I can assure you. Furthermore, caseloads were exceptionally high due to the increased demand and the lack of capacity. Haringey struggled to recruit experienced social workers due to perhaps professional fear of being associated with its poor reputation. At many points, my caseload far exceeded guidelines, and this was the norm. Due to what is termed the "no delay principle," care proceedings now have strict court timescales to adhere to, involving a phenomenal amount of paperwork and subsequent meetings to attend. Alongside this, most importantly, the children must be visited, again adhering to timescales. It was, at the very least, psychologically and emotionally draining.

Despite the challenging circumstances, I found I excelled in this area, and it was not long before I began to achieve recognition for my practice. While overall being extremely child-focused, I was also sensitive to the needs of children's absolute right to be cared for in their birth family, wherever possible. I found I had innate positive communication skills when working with parents in what can be concluded as a most adversarial position. I was often commended in court by high-ranking judges, family law barristers, and court-appointed children's guardians for my practice. I have to say, now having worked across most of the services, I believe this is the most stressful area of social work, as it is here where the most at-risk children require protection and care. Further, decisions that are made often have lifelong implications. Whatever the layman's view, it is never an easy decision to remove children from their parents, as most often, despite their pain and suffering, most children want to be with their parents as this is all they have known, and overall, no matter what, they love them. I have worked on some extremely sad and traumatic cases involving sexual abuse and extreme physical and emotional abuse. I have never become de-sensitised to the pain and suffering some children go through.

When the evidence was stark and children needed to be kept safe, these were the clear-cut cases. Decisions to place them away from their parents' care on a permanent basis was easier to reconcile with, as overall, a child's safety and well-being must always be paramount. The more emotionally challenging cases were the ones where parents were not deliberately hurting their children or abjectly neglecting them because they didn't care, but that harm was being suffered due to parental lack of understanding of the concerns and/or the impact of their behaviours. This is often linked to mental illness, substance/alcohol abuse, domestic abuse, and parents' own experiences of being poorly parented. Here, often significant intervention must take place to develop parental insight into making the necessary sustainable changes, while maintaining the parent/child bond, while also ensuring the child's needs are being met as best as possible, and all within a timescale that would not cause more harm due to delay. It was really complex work, and not for the fainthearted or non-resilient. I found I developed a caring and empathetic working relationship with parents, and they responded well to this approach. I tried my best to afford parents my time to carefully explain the concerns and what they needed to do. I tried my best to contain the children's and their parents' natural distress at being separated, and I was very aware of the power imbalance. I always endeavoured never to take advantage of this.

I also found I was confident at giving evidence, something a lot of social workers find extremely nerve-wracking and difficult to do. I think it was because I understood the importance of knowing my case and the evidence. When I believed in the plan, I was able to speak about it and be challenged upon it. I also knew that even in the saddest of situations, where the parent, often the mother, simply could not make the changes within the child's timescale and the plan was for long-term fostering—or even more tragic, adoption—there were some kind things that could be said. I found it difficult to understand the social work practice that if the plan was permanent removal, then the parent had to be demonised in court in order to emphasise why the preferred plan was being sought. This was never my way, and I was positively recognised for my humanitarian approach. Even when, at the most crucial points in a case, where it was clear that the writing was on the wall and a permanent decision to remove would be made, I would try to support the parent in their distress. It is one of the saddest things to witness a parent who does love their child but cannot care for them, keep them safe, or meet their needs lose custody. In fact, it is heart-breaking at times. Some of these memories will stay with me for life.

It also takes a great deal of courage and resilience to be the face of the local authority in these instances. I and many other social workers have faced death threats, been abused and vilified by parents, and at times, devalued by the public. While this is not right, who can say how they would react when faced with the overarching arm of the law saying you cannot care for your child. In these instances, I completely understand why some parents mistakenly feel that it is the social worker who is the overall driving force. While immensely stressful, there were many positive outcomes that I often reflect upon. It is most satisfying when the best outcome has been achieved, and this is accomplished when parents have understood the concerns, worked with support to make appropriate changes, and have had their children returned to their care. I found I had a passion to do my best to try to get it right for the children and their families. Of course, I am not perfect and invariably, some mistakes have been made along the way. However, I have come to learn that when making mistakes, it is important to reflect on what could have been done differently in order to endeavour to improve upon future practice.

Within two years, I was promoted to senior practitioner. I also developed some wonderful professional and personal relationships with my colleagues. One of them is now one of my dearest friends, whose daughter I am now a proud godmother of. I also trained to become a practice educator and was responsible for training students and assessing newly qualified social workers through their first year. I was exceptionally busy and often working in excess of a fifty-hour week, including the weekends. During this period as I was working hard on my career, my relationship with Keith began to flounder again. Now, looking back, I can see I had completely outgrown him intellectually and emotionally. I think he must have felt very insecure in this, and as a result, sought comfort and encouragement elsewhere. It probably would have been best to end the relationship somewhere in 2010, but I did not want to hurt my children or Keith again, and I was fearful of not being able to cope financially, so I attempted to keep it going. I believe we both tried our best to paper over the cracks with holidays abroad and family outings, but it simply just did not work. The gulf between where we were and the beckoning future widened with each passing day.

It was also around this time that I began to think of writing this book, and I went on a week-long Arvon writing course to a place called Totleigh Barton in Devon. The course was specifically aimed at memoir writing, and I met some amazing would-be and published authors whom I have derived great inspiration and encouragement from. I cannot quite believe this was now over ten years ago, and it is only now that my book is coming to fruition. However, I now know and truly believe that nothing happens before the right time.

I was in my early forties, and I began to re-engage with the Law of Attraction. I avidly studied books by Tony Robbins, Joe Vitale, Jack Canfield, Les Brown, and many others, and I felt my energy shifting. I began to realise the power of thought and feeling and how these have an impact upon, or should I say, affect and influence desires and dreams. Keith did not believe in such ideas, and I think he thought I was slightly deluded. His lack of willingness to open his mind, develop himself, and believe in me, my book, and my passion only served to increase the divide between us. I know he did not consciously want to sabotage our relationship any more than I wanted to be the cause of any more pain. It is just how it was at the time, and why it eventually had to come to an end.

While my career was taking off, my relationship with Keith collapsed, and I found I was once more in need of therapeutic support to cope with the difficult situation and devastating feelings I consequently felt. Therefore, sometime around early 2011, I contacted my trusted therapist Amelia and asked if it would be possible to see her again. As had always been my experience of Amelia, she was kind, sensitive, and very open to helping me think about what was happening in my life, and wanted to support me to find some resolution. She helped me to feel less guilty, as despite what I felt had been my best efforts to maintain my relationship with Keith, it was healthier for him, me, and the children to find acceptance and the strength to end it for good. Following a further period of turbulence, despite me clearly not being the person Keith wanted and needed, he struggled to let me go. Emotionally, it was again an exceptionally difficult period. We also had the house, which we had a joint mortgage on, and this posed its own problems. While this was a difficult time, I had more emotional strength and I was better psychologically equipped to cope with it. We even spent over a year in the same house, basically not speaking to each other. I did not let this drag me down and focused on my children, myself, and my career.

Although this book was very much on my mind, I did not write much of it as I did not have the physical time or emotional and thinking space to do so. I was able to focus on my personal development, and I worked on feeding my mind all that I could to affect a more positive change and better outcome for myself and my children. I read books and teachings around healing and developing myself, including Louise Hay's *You Can Heal Your Life*, Les Brown's *It's Not Over Until You Win*, and Tony Robbins' *Awaken the Giant Within*. I watched the film *The Secret* again and again, and I began goal setting and visioning using Joe Vitale's

The Attractor Factor method. Keith and I had accepted that our relationship was over and that we had to sell the house. Initially, I did not want to as I felt it would again be destabilising for the children. Moreover, Jessica was still at school at the time. However, Keith was not having any of it, as in his mind, he was not going to lose his home a second time. If he was not having the house, then neither was I. Depleted of energy to battle with him, I resigned myself to the fact that it had to be sold if I was going to be free, and freedom from the suffocating relationship was what I yearned for.

Using a combination of goal setting, visioning, and attracting, I wrote a letter to the Universe that, in line with the law of attraction, came to fruition. These included my house being sold for a certain figure (enough for both Keith and I to move on), to rise further within my career (I had my sights on progressing to be a team manager within the court team), and to hopefully meet my soulmate one day. I was very specific about my soulmate's characteristics and personality, and I hoped one day he would come into my life. Of course, I was not ready at this point, but I knew one day I would be, and that it would be different to any other relationship I had had. While I was attempting to incorporate the ideas I was learning, I would say I struggled with maintaining consistency. However, although I dipped in and out, I remained focused on getting out of the relationship and moving forward with my life.

As the situation between Keith and I became even more intolerable, we put the house on the market. It sold within a few months and both he and I walked away with more or less the sum I had envisioned. Not long after this, I went for the post of team manager in the court team. It was a lengthy process involving tests and panel interviews, and I was successful. In my role, I supervised a team of seven experienced social workers and two newly qualified. Despite the challenges, I enjoyed my work immensely. I understood the importance of our role in the lives of children and their families, and I was proud when we achieved positive outcomes. I enjoyed supervising my team. We had a cohesive and mutually caring bond with each other and often, it felt like we were in it together, which of course we were. With more responsibility comes more work. However, I continued to excel and achieve recognition for my child-focused practice.

I was so relieved that my relationship with Keith was finally over, and I finally felt free to pursue my life. Jessica and I moved to a little flat. We were happier than we had been in a long time, and I felt more than hopeful for the future. I used a portion of my money to pay off the debts that I had accumulated, and once again, I have to say, I overly lavished my children and myself. The older I am becoming, the more I am realising that part of my history of trauma and adversity has led to a trait within my own personality whereby I have needed instant gratification. This has resulted in me having often lived beyond my means, and this is something I have had to get a handle on and work towards making some sustainable changes. I continued to see Amelia, as I found it immensely helpful to have a trusted person whom I could be open with about my difficulties. For a long while, I did not want to let go, and Amelia never made me feel as if I had to end our therapeutic relationship. She was always supportive and helped me to be proud of the progress I had made in my life. This was something I continued to build upon.

The lovely bright and airy flat I had moved to was in Walthamstow (East London) and was literally just across the road from my dear friend Sarah. I started to have more fun than I had in a long time, and Jess and I happily settled into our new life. Reace visited often, as did my brother, who, funnily enough, lived on the same road, just at the other end. I no longer felt conflict at home and was free to pursue my work and my personal development, and to enjoy my relationships with my children, family, and friends. Life was more much stable, and I felt very confident that I would never tumble as I had done in the past.

CHAPTER 22

It was the year 2013. I was in a good place, and little did I know, my life was about to take a new turn and get even better. I was free from the past, healthy, fit, and I looked and felt great. Having now progressed to being a manager within the court team, what is termed the revised Public Law Outline (PLO) had come into full effect. This brought more changes to social work practice, most specifically within the court arena. A significant change was that all care proceedings were now expected to be concluded within twenty-six weeks, where possible. This was due to the inordinate delay in which they were previously being completed, which in turn resulted in even more harm to children in terms of their development and needs not being effectively met, which ultimately impacted upon overall life outcomes. The aim was to effect a more streamlined case management system within the court process. While I understand the need to avoid delay, this meant the pressure and challenges upon social workers also vastly increased. The volume of work involved in care proceedings is phenomenal, and now it had to be completed within a mostly unrealistic timeframe. Even with the significant challenges, I was committed to my work, and I continued to achieve respect and recognition for my practice.

Despite the hard work, I was happy and focused on making time for my self-development. I was building upon my progress by working on my physical, psychological, and spiritual growth. I continued to read extensively, exercised, wrote a journal, and stayed focused on what I wanted for my future. I was still having sessions with Amelia as they were always helpful; however, by now, I was reaching the point of acceptance and forgiveness both towards others and myself. I knew I had done the very best I could with what I had at whatever given time, and in this, I was aware of the importance to love and like myself. I was finally happy to be me.

My relationships with my significant others were also very good. Reace, now in his mid-twenties, was living close by with his partner of that time. He was working as security alarms engineer with Keith and was happily living his life. Even though Keith and I had separated, the children remained close to him. Despite the difficult preceding years, I was happy they still had positive relationships with their father, and whilst not perfect, it was supportive, and this was important. Jessica was in the last year of her secondary education, and after having a difficult period during her adolescence, which, no doubt, had been impacted by the difficulties between myself and her father, she was making good progress. She was growing into a beautiful, intelligent, and kind young woman, with sincere compassion and a deep soul. She had overcome some difficult challenges and was now a champion of young people's rights as a Waltham Forest young advisor—a role she took very seriously and for which she achieved wide recognition, including meeting with the Mayor of London. I was deeply proud of both my children.

Mark continued to struggle with his psychological and emotional well-being. He had never managed to forge a romantic relationship with anyone, and he was lonely. A major hurdle for him was that he didn't really like himself and he felt unworthy and unlovable. This was the sad consequence of being an abandoned child, and of the trauma he had suffered. My father did what he could within his own capabilities, but in many ways, Mark was far wiser than my father, and while he loved him, he did not really warm to his clumsy and, at times, lacking in warmth approach to survival. My brother did, however, have an unwavering support in myself and knew that no matter what, I would always be there for him. I believe that in this, he drew some strength. He also had the support of my children, who loved their uncle and helped him wherever they could.

My relationship with my father had grown more positive with each passing year. I did not hold his emotional and psychological limitations against him as I knew he had done his best. I had come to accept him for the man that he was—outrageous, funny, and sometimes rude, but overall strong and determined, and whom almost always had my back. We were now good friends, and he had been a massive support during the difficult years leading to the final breakup with Keith. As a family, we often congregated at my father's house for dinner as it remained the family home. He enjoyed having us around and he had mellowed significantly over the years. He told me often that he was proud of me, and I also appreciated that despite all we had gone through, he was big enough to own his truth. Over the years, he had apologised for his own failings. His relationship with Pam was dead, and while they still lived together, it was more out of habit than anything else. They would also soon split for good. This, I believe, brought us even closer, as I could see he was aging even if, at times, rather disgracefully.

I was enjoying some amazingly supportive friendships, and while some that I held so dear had sadly come to an end, I accepted that this was part of life, and I held no grudges. I was busy enjoying my life. However, there was something missing that had been for many years, which kept leading me back to thinking about the letter I had written to the Universe when I was seeking a way out of the difficulties I was experiencing, and when I had asked for my soulmate. I had been specific about the man I felt would be my match. I had asked for a man with emotional and psychological strength, who would unconditionally love and understand me, a man whom I could be honest and real with. He also had to be good looking, intelligent, funny, and caring. It was a tall order, and if this still was not the right time, I would be strong, as I was determined I would not settle for anything less.

It was summer, and my father, even at the grand old age of seventy-three, was still a soul mover and groover and often went out clubbing, hence growing old disgracefully. Although, it must be something in the genes, as he was still getting away with it and most certainly did not look his age. I think he must have thought I was lonely, as one weekend he said that I should tag along with him to a soul night that took place on a riverboat docked near Canary Wharf. Not really wanting to go out with my father (I mean, who does?), I invited my friends. However, they bailed at the last minute, leaving me to go to the soul night with my father and his lady friend (not Pam), to accompany him. Even though I felt some sympathy for Pam, I knew their relationship was dead and I was glad he had someone with him. I was worried people may have mistakenly thought he was my partner, which would have been more than cringeworthy. I was disappointed my friends were not going, but I did not let it put me off. So, dressed in my glad rags, and as my father always says, "I looked good." The boat was fabulous, a real disco boat with a great atmosphere and fantastic soul and disco grooves. It was not long before I was dancing away in my element, and having always been an avid dancer with my own style, I clearly caught someone's eye.

I was in my own world, cutting some sharp moves on the dance floor when, in a flash, this most handsome man with long, curly, shiny black hair, gorgeous golden-brown skin, and a beautiful, cheeky, twinkling smile that matched his eyes swooped in like a flash to dance me right off my feet. As we looked into each other's eyes, there was a deep familiarity and a sense of knowing that I could not put my finger on, but felt most deeply within. We danced the night away that evening, laughing, swirling, and gazing at each other with intrigue. When we did stop to talk, we completely hit it off. He was smart and very funny, and I was even more enthralled when he told me his name was Pierre. I thought, how cool.

That night, he pursued me with an intense, chivalrous passion, and with an earnest, cheeky smile, he boldly declared that we were going to be together and that he was going to totally spoil me like no other. While, of course, I could not be certain at the time whether this was a great chat up line or not, I was most intrigued and caught up in the moment. We laughed, danced, and chatted away, and before I knew it, my father said it was time to go. Feeling somewhat like Cinderella being dragged from the ball, I explained that my father was leaving and that I couldn't possibly stay there on my own. He was as disappointed as I was, but clear in his intentions that we would meet again soon. My father, with his mind made up to leave, was ushering me to hurry up. So, in my haste, I scrambled in my handbag for my phone, only to find the battery was dead. I was worried I was not able to take Pierre's number, so instead, I found a piece of paper on which I scribbled my number with my black eyeliner, reminiscent of the '80s era. With that, I made a sharp exit, hoping I would see this handsome, dashing man again.

It was a few hours later, perhaps around dawn, when in my bed, I heard my phone ping with a text message that read *"I am missing you already, Pierre."* Initially, I felt some reservations. I did not want to waste my life on any pointless relationships, and I could not be sure the feelings I had experienced were anything more than being swept away by the moment. So, I held off from meeting with him for some weeks, but we spoke often and messaged. Pierre was not going to be put off that easily, and he pursued me in a most gallant manner that I could not resist, and I finally agreed to a date. Our first date sealed it. We talked for hours and hours, sharing our lives with each other over champagne and dinner. The electric energy between us was like nothing I had ever experienced in my life, and he told me he felt the same. I found I could be completely open with Pierre, which was most freeing. We both knew that we had a deep connection and a deep affinity, and we shared many similarities, including our quirky sense of humour.

We found that over the years, since our respective childhoods, we had lived literally within the same areas, as in Essex and East London. We were blown away when we discovered that we had lived on the Cathall Road estate during the same years, just in opposite blocks to each other. Further, our daughters had gone to the same school and knew and liked each other. We even had our old raving days in common, and worked out that we would have been at many raves probably at the same time. Over the course of the following months, I discovered Pierre to be a confident and very popular man who is well-known in our local area. We both knew many of the same people; we had just never met each other. I came to understand that this was for a very good reason. Had we met at any point over the years, of course we would have been deeply attracted to each other. It just would not have been the right time for either of us, and the Universe had a far grander plan.

Our budding romance was beautiful, and I loved everything about Pierre. His dazzling, electric personality matched his name, and I was more than impressed by his amazing skills. By trade, he is a builder with multiple skills that most people I know, and others who are in his trade, are in awe of. On top of this, he could cook like no one I had ever met. Now, many years later, I know I am not biased, as everyone who is fortunate to have him cook for them raves about him. He has the talent of being able to cook for anyone's palate and to their specific desire. He totally lived up to his promise when he told me that he was going to spoil me like no other; he truly meant every word he said. He lavished me with flowers and amazing presents, he wrote me poems and love letters, and he even created a disco/cocktail bar for me, as he knew I just love disco. He made me feel like I was the most important and special woman in the world. He was so romantic and sincere, I fell, hook, line, and sinker. Everyone around me could see how happy I was, and they were happy for me. We had the most fabulous romantic times. We loved to dance with each other, and we seriously impressed wherever we went.

While we loved to go out and we enjoyed many trips away, we enjoyed staying in even more, with Pierre cooking, of course. We loved each other's company, watching movies, box sets, and talking for hours on end, sometimes throughout the whole night.

We talked about everything and found we could trust each other with our deepest feelings, something neither of us had ever experienced in any of our previous relationships. While clearly a strong man, Pierre also had a vulnerable side that I came to find he rarely showed anyone, but felt able to share with me. He had his own childhood traumas and had suffered maternal deprivation. He was born in Mauritius and had lived there until he was ten years old. His mother and father had left him when he was two to start a new life in the UK. He was also the second youngest of eight siblings, so even before his mother left him in Mauritius, she was preoccupied nursing his younger sibling. Therefore, he had not been mothered as an infant, and this relationship never recovered. Even when he came to the UK, he did not live very long with his parents before being placed in a boarding school in Essex for the remainder of his adolescence. I quickly came to realise that despite a bold front, his own childhood trauma had had a profound impact upon him, and as his way of coping, he mostly hid his true, deep emotional side from others. We found understanding and comfort in each other.

Like myself, Pierre had been through the emotional mill in the recent years before we met. His long-term relationship with the mother of his children had ended a few years before we met, and he had some difficult times in picking himself up. In the early days of our relationship, he loved to tell me how he reached the point where he, too, had asked the Universe for his soulmate. He was so sincere in telling me how one day, about eighteen months before we met, he had looked up at the sky and asked God for his wife, a woman he would settle with, adore, take care of, and be taken care of by. He was clear he was not going to settle for anything less, and he told me when we met, he knew instantly that I was the one.

I fell deeply and passionately in love with my strong, handsome, intelligent, and funny Pierre. He did everything he could to make my life comfortable and fun. I was his focus and he never got tired of telling me that he was also most impressed with my achievements. He understood how hard it had been for me, and he thought I was amazing. A few months into our relationship, he looked me deep in the eyes and said, "I am going to marry you." I stiffened as he said this, as this was something I had not thought of, especially after my failed brief marriage during the turbulent years—a marriage I had put to the back of my mind and mostly did not even think about by then. It was at this point when I had to confront the fact that I had not even gotten divorced. Whilst I was sure I was never going to get married again, I did feel I needed to get a divorce, given that it was over ten years later. Once the wheels were set in motion, the divorce was finalised quickly and uneventfully. I was now free in all senses of the word.

I was more than pleased that my children had really taken to Pierre, and when we moved in together, they were happy that I was being very well cared for, as was my brother. Mark, being the perceptive man that he is, despite his difficulties, could see that Pierre was the right man for me. Even my father, who is not the easiest of men to win over, was impressed and warmed to him. Although, I think Pierre being the master chef that he is had some part to play in it during the early days. However, as time passed, my father's affection for Pierre grew to love, and he even said to him that he viewed him like a son, something he had never said to anyone else. I was the happiest and most nurtured I had ever been, and life just got better and better. I was equally well received into Pierre's family, who warmed to me, and they were also very happy for him. Pierre, being seven years older than me, was very assured in himself and as a father. However, as with all families, it was not without some difficulties. Despite this, I loved the way he was with his own children, which was another plus in our relationship.

It was around this time that I decided to end my therapy. I had reached the point where I had accepted and come to terms with my past. Through my therapy, I had worked through much of the trauma I had suffered. I forgave my mother, as I knew she had her own entrenched difficulties that she had never been able to overcome. I had even come to terms with the abuse I had suffered, and while I would never forget it, I chose not to let it rule my life anymore. I had forgiven myself and I was happy in my life—so much so that it had reached the point where I did not really have time for therapy, and this was a good thing. When I said goodbye to Amelia for the last time, I knew I would not be going back. She was as supportive as ever, and I hope that she knows she was instrumental in my coming to terms with all that happened. I am forever grateful to her for this.

With my relationship with Pierre going from strength to strength, I was also making great strides as a court team manager. However, the work continued to be demanding and gruelling, and with all the amazing things happening in my life, I found I had never had any spare time to even consider writing my book. Pierre was keen to support me to write my story, and we began to make it happen. For some time, I had been thinking of becoming an independent social worker and knew if I could make this work, this would be a fantastic move forward and would help me get off the frontline. An independent social worker is self-employed and undertakes parenting, fostering, and adoption assessments on behalf of local authorities, providing expert opinions within the court arena. I had also, for a long time, dreamed of moving from London to live near the sea. When I had sold my house, I had hoped to buy a house and had thought about moving to the Essex coast. I was still close with my dear friend Caroline, and she was now living in Clacton. For various reasons, I did not fancy Clacton. However, I did like the surrounding areas, so for some time even prior to meeting Pierre, I had this as a goal. The main thing stopping me had been Jessica, as she had to finish school and she had made it clear she did not want to move out of London.

Pierre shared my desire to move near to the sea, and it became more achievable with a sincere and supportive partner by my side. It was not long before we discovered Frinton-on-Sea, and a house came up for rent that looked exactly like the one I had on my vision board at the time. We decided we would go for it to see if we liked living by the sea and if it would help me focus on moving into independent social work and the writing of my book. Jessica had now finished school and was at college. However, no matter how attractive a proposition I tried to make it, she was adamant that she was not leaving London. Being the strong-willed young woman that she is, nothing I said could persuade her. She was clear that she would live with her father, my father, or my brother, but she was not moving from London. Even though I did not want to leave her, I felt I had to do what was right for me and resolved that I could still look after her and do what made me happy. She decided she would prefer to live with Mark, as he had space and I think she felt she would have less restrictions than if she lived with her father, who was close by, or my own father, who had offered for her to live with him. Pierre, being the builder with the skills that he has, turned my brother's home into a two-bedroom flat and renovated his garden to make them both comfortable. Jess was in her element and Mark was happy too, as he had company. They got on very well and were supportive of each other.

With the move in motion, the time came for me to say goodbye to Haringey after nine years. It was an emotional farewell, but everyone was happy for me, as my work colleagues had come to know Pierre and could see how well he treated me. Although my aim was to move into independent social work, this was not possible at first as I needed to build a portfolio, register with agencies, and undertake some further training. So, upon moving to Frinton, I went back on the frontline as an agency social worker for Essex County council in a duty and assessment team in the Clacton area. Essex had a blanket policy at the time to not employ agency workers as seniors. This was more to do with budgetary implications than anything else, so I had to go back to a social work position. I was so happy in my life and could see the way forward for the future. It really did not matter that I was stepping down, as I was doing so to move forward. I enjoyed working in a different local authority with differing challenges, and as they say, a change is as good as a rest. I did not miss the phenomenal amount of work that came with being in the court arena. The demography of Clacton and the surrounding areas such as Jaywick and Harwich involved many large family groups who were experiencing high levels of deprivation. The toxic trio of mental health, substance misuse, and domestic violence was prevalent, and I had a caseload as high and as challenging as ever. I enjoyed being back in a duty team. I made new friends with my colleagues, and my previous experience did not go unnoticed by senior managers.

Pierre, with his abundance of skills, was able to secure lots of building work, and he became a hit with various building contractors in the area. We settled and enjoyed our new life. Jessica was happy at college, and she would often come for weekends to Frinton for rest and relaxation as did Reace, Mark, Pierre's children, and our friends and family. We were never short of guests, and we enjoyed hosting and entertaining. It is no exaggeration when I say that Pierre is the best untrained chef I have ever known. I was never a great cook, and he made it clear I never had to cook again if I didn't want to. I am a firm believer that it is possible to taste food that is cooked with herbs such as love, passion, enthusiasm, and inspiration. Food does not taste so nice when it is dashed with a bit of stress, resentment, and/or is distinctly uninspired. So, I took him up on his offer and I have not really cooked ever since we met.

I was so happy that when Pierre proposed with a beautiful diamond ring, I was so won over that I did not try to resist his charms. I was free to do whatever I chose to do, and I chose Pierre. Once I had made the decision, I was completely bowled over by the idea, and we decided we would get married in his birth country of Mauritius. It was more my idea than his, but he was very happy that this was what I wanted, and we set about making sure we had the best wedding ever. While I had travelled the Caribbean extensively and had been to numerous parts of the Mediterranean and Europe, for some reason, I kept gravitating back to the Caribbean as I loved the warm, tropical sun, beautiful crystal-clear seas, and the vibes. Prior to meeting Pierre, I had never thought of going to Mauritius, although I was aware of its beauty and that it was highly regarded as heaven on earth. As our wedding got closer, I could not wait to go there with my love.

We arranged for our wedding to take place at La Pirogue, a beautiful hotel in the Flic en Flac area of Mauritius. The location for the ceremony was simply stunning, and our wedding took place on the edge of a clifftop overlooking the beautiful Indian Ocean with some of our family and friends in attendance. My dear friend Martina was my maid of honour, and my father proudly gave me away. I was filled with love for my husband-to-be and bursting with happiness as we said our vows. I trusted him with my heart and soul, and I knew he felt the same about me. On January 11, 2016, I married the love of my life, my twin flame, my best friend, and my protector. To this day, no one has ever loved and cared for me like my Pierre, and I simply could not imagine my life without him. Our wedding was amazing and is still talked about amongst our family and friends. Our wedding reception, if I do say so myself, was one of the best I have ever been to and we danced the night away under the stars with a live band, Sega dancers, so much love, laughter, and fun. My Mauritian family and in-laws really helped to make it a most memorable occasion. I always smile whenever I think back or look at our stunning photos, and we have the most amazing memories of our wedding and honeymoon. We settled into married life and we started to think about our future. At fifty-three and forty-six, while not over the hill, we were not getting any younger.

CHAPTER 23

On May 1, 2017, I received the news my mother had passed away. In many ways, it was finally a relief, as she was out of her torment, and I would never have to explain why I was motherless to anyone ever again. While we had no relationship and neither did Mark or Ros, we all decided we would attend her funeral. It was a sombre yet bittersweet affair. Her only mourners were her children, my husband, my father, and her grandchildren. While a most sad occasion, it was also positive, as we laid her to rest in so many senses of the word. I had already forgiven her, but it was now that I really understood her life had been tragic and I would never again feel bitter or resentful towards her. The loss of a mother through death is a profound and devastating experience for most people. However, having lost mine at the age of four through abandonment, I believe I had already grieved for my loss. Therefore, in many ways, I found the actual death of my mother, while poignant, a rather freeing experience. I now feel more at peace than ever before, and I can truly appreciate how traumatic her life was, and in this, I feel deep sympathy for her. I cannot say empathy, as I have managed to make so many changes to my family narrative, changes that she was not able to, and I am grateful to be in this position.

Strangely, at the time of her death, I did not tell anyone at work that my mother had passed away, mainly because I had not even shared anything of my past with my Essex work colleagues at that time. So, while it was emotionally challenging not to say anything, it would have been even more challenging if I had to fill in the gaps. It was easier to say nothing, and fortunately, I had Pierre who has been a massive support in my recovery and healing. Having suffered maternal deprivation of his own, he has always shown a depth of understanding I had not known in any of my previous relationships.

I was working part-time as an independent social worker and as a part-time child protection social worker. I was finding it extremely difficult having to be, in effect, two different kinds of social workers, constantly changing hats to suit the particular task at hand. Even though I was only working part-time for Essex, I had a heavy and complex caseload that often required me to work more than my part-time hours. It was very stressful at times, and while I did not want to give up my goal of moving to full-time independent social work, it was starting to feel and become apparent that this would not be possible in the near future. When I had started along the independent route, the plan had been to specialise more in parenting assessments, but I found this area was extremely competitive and that more often, local authorities and lawyers had a pool of tried and trusted experts they would consistently commission. Therefore, I found that while I was being commissioned for some parenting assessments, I was more often being offered fostering and special guardianship assessments. Of course, these are extremely important, but at the time it was not where my passion lay. For financial reasons, I could not give up my part-time post, as with independent work, payment for any assessment was not made until after it had been completed and had either gone to court or a relevant panel for approval. This meant there would often be weeks without any payment for my independent work.

While I attempted to soldier on, it got to the point where it was simply not feasible to continue to juggle both roles. Further, I was also feeling more and more frustrated that I was not making any headway with my book, which I had hoped to have completed by then. The reality was, I had barely made a start aside from drafting the chapter outlines and making a copious number of notes. Thinking about it now, of course, it was impossible to be a frontline child protection social worker and a part-time independent social worker, alongside writing a book that would delve into my deepest experiences of trauma and adversity. I did not have the time or the emotional and mental headspace. However, I never gave up on it and I knew it had to be completed. Feeling somewhat deflated, I went back to the drawing board and refocused on my self-development to help me work out a way forward.

Following the summer of 2017, I made the decision to throw in the towel and decided to obtain a social work post that would enable me to achieve a better work-life balance where I would be able to focus on my writing. Pierre, as always, was supportive of my decision. So, when I folded my limited company and made the decision to go back on the frontline full-time, he was right behind me, encouraging me to go for what I wanted. While I was disappointed not to have made a success of the independent social work route, which was made worse by the fact that I was also left with a high-income tax bill, I still knew I was going to achieve my goal of writing my book. Pierre's support and confidence in my abilities was most encouraging, and he always spoke positively and confidently of my abilities, which gave me confidence to continue. He knew my book was a burning desire and that I would not be satisfied until I had written it. He never made me feel that I had failed even when I felt I had, and he always made sure that all my needs were taken care of so that I could focus when I needed to.

I decided I needed to make a clean break from both roles, so I handed in my notice with Essex County council and informed my agency that I was looking for a full-time post where I could realistically achieve some sort of work-life balance, specifically within the area of a Multi-Agency Safeguarding Hub, mainly known as MASH. MASH teams were developed following the Munro review of safeguarding practice that I spoke about earlier (in 2011). Further, in the revision of Working Together to Safeguard Children, statutory guidance in response to poor multi-agency working was, as already stated, widely accepted as a significant barrier to keeping children safe. Both serious case reviews and the inquiry following Peter Connelly's tragic death concluded that the inter-agency working was woefully poor and had to be addressed. The concept of MASH teams has evolved significantly since they were first introduced; however, the ethos remains the same, i.e., to improve the sharing of information and decision-making between all agencies to ensure the safety of vulnerable children and adults.

MASH teams within children's services are comprised of social care, police, probation, health, education, and housing, who all work together to collate information to respond to child protection and child-in-need referrals or concerns. All referrals are screened alongside relevant proportionate information checks and enquiries to make threshold decisions regarding risk. The initial difficulty I faced in securing a position was that I had no MASH experience, although I did have significant child protection and assessment experience. Therefore, I was confident that my skills and expertise were transferable. However, I was soon to find that MASH positions did not come up often and when one did become available, it was snapped up quickly. This is because while still complex, challenging, and demanding, there is no case holding within MASH. Hours are, overall, meant to be nine to five, which, in theory, makes having a life outside of work a lot easier to achieve. Once I had made the decision that MASH was the way forward, I was not going to be deterred by lack of experience and/or limited availability. I advised my agency of my plans and accepted that in the meantime, I would have to take an alternative post.

As stated, due to Essex's no agency senior social workers policy, I had taken a step down. I had not been bothered by this, and it did not really matter to me, as it had been right for my situation and needs at the time. However, if I was going to move to a MASH team, I knew I needed to rise back up the ranks to a more senior role. Living in Frinton, the next neighbouring local authority was Suffolk, and while they did have a MASH, they had no vacancies. I accepted that it was not going to happen overnight, but knew I would get a post when one became available and that I just had to be patient. London had a much wider availability of roles, so when my agent said there was a senior post within a Wandsworth locality team with the opportunity for fast progression, I thought, why not? I started at Wandsworth in September 2017 as a senior practitioner. As I was living in Frinton-on-Sea, the commute would have been unthinkable, so I decided to live at my father's house during the week, returning home for weekends. Pierre's work often took him to London, so he would come and stay with me. My relationship with my father was the best it had ever been. He was supportive, and he enjoyed my company and that of Pierre's. When thinking back to the past, I am happy to say we have come a long way. It also meant I was able to see more of Reace and Jessica, as I was based in London for the week. I joined a locality team with Wandsworth and excelled at my work. I was soon offered a deputy manager post, and just as I was about to accept the position, thankfully, in June 2018, an agency MASH position became available at Suffolk. Although this was not a senior post, it meant I could live at home in Frinton and finally focus on my book. Therefore, I happily accepted.

I really enjoyed working in the MASH in Suffolk. It was like a breath of fresh air. It was very different to any of my previous roles, as there was no direct working with children and families. I enjoyed learning the way of the MASH and working alongside various partner agencies. I also made friends, including a dear one, with whom I felt confident in sharing my life story and hopes for the future. This was very special as it was not often that I felt comfortable discussing my past with my work colleagues, but with this special friend, I felt I could be open, as she could with me. We found we had similar hopes and views in terms of supporting children and families away from statutory social work. We both felt constrained, as many social workers do, by the ever-increasing bureaucracy and lack of resources. It was not getting any easier working within the system, and I found my passion was waning. My aim was to finish my book, and it would be my way out of statutory frontline social work. I focused my weekends on busily writing and found I was making more progress than I had ever made previously. This motivated me greatly and encouraged me to continue.

During this period, I was overjoyed to become a grandmother, as Reace and his partner had a beautiful baby boy. My little grandson has fast become a wonderful light of my life, and he is an absolute bundle of gorgeous loveliness and fun. It was shortly after my darling little grandson's arrival into the world that Pierre and I decided it would be in our best interests to move back to London and into my fathers' house. We felt to move forward, and overall with networking in regard to my book, this was our best option. Whilst living in Frinton had been wonderful, I knew networking opportunities would be more readily available in London. By now, my father was approaching his eighties, and with his relationship with Pam over, he welcomed the support. I was happy as long as I had Pierre by my side. Being the master builder and renovator that he is, he set about making my father's home comfortable for us, and my father was generous as he allowed us the space and rooms to make our own. While I was a little sad to leave our lovely house after five years, it was also exciting, as we were moving in the right direction. I was also happy as it meant I was able to spend more time with Reace, Jessica, Mark, and my gorgeous little grandson.

My plan was to secure a senior MASH post in London, finish my book, and thereafter consider the next steps in terms of my vocation and service. As my life was progressing and evolving, I became even more energised to use my book as the platform to form a company. AnAID will be the umbrella under which I will start to fulfil my vocational and life purpose, of which I will speak about shortly. Once we had made the decision to move back to London, to my surprise, within days, my recruitment consultant advised there was a MASH senior post in an East London local authority. I thought it was perfect until he dropped the bombshell of where it was. I could hardly believe that what I thought would be an ideal post was in the local authority I would never have dreamed of wanting to work for, Tower Hamlets—the same local authority that had failed me as a child. I wondered if I could even do it. Funny enough, the more I thought about it, the more appealing it became. I fully intended this to be the last local authority in which I would work as a statutory social worker, as I wanted to complete my book and get off the frontline. At the time, I could not think of a better way to end my statutory social work career and to chase away any lingering ghosts. I felt it would be an extremely cathartic personal and professional experience, and the more I thought about it, the more I wanted this post. So, when I attended the Tower Hamlets social services offices for my interview, in my mind, there was no way I was not going to be offered the post. Interestingly, the team manager who interviewed me was a lovely man with whom I had studied my social work master's with at Middlesex University.

The day I started with Tower Hamlets, I was feeling buoyant and full of motivation, so you can imagine my surprise when I was informed that the lovely team manager had left the week before to go to Haringey to take up the post of a service manager. I am sad to say that immediately, I experienced bullying by the other team manager who had been at my interview, but who had rather strangely not said a word to me throughout. By the end of week two, I knew I could not stay there. Although I was extremely disappointed, I knew I could never allow myself to stay. I felt like I was being abused as an adult in the very same authority that I had suffered abuse as a child. That is how deep I felt about it. I think it was due to the fact that I had held such high hopes and was prepared to give it my very best, even though I had suffered such trauma in the local authority's care as a child. Nevertheless, having decided I would not tolerate such treatment, I got ready to hand my notice in even though I had no other post lined up.

As coincidence or even luck would have it, one of my new colleagues with whom I had struck up a lovely working relationship with advised me that the new service manager of Haringey MASH had contacted her about a management post in his team. She felt Haringey would be too far for her to move, so asked me if I was interested. Within MASH at Haringey, as a manager; destiny had once again prevailed. I was going right back to where I had started my social work career. To say I was happy and relieved would be an understatement. However, I was not going to leave Tower Hamlets without making my feelings known and bringing the oppressive behaviour I had suffered to senior management's attention, of which I am happy to say I did. Thereafter I left, and I did not look back.

I was very happy to be back in Haringey. It had been five years since I had left and having the affection that I do for the local authority, I likened it to a feeling of having gone home. I had trained with Haringey and had gained considerable skills alongside developing a measure of resilience that has stood me in good stead for child protection practice within other local authorities. While there were many new faces and the whole senior management team had changed, I still had and continue to have many dear friends and colleagues across the services who have remained.

At the time of writing this, I have been back at Haringey in the MASH for almost three years. As stated earlier, the MASH is the front door where all referrals, contacts, or any concerns regarding a child or young person residing in the local authority are screened. It is where crucial decisions regarding the level of risk and need are made. It is fast-paced and often highly pressurised. I am happy to say I have a fantastic and supportive team and that I work with many conscientious and committed social workers who are as determined as I am to keep children as safe as we can and to ensure appropriate support is implemented when necessary. However, social work is more demanding and more complex than it has ever been.

Arguably, these are some of the most challenging times in recent British history, making social work practice even more difficult than I have ever known. After many years of austerity and savage cuts, the immediate and wider system has gone beyond crisis, and I am not alone in thinking that it is at breaking point. Social care budgets continue to be cut year upon year even though social problems are dramatically rising. As a result, resources are even more scarce, and it is only going to get worse. The demographics of Haringey and many other local authorities are vastly different to when I qualified, and the population is more transient than ever. The nature of social problems continues to evolve, and we have seen the distinct rise of child criminal and sexual exploitation, youth violence, gangs, county lines, and modern slavery. Communities are growing more desperate, leading to the rise in mental health difficulties and substance abuse, as people try to either self-medicate or obliviate themselves from their problems. In turn, this has led to the surge of domestic abuse, which has seen a sharp increase of related killings over the last few years. All of the above, and the cumulative effects of poverty and deprivation alongside the chronic national housing shortage, rising crime rates, the crippled police, NHS, and education services are impacting upon social work and the ability to keep children safe. Even as I write this, I am aghast to say a Haringey colleague was stabbed recently in the line of duty, trying to keep children safe.

Furthermore, there is now the social phenomenon of Coronavirus, which has changed the face of social work beyond anything I would have imagined even eighteen months ago. The sense of isolation faced by the social workers is increasing, as working from home is now the norm. Of course, visits still take place, but after this, most social workers go home, with meetings most often taking place via Microsoft Teams and Zoom. This impacts upon team cohesion and the invaluable support that is obtained by working directly together. It makes having impromptu case discussions and the sharing of knowledge difficult, though thankfully not impossible, as with all situations, we learn to adapt. We now realise Coronavirus is not going away. Therefore, working arrangements are not going to change anytime soon, and the new hybrid way of working is likely to prevail.

Despite these unprecedented times, I refuse to be pessimistic, as I know there are lots of amazing people with good intentions, providing fantastic services across the UK and the world over. People are trying to ameliorate these crises, and will never stop trying. I am one of these warriors. Therefore, this is for sure my last statutory social work role, as I have so much more to offer and give, and in this, I very much look forward to my next phase. Although the role of a MASH team manager is demanding, I have found the time outside of work, with the loving, consistent support of Pierre, to finally finish this book. This has been a massive achievement of which I am most proud and of which I am certain is going to be a support to many others.

Having bared my soul, I consider it important to talk about how I have overcome the trauma and adversity that I have suffered—to show how I have moved to my current place, where I have recovered, I am healed, and I am making continued progress in all areas. This is how I would like to end this book, along with some ideas in the last chapter about my intended service and personal goals.

EPILOGUE

At the start of this book, I wrote about my feelings around how long it has taken me to complete the telling of my story. I can now joyfully and thankfully say that I am at peace with this, as I happily accept that this book would not have been completed before its time. Had I finished writing this a few years or even a few months ago, it would not have had the same meaning it has now. Over the last few years, and especially the last twelve months, I have come to realise the importance of self-development and self-care, and even more so when working upon one's own recovery and healing. This is especially important regarding overcoming childhood trauma and adversity.

When thinking about how I have survived, and more importantly, moved through the pain to make the changes to my family narrative, and to achieve academic, professional, and personal success, I've found that it has been through the continuous cultivation of seven crucial principles: Acceptance, Forgiveness, Gratitude, Hope, Faith, Determination, and Self-development.

I have come to truly understand that to recover from trauma and to move from life happening *to* you, to life happening *for* you, it is absolutely necessary to find acceptance for what has happened to you. Acknowledge and accept, whatever the traumatic experience, that it was not your fault, that it has been part of your destiny, and that it cannot be changed. Truly accept that if it cannot be changed, there is simply no point in fantasising that it could be and wasting precious moments of your life in doing so. To accept the realities of your life—and any trauma that has been suffered—can be extremely freeing, can help you to grow as a person, and can ultimately support the process of moving on. To find acceptance means to have consciously decided to not let bad memories of childhood or any trauma dictate how you feel about the rest of your life. It may seem easier said than done; however, the choice is quite simple. Without acceptance, the only option is a life of perpetual wishing about what might have or could have been different, and the devastating impact of this, sadly for some, can last for life.

To find acceptance, it is first necessary to confront and acknowledge what has happened. It is important to find ways to understand the nature of the trauma, to face it, and to work through the range of complex emotions and behaviours that often come with it. Once you begin to understand the trauma, you can start the process of implementing changes as to how it affects you. To do this alone is almost always impossible, and I can say that I have not reached my own point of acceptance without help and support. It will be important to find what works best for you in this process, as in all of our differences, there is no one size fits all. It can involve therapy (all kinds), support groups, self-help books (printed and audiobooks), mindfulness/meditation, or removing toxic people, negative energy, and bad habits from your life. These are just some of the ways in which support to achieve the state of acceptance can be reached. The most important step in this process is to actually want to begin on the road to recovery and healing, which is by no means easy, but it is possible. Once acceptance has been achieved, you no longer waste precious moments of your life wishing things had been different. You choose to think different things and focus your energies on things you actually have some control over. Through the journey to acceptance, you can find peace, and as Oprah Winfrey so eloquently says, *"Turn your wounds into wisdom."*

Finding forgiveness has been another essential component of my recovery and healing. When thinking of my significant others, I forgave my mother, for I have come to understand and accept that she had her own traumas which she was never able to resolve or recover from. Sadly, her life was one of rejection, loneliness, shame, and abuse throughout. She endured a pitiful existence right to the very end. How can I not forgive her, and more importantly, not be grateful for my life that without her, literally I would not have had? I hope and pray she is at peace and that she knows that I forgive her. Without my dear father, I would not be the person I am today. He never ever gave up or gave in. Yes, he did make mistakes, which he has accepted and owned. He has sought forgiveness and has been a true constant throughout my life even when I could not see it. I know that he did his best with the emotional and psychological tools and life skills he has. Overall, my father never gave up on me and my brother, and I will love him forever for this. Today, we are the best of friends, we support each other, and we will walk this road of life together to the very end.

To all those who had the responsibility to protect and keep me safe and ultimately caused myself and many others significant harm, I forgive, because I choose to. They have had to live—and perhaps some still live—with the shame of their actions, not I. Forgiveness does not mean that whatever trauma was perpetrated against you was not wrong, or that you must condone heinous crimes or abusive actions, and it definitely does not mean you have to forget. It is the overall understanding that hate and resentment hurt the holder more than the person it is directed at. Quoting Buddha, *"Holding onto anger is like drinking poison and expecting the other person to die."* As with acceptance, forgiveness is not always easy to find. However, it is important to note that without this, you are unlikely to find peace of mind and ultimately freedom from the past, which has to be the goal, particularly if it has been traumatic. In the words of the late great Nelson Mandela, *"Forgiveness liberates the soul, it removes fear. That's why it is such a powerful weapon."* I sincerely do not hold any hate or resentment for anyone who may feel that they have hurt me, as I truly understand that life is a journey and that everyone makes mistakes, including myself. What is of utmost importance is how we address those mistakes. On this note, and perhaps most importantly, I forgive myself. I understand why I have made the mistakes that I have, and I have made a promise to myself to endeavour to live a life that does not cause hurt to others. Forgiveness is the best gift that I have given myself, and in this, I am at peace.

> "Gratitude *makes sense of our past, brings peace for today, and creates a vision for tomorrow.*"
>
> —Melody Beattie

Upon my journey of recovery and healing, I have cultivated an 'attitude of gratitude,' and I surely can testify to the healing powers of this. I am most grateful for my life and for being able to overcome significant trauma, and for my achievements. I am grateful that I am able to love unconditionally and that I am loved equally. I am grateful for darling Pierre, my family, and for having loving relationships with my older sister Ros and my little sister, both of whom came into my life during adulthood. I am grateful that I am free to express my feelings and that I live a life of abundance in so many ways. I am grateful for my past as without this, I would not know how to help and support others who have suffered similar experiences, and this is my life's purpose. The list goes on.

Numerous research studies have shown that expressing gratitude positively impacts mental health. It can help improve mood, reduce stress, and alleviate depression. I have found it nigh on impossible to be sad when I am expressing gratitude. When I practice mindful gratefulness, I feel happy and motivated, and I love to feel this way. I like to begin my mornings with a routine that sets me up for that day, helps me to focus on my goals, and helps to keep me grounded. I always start my routine with a guided gratitude meditation. Thereafter, as often as I can, I write in my gratitude journal. When I miss a few days for whatever reason, I feel out of sorts and not energised in the way that I am when I do practice mindful gratefulness. However, even if I cannot always do my morning routine, I always give daily thanks in my mind for most things. Of course, I have my off days, but who doesn't? However, overall, I am very much aware that whatever has happened to me, I am fortunate. I have much to be thankful for, and for this, I am truly grateful. *"Enough is a feast."* - Buddha

In the words of Dale Carnegie, *"Most of the important things in the world have been accomplished by people who have kept on trying when there seemed to be no hope at all."* The more self-aware I have become, the more grateful I am that I have always managed to remain hopeful and optimistic. In the past, when I had been so down that it had been almost impossible to see the light at the end of the tunnel, it was hope that had kept me going. As a frightened, abandoned, neglected, and abused child, I would lose myself in the world of books, and in these, I found courage and hope. As I progressed through what can be described as a most turbulent adolescence, I did not lose hope. Even at the point where I felt my life was over and I attempted a pitiful cry for help, I still hoped and yearned for better days. I hoped for a better future and for unconditional love, and it was then that I was gifted with my children. When I made terrible mistakes and hurt myself and others, I hoped and prayed for forgiveness, and this has been achieved. It was hope for the future, for security, and to feel proud of myself that led to my academic successes. It has been the desire and hope to help others who have suffered in similar ways that has led to my professional success. However bad life may seem, there is always something you can do and succeed at. *"Where there's life, there's hope,"* said the brilliant late scientist, Stephen Hawking. Today, I am hopeful for this next phase of my life. There is still so much to do, see, and achieve—how very exciting!

Along with hope, over the years I have developed a deep faith in myself, not only to survive and overcome the trauma and adversity I have suffered, but faith that I would achieve. Even now, I have faith that I will go on to achieve even greater things in line with my life's purpose, which I will outline shortly. Faith is the intrinsic ability deep within to trust in what cannot be seen; it is the steadfast knowledge that deep down, you know and believe things will work out and get better. It is putting one foot in front of the other when you cannot see what is ahead. It is widely acknowledged that Albert Einstein, who is one of the most influential scientists that has ever lived, spoke much about what cannot be seen but is known and felt. It is this which can be concluded as faith. He said, *"I believe in intuitions and inspirations. I can sometimes feel that I am right. I do not know that I am,"* and *"Imagination is everything. It is the preview of life's coming attractions."* It is faith that has kept me planning, goal setting, visioning, and moving forward, and it is faith that has helped me understand what my life purpose is. It is what helps us find ways to move through the fear to find solutions to our problems. At the most difficult time in my life, hope and faith have seen me through and always will. *"Faith gives you an inner strength and a sense of balance and perspective in life,"* said Gregory Peck. John Paul Jones said, *"If fear is cultivated it will become stronger, if faith is cultivated it will achieve mastery."* I know which one I prefer to lean on.

We are all individual and unique. When reflecting upon my strengths and the principles I have cultivated in order to survive and achieve, it must be said there is no right or wrong way. What I do know for absolute sure is that there MUST be a way, and I have been resolutely determined. By this, I mean that whatever happens, to survive, you cannot and must never give up. I have been down and at times, especially when I was younger, I could not see light at the end of the tunnel. However, I have never given up. It was during these times that I knew it was sufficient to take each day at a time. Even if it meant that I was just putting one foot in front of the other, this was enough until I felt strong enough again to walk, and then run. I have been determined to not let my past define me. As a teenager, I often thought that if I had succumbed to a life where trauma or depression were the main features, this would probably have been understandable. However, I was never going to have this for myself. Then I had my children, and I became determined to be the best mother I could, even though I had no maternal reference to go by. I was determined they would not suffer like I had, and I am proud that I have achieved this and more.

Through determination, I changed my family narrative, and becoming a mother made me determined to achieve an education. It is my determination that has been the foundation of my survival and has fuelled everything I have ever done and achieved in my life, and it always will. *"If you set goals and go after them with all the determination you can muster, your gifts will take you places that will amaze you,"* said Les Brown. This book has most definitely been the hardest thing I have ever written. Going back and going over the traumas and adversity I have experienced has taken so long, and at times, I have become weary to get to the end. However, I could never have given up once I started. The older I become, the more I value the gift of determination that keeps me moving forward and towards my future goals.

Finally, the importance of working to improve oneself through self-development, not only in terms of healing from trauma and adversity, but in all areas of life, cannot be underestimated. The great thing about self-development is that you have absolute control and choice in this, and if you choose so, no one can take this away from you. As a young person, I would not have been able to articulate or understand that I was a keen self-developer, but this, I have always been. I would say I began through reading as a young child as a form of escapism, and that it helped me to develop an awareness of the world outside of where I was. I have come to understand that it was essential to my survival. Having survived adolescence, becoming a teenage mother, and upon re-entering education during early adulthood, I was self-developing. I progressed on to higher education, and since then, have continuously worked on developing myself. For sure, there have been numerous points in my life when I have not always had the strength, or I have lacked a consistent approach. However, through the continuous cultivation of the above principles, I have found a way to keep going, and in this, I have progressed and achieved. When thinking about recovery from trauma, self-development is important, as without this, it is difficult to escape being captive of the past.

As I have said, another essential component of my own self-development has been to create a morning routine, whereby I focus purely on my physical, mental, and spiritual well-being, alongside working on my goals and aspirations. Research has shown time and time again the benefits of a regular morning routine, and that it helps to prepare for the day, increases productivity, decreases stress, improves relationships, assists to develop healthier habits, energises, motivates, and it most certainly helps one to achieve goals. Over the years, leaders in the area of self-development, such as Tony Robbins and what he has termed the "Hour of Power," along with Hal Elrod's *Miracle Morning* have greatly helped me to develop a morning routine that includes gratitude meditations, journaling, affirmations, visualisation, exercise, and reading. My ideal morning routine will start around 6–7 a.m. and will last for at least one and a half hours. When I gift myself my morning routine, I feel energised, motivated, and focused. When I do not do it, or I have a break, the impact on my motivation levels, energy, and productivity is significant. Therefore, I try not to have too long a break, as I do not like the way it makes me feel. I wholeheartedly recommend a morning routine, not only in terms of healing from trauma, but also in helping to keep up motivation and to focus on goals. As with most things, it will be important to identify what works best for you, but once you've worked it out, just go for it.

Today, I am in a great place in my life—the best, in fact. I am now focused and working towards my future goals. As the late and wonderful Dr. Wayne Dyer said, *"I am working on not being better than anyone else but being better than I used to be."* There are so many ways to develop oneself. The important thing is to continuously work *"to keep your cup filled up,"* as Oprah says. I will always strive to improve, and in this, I read, study, and work with others to achieve this aim. Currently, I have a fantastic life coach whom I consider to be a good friend. He is helping me move on in leaps and bounds in terms of my self-development, and he has been a great support in helping me finish this book. Most significantly, he has helped me to articulate my life purpose, which is key to moving beyond surviving to thriving, as with a purpose, there is hope and a point.

> *"A purpose will ensure you feel motivated and help you decide how to spend your time."*
>
> —Mark Wilkinson

Through my coaching with Mark, I am now able to confidently inform that my purpose is to support, empower, motivate, and inspire—particularly those who have suffered trauma and adversity—so that healing and positive, sustainable changes can be achieved. I am most grateful to Mark for his help, and I look forward to working with him in the future.

This book is pivotal in terms of the start of my path out of statutory social work, and I am so enthused and energised for the future. Through my company, AnAID Empowerment, I will write more books, become a motivational speaker, and a life and overcoming adversity coach. I will also focus on my independent social work and consultancy service. I intend to undertake a PhD, a long-held dream of mine, of which I know I will achieve in due course. Alongside this, I would like to create a Parent Empowerment Programme (PEP for parents). The aim of this programme will be to support parents going through the child protection process, to empower them to make sustainable life changes and changes to their own family narrative, to heal their lives, and ultimately keep their children safe and with them. Pierre and I also plan to create a wellness retreat for all, but with a focus on social workers, to escape the pressures of the work and to find some rest, rejuvenation, and to refocus. I am most passionate about the future, and in the words of the wonderful late Maya Angelou, *"My mission in life is not merely to survive, but to thrive; and to do so with some passion, some compassion, some humour, and some style."* I have many more ideas and goals, but I must end this story somewhere. So, with a deep, sincere, and heartfelt gratitude, I thank you for taking the time to read my book.

AFTERWORD

I'm truly grateful to Diana Hylton for asking me to write the afterword to her powerful book.

Diana is a real force of nature. When you're in her presence, you can feel her energy, spirit, and enthusiasm, as these qualities simply shine through her and inspire all those around to achieve greater things. Diana also cares a great deal. Putting it simply, you can't have a career in social work such as she has had, without caring a huge amount about other people, and in Diana's case, her focus is the children of the UK.

I've had the pleasure of getting to know Diana over the last eighteen months. During this time, she has developed hugely as a person and is now ready to become a best-selling author in her own right.

In her memoir, *Both Sides of the Track*, she openly shares her traumatic childhood, which would have been too much for many, and is poignantly honest about the struggle of her mother leaving while she was young, leading to Diana and her brother being taken into custody of the UK care system. This is something that many of us cannot even imagine living through. However, Diana's description and subsequent commitment to not only surviving, but also thriving, is in no small measure a testament to her character, determination, and personality style.

I first met Diana after she contacted me about my Life and Business Coaching program, 12 Months to Remix Your Life, where we discussed what she would like to achieve. She told me she had a choice. One was to attend Tony Robbins' Unleash the Power Within (UPW), which I know she will do someday soon, and the other was to reach out to a Life and Business Coach such as myself for guidance on the journey that she is now on. I'm grateful that Diana chose to work with us, and she's also told me that she's received '10 times the value' that she's paid us!

At the time when Diana reached out to me, my debut book, *Life Remixed*, was ready to be launched and has since grown into an international best seller and award-winner. Diana will 100% follow in my footsteps with her memoir as a best-selling author, and onto the Life Remixed Live stage next to me as she is a natural relating socialiser, and knows, using her own experiences, that she has the ability to change people's lives for the better.

At the start of our coaching journey, we ask our clients to complete an E-Colors Personality Diversity Indicator (PDI). Diana came out as a Yellow/Blue, the Relating Socialiser, and a lot of her choices as she became an adult are in line with what we describe as a personality style with those Yellow/Blue tendencies.

Yellow/Blue personalities are typically focused on people rather than tasks, have a strong desire to help others, like to be liked (or even better, loved), are emotionally driven, don't like confrontation, and struggle to say no for fear of upsetting someone.

Diana's E-Colors results are very similar to my own, and we also share a love of house and dance music, which keeps our energy strong even as we mature. Interestingly, a couple of the potential limiters for myself, for Diana, and for many others with the top colour of Yellow is that we can become easily distracted, and on occasion, lack focus and decisiveness. When working as her Coach, we identified her strengths and these potential limiters early on and set to work.

The next step was to help Diana define her purpose; it is such an important thing to do, and yet most people don't have a clearly defined purpose for their lives. Diana grasped this aspect quickly and has stuck to it diligently ever since. I'm reminded of the quote, *"What a different story people would have to tell if they would only clearly define their purpose and stick to it until it becomes an all-consuming obsession."* This is true for Diana, myself, and all the Life Remixed Coaching clients.

Diana has worked hard to become more focused, and the result can be seen in this compelling book. I was fortunate enough to read an early version of *Both Sides of the Track* in which Diana shows her resilience and persistence to grow through those traumas. Never giving up and achieving ongoing success is the result. She has also clearly defined her seven principles, namely, acceptance, forgiveness, gratitude, hope, faith, determination, and self-development, that have helped her grow.

Ultimately, this is an inspiring story of a journey of forgiveness and freedom, and one that we must all understand in order to embrace self-development and then use the parallels to grow further in our own lives.

I'm so looking forward to Diana joining me as a Life Remixed Coach, as I know she is going to help a lot of people.

Well done, Diana! You're a wonderful soul and now a published author. Here's to your ongoing success, onward and upward.

Thank you,

Mark Wilkinson
Life and Business Coach
Best-Selling and Award-Winning Author of *Life Remixed*
www.markwilkinsonofficial.com

ACKNOWLEDGEMENTS

Dad, I am so very grateful for your enduring love and support, even when I did not always know or believe it. We have overcome immense difficulties and challenges, and I am so happy that we are much more than father and daughter; we are true friends. I love you and I thank you always.

Pam, I thank you deeply for your support, especially when I was very much in need, and for being my children's Nan. I love you.

Ros, words alone cannot express how happy and grateful I am that you found us. I love you and I am so proud of you, my sophisticated big sis.

To my little sis, I am thankful that you came back into our life, and for our relationship. I love you.

Caroline, I love you as my sister and I thank you for the love and care you gave me as a little girl. I am so grateful that we were brought together again. You mean the world to me. Without you, justice may not have been achieved, and ultimately, this book may not have ever been written.

Sarah, we are Yin and Yang (twinnies), sisters. Over the last thirty-seven years, we have grown up and been through so much together. Through the laughter and the tears, we have had a blast and so much fun. I love you always. Stacey, I love you too.

Martina, I got there thanks to your love, never-ending support, and constant encouragement. We are true birdies, we are family. I love you dearly.

Andreea, I thank you for your love, support, and of course, the deep belly laughs. We are way beyond MASH Minions; we are dear friends for life.

Wendy, Donna, Jean, Michelle, and Johnny B, though we may not always see each other, I am sincerely grateful for your love and support during the early days. I love you and I thank you.

To my goddaughters, Symone and Fina, and my niece, Carrie Ann, I love you all.

Bob and Maureen, you were such a massive support and I thank you.

To the three other musketeers, Angela, Annette, and Lorraine, love you guys.

I am most grateful to my wonderful therapist and psychological mother. Thank you for helping me come to terms with and break free from the past.

Dr. Paul D, Chris P, Leonie P, Sylvia H, Mairead O, Barnaby D and Annie W, thank you for believing in me.

I would not be the social worker and children's advocate that I am, had I not met and been inspired by you all. I admire you and I thank you all for your encouragement and for teaching me the ropes.

Mark Wilkinson, thanks to you, coach! You have been such an immense help in my getting to this point and beyond. Thank you so very much for writing such an amazing and inspiring afterword. Also, big thanks to Emma Wilkinson for my beautiful logo, website, and for bringing AnAID Empowerment to life. Team Wilks, I am grateful for all you both do and for our wonderful Life Remixed community.

To ALL my wonderful friends within the social work and legal professions, while far too many to mention individually, you are all very special nonetheless. I thank you for all you do, and I sincerely value our friendship.

To my dear fellow comrades from St. Leonard's, I wish you all love, peace, and happiness always. To Paul C, thank you for protecting me. *Liam Carroll – RIEP.*

My dear friend, Vincent Simmons, thank you for your encouragement of my writing over the years and for being such an inspiration. You are the epitome of true faith and of what one's mind can achieve with belief. I am beyond happy for you, and I look forward to you sharing YOUR story with the world.

Thank you, Judy, Ashley, Michacla, Anne, Harshita, Allison (Hasmark Publishing International), and Joel Capillaire (Dream Capture Ltd). It has been a wonderful journey.

Finally, to all who I love and those who love and support me, but whom I have not been able to mention here, my heartfelt thanks to you all. *Paul, Deena, Stephen, and Jayne, I will always love you, and I miss you. RIEP*

Victoria Climbié and Peter Connelly, forever angels, never to be forgotten.

ABOUT THE AUTHOR

Diana Hylton is an independent social worker and is the founder and director of AnAID Empowerment, which provides a range of social work services across the UK.

Diana is an expert within her field, and she has twenty years of experience working with vulnerable children and their families. Seventeen of those years have been spent working within challenging and diverse local authorities. She is a qualified practice educator and has supported numerous social work students through their training and into the profession. She is passionate about child protection and supporting families.

In her debut book, *Both Sides of the Track*, Diana shares her experiences of being on both sides of the care system. In this, she demonstrates her purpose and mission, which is to support, empower, motivate, and inspire—particularly those who have experienced trauma and adversity—so that progress and positive, sustainable changes can be made.

Diana has recently left statutory child protection social work and her role of team manager within a MASH

(Multi-Agency Safeguarding Hub). She is focused on developing her company, her social work and consultancy practice, life coaching, and motivational/keynote speaking. She is planning to write more books and to study for her PhD.

REFERENCES

Batty, D. (2001), 'Key Figures in the Climbié Case', The Guardian, 10 December.

Batty, D. (2001), 'Timeline for the Climbié Case', The Guardian, 24 September.

Jones, R. (2014), 'The Story of Baby P: Setting the Record Straight', Policy Press.

Munro, E. (2011), 'The Munro Review of Child Protection: Final Report: A Child-Centred System', Department for Education.

NSPCC, Child Deaths Due to Abuse or Neglect: Statistics briefing, 2021.

Storey, T. (2010), 'Care Proceedings and the Baby P Effect', Irwin Mitchell

Children Act 1989 (legislation.gov.uk)

St. Leonard's | IICSA Independent Inquiry into Child Sexual Abuse

The_Protection_of_Children_in_England.pdf (publishing.service.gov.uk)

Victoria Climbié Inquiry - GOV.UK (www.gov.uk)

Printed in Great Britain
by Amazon

87363495R00192